Francis Davison

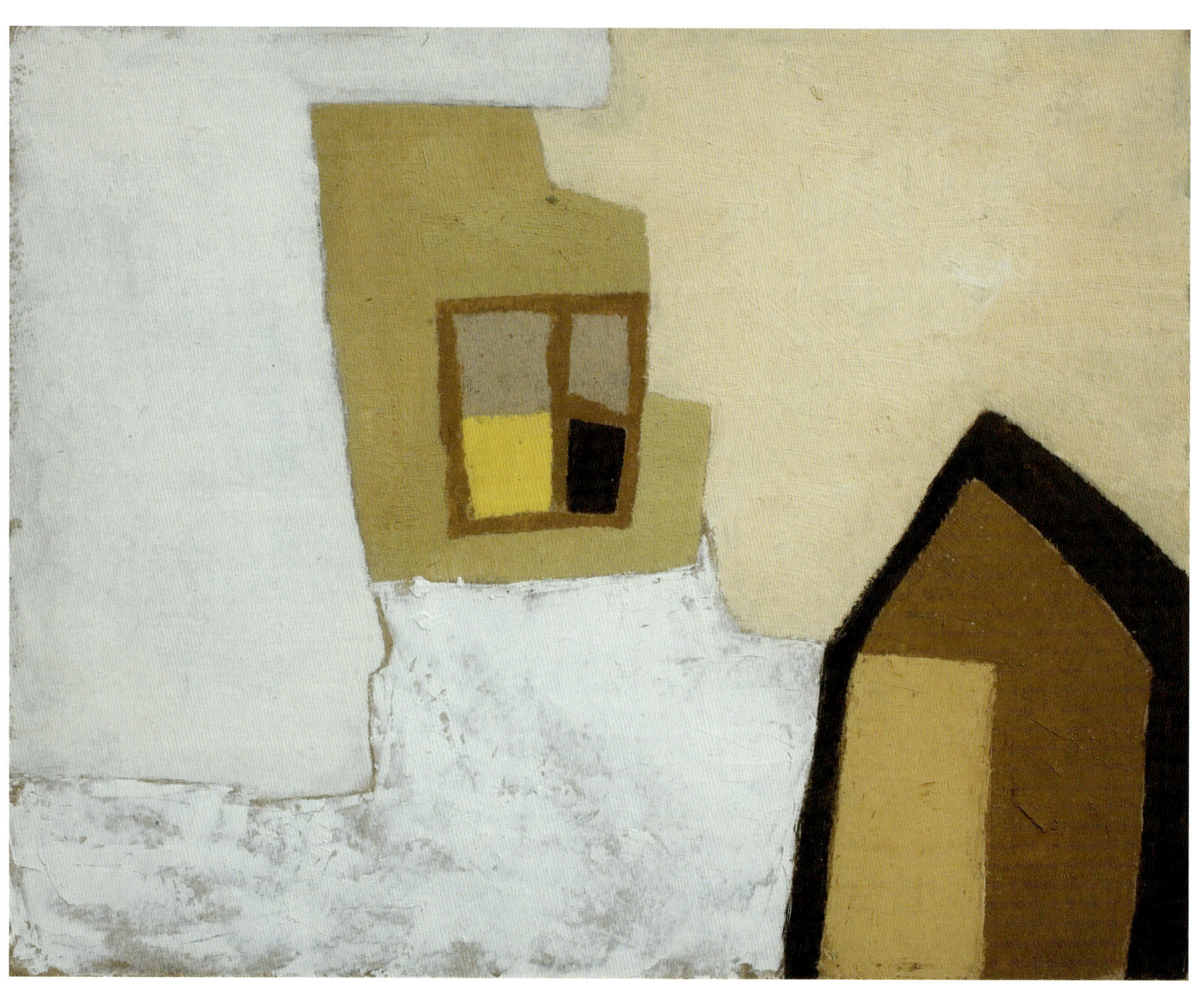

Francis Davison

Andrew Lambirth

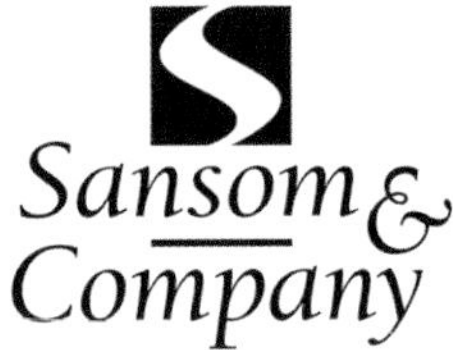

Sansom &
Company

Published by Sansom & Company
(a publishing imprint of Redcliffe Press Ltd)
81g Pembroke Road, Bristol BS8 3EA

Updated edition published in 2020
First edition published in 2013

info@sansomandcompany.co.uk
www.sansomandcompany.co.uk

ISBN   978-1-911408-72-7

British Library Cataloguing-in-Publication Data
A catalogue record for this book is available from the British Library

Design and typesetting by Nick Newton Design

Printed and bound in the Czech Republic by Akcent Media

Cover
C-149 (see page 18)

Frontispiece
O-37   1951 Oil on board 30.4 × 41 cm (13.25 × 16.5") Private collection

Contents

Preface to the Updated Edition 6

Introduction 22

1 **Early Life and Writing** 29

2 **Meeting Margaret Mellis and Painting** 38

3 **Collage** 81

4 **Late Work** 101

5 **Posthumous Career** 141

Conclusion 172

Sources 174

Notes 174

Bibliography 175

Acknowledgements 175

Preface to the
Updated Edition

This book recounts the career trajectory of Francis Davison from poet to painter and finally to abstract collagist. Collage marks the high point and crystallisation of his vision, and it is as a collagist that he is principally valued and celebrated. This preface contains a digest of my most recent thinking about his work, and draws heavily upon my essay on Davison's collages in the exhibition catalogue for his 2017 show at the Redfern Gallery. The present essay should be considered as supplementary to the main text of the monograph that follows, and in no way a substitute for it.

After just a few years experimenting with drawing and painting, encouraged by his wife Margaret Mellis, herself a distinguished artist, Davison made his first collages in 1952. Their subject was a continuation of the cottage and field paintings that preceded them, but taken to a further degree of abstraction. It soon became evident that complete and self-contained abstraction was the goal towards which he was headed. The forms of his early 1950s collages became more hard-edged and geometric though they still bore references to things seen: to a boat on the seashore, aerial views of fields and farms, or the profiles of houses. Gradually, however, over the period 1952–63, the shapes of cut or torn paper began to be released from depiction and to take on their own identity as shaped colour and tone. During the next period, 1963–70, Davison reached maturity as a collage maker, and found his voice. The imagery became more organic, the paper torn rather than cut. His work achieved a much higher level of formal attainment, consolidated and augmented over the remaining years of his life.

Davison's distinctive collage style of interlocking patterns floating in space is a clear development of Britain's linear tradition which stretches back to the great age of Celtic ornament and manuscript illumination. In his mature work, he had the remarkable ability to make torn paper look like brushstrokes of paint, a most appropriate skill at a time when many of his radical contemporaries were exploring the farther reaches of post-war abstract painting. In some respects, Davison can be seen as a painter manqué, though the term implies that he would have preferred to have painted, when it's evident that the medium of collage suited him entirely. (When he found his true métier in collage, he ceased to paint.) And it could be convincingly argued that the language of collage he created was more individual and powerful than anything he could have done in painting.

Davison exploited not only the physical possibilities of the material, but how it might be closely structured without affecting its immediacy. He recycled plain paper, coloured but not printed, unlike say Kurt Schwitters who revelled in the detailed evidence of the previous life of his collage elements (the markings on newspaper, bus tickets, tin foil, franked envelopes) and invited the strangeness of new juxtapositions. Davison's approach was altogether more focused and in some ways more exploratory than this. Schwitters brought everything together almost haphazardly to create a new and startling reality, in line with the classic Surrealist juxtaposition of an umbrella and a sewing machine on a dissecting table, whereas Davison tested every disposition repeatedly until he got it right.

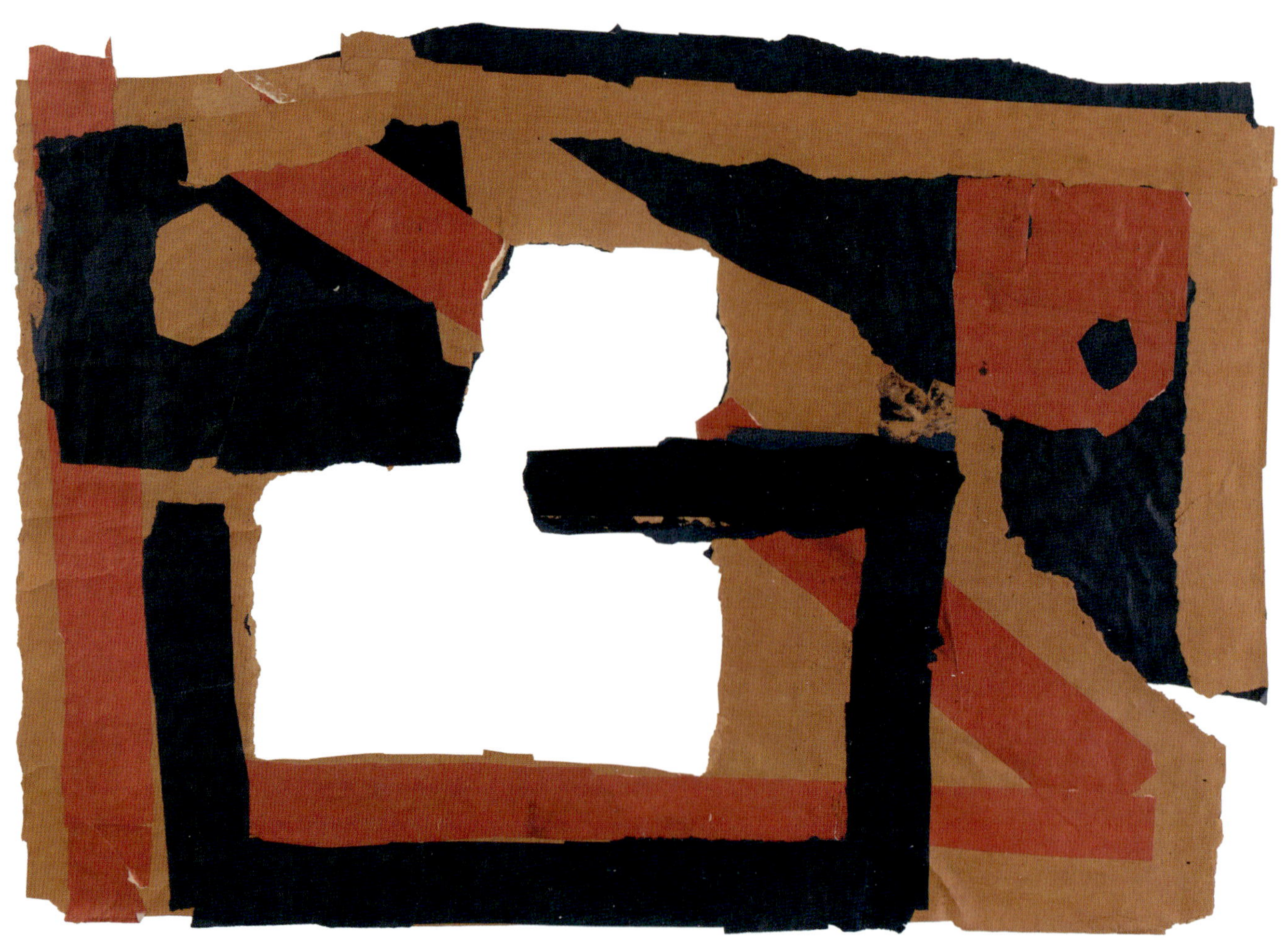

C-182 1970 Collage 72 × 98 cm (28.3 × 38.6")

His employment of mass-produced coloured wrapping paper gave the initial impression of informality. Its worn and distressed look was evidence of human involvement, human usage. The humped, wrinkled and sometimes folded paper is simply glued together, with no attempt to smooth it out or flatten it, or present it tidily. Occasionally there are visible glue marks where a piece of paper previously stuck down has been summarily removed. A picture is a sum of decisions and revisions, and these are no exception. Davison's collages are the reverse of precious, but they generate their own currency by accepting this very inelegance as a strength and building upon it.

The colour, though intentional, is found colour – he worked with the given colours of the papers he collected, and although they often look as if painted, he never actually painted them. (For if you paint paper you alter its whole texture and lose the subtlety of surface.)

A feature of Davison's mature work is the preponderance of big blobby *taches* of colour such as you might find in the abstract paintings of Bert Irvin. Comparison may also be made with the shapes in Roger Hilton's early paintings, while Hilton's friend and colleague Sandra Blow should also be mentioned in this connection, a vivid and prolific collagist herself. Similarly, some of Davison's shapes have a kinship with the ragged colour areas in Patrick Heron's paintings. It wouldn't be surprising if such close friends as Davison and Heron were to influence each other, and interestingly, Heron's late work, particularly of the 1990s (made when Davison was already dead) seems to share a similar complexity of formal language, and a comparable use of colour.

Colour really took off for Davison when the range of found paper available to him suddenly broadened out in the 1960s. Subfusc browns and ochres were replaced by red, blue and green. His collages are remarkably painterly in their manipulation and application of colour, particularly in the way small bits of paper are attached to larger ones. It sometimes takes an effort to recall that all these marks, shapes and groupings are made from nothing other than torn paper. The lines and blocks of colour so resemble brushstrokes and painted dispositions that the eye can be briefly tricked – particularly where Davison has torn away areas of paper previously stuck down, leaving only a trace or echo, like a smear of pigment.

Davison was a master of the edge: not simply in the ragged outside edges of his collages which, while remaining roughly square or rectangular, frequently take on a new and radical dynamic through an unexpected rhythm of projections and protrusions matched by gaps and absences; but also within the collage, as different edges of paper are lapped and abutted in lyrical and often complex patterns and layers. Davison used tone to great advantage, varying the browns and blacks and reds with instinctive subtlety, and employing blue with particular verve. The artist also made telling use of white, though in his later work white is often replaced by absence – a gap in the weave, a hole through which the backing board on which the collage is mounted may appear. The gaps act like breathing spaces, bringing a new sense of transparency to the work.

These breathing spaces also lift this predominantly two-dimensional work into three dimensions. As Davison developed his collage practice, he moved increasingly towards the sculptural and would talk about his work in those

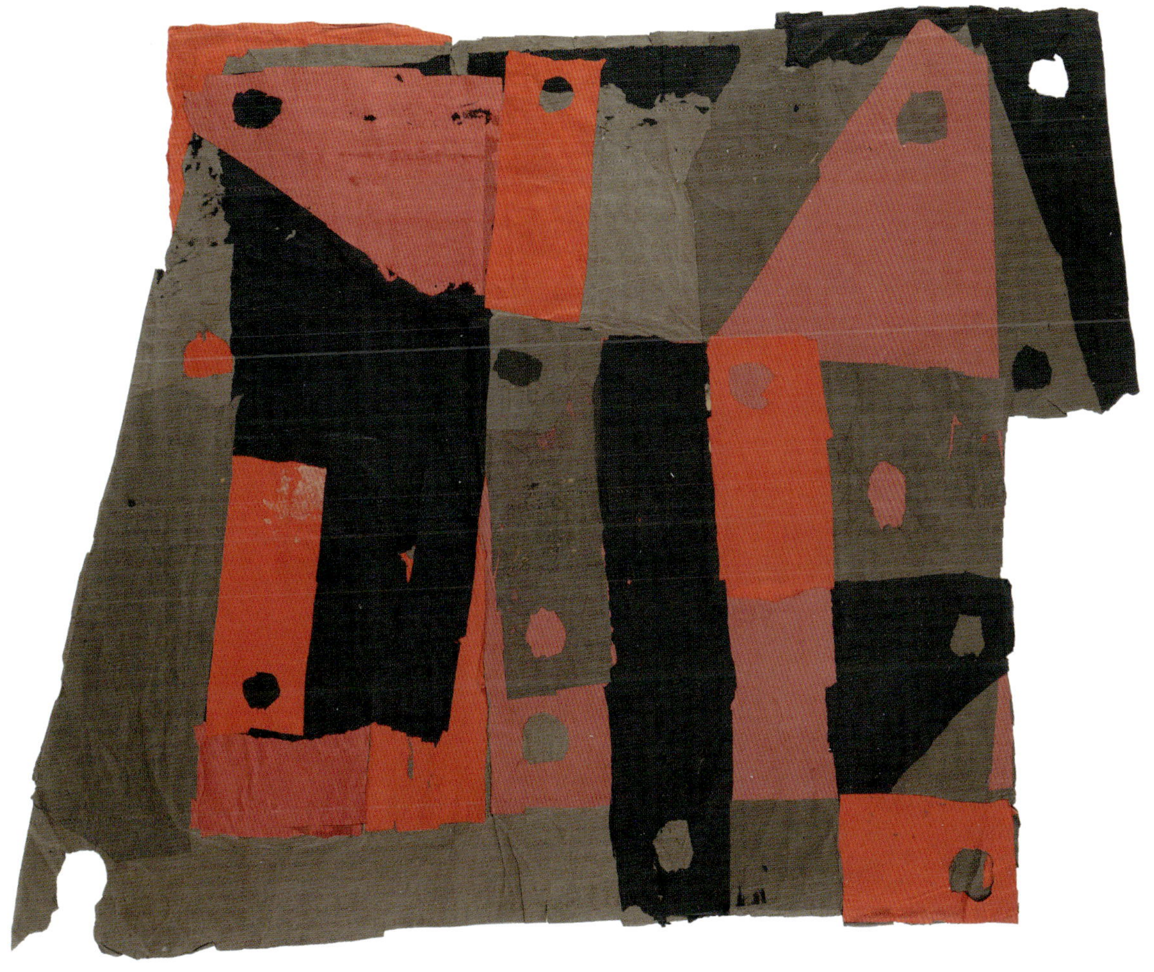

D-36   1970   Collage   107 × 133 cm (42.1 × 52.4")

terms. Presenting the collages on the white ground of the pages of this book helps to show what he was aiming at. The paper elements were no longer stuck down to a backboard but supported each other with a minimum of glueing. Edges and openings became more and more important, intervals and apertures were now as crucial as overlays and alignments.

The ragged edges help to project energy outwards, rather than containing it within a rectangle, but if this suggests a dispersal of effect, the opposite is in fact true. Somehow Davison's collages become more potent and intense despite their rough and permeable edges. These collages are multi-directional, like tapestries, or like Adrian Berg's big Regent's Park paintings of the early 1980s. They could be hung any way up and still hold their space forcefully on the wall. What could be viewed as an uncertainty about the orientation of his images was actually a hard-won freedom.

There are two key contexts in which Davison's collages may be usefully surveyed. Firstly, in the company of his painter contemporaries, such as Heron, Hilton, Irvin, Berg, Blow, William Gear, and William Scott. And secondly, in a wider more international context, situating his work alongside such artists as Schwitters, Hans Arp, Robert Motherwell and Nicolas de Staël. (Davison distrusted the paintings of de Staël, but I'm thinking of his late collage work.) To these may be added the mostly anonymous creators of African textiles. In particular, the marvellously free improvisations on African bark cloth, a potent mixture (like Davison's) of the organic and geometric, and the distinctive patterns of Kuba cloth from the Congo, made from raffia palm leaves.

Although there are occasionally cut edges to be seen in his work – especially in the early years – for the most part Davison tore his paper, thus avoiding the kind of fluency with scissors that Matisse developed, and which itself could become a mannerism. One of the great American practitioners of collage was the Abstract Expressionist Robert Motherwell. He claimed that collage was a modern substitute for still-life, citing the debris left on the tablecloth at the end of a meal. But for Davison, collage was the antithesis of still – it was all about movement and the passage through life, about active experience and a celebration of living, not *nature morte*. However, Motherwell himself also admitted the potentially vigorous nature of collage, writing in 1946: 'The sensation of physically operating on the world is very strong in the medium of *papier collé* or collage…'

In fact, Motherwell, who made his first collage in 1943, a decade before Davison began to explore the medium, considered the torn edge to be his own original contribution to the art of collage. Who did what first is always a vexed question among artists. As early as 1916 Arp had made torn paper collages, and his work bears an unexpectedly close relationship to what Davison was doing. Motherwell used collage on canvas and most often in conjunction with paint, whereas for Davison at the height of his achievement it was an altogether more restricted form, entirely composed of and reliant upon paper. Intriguingly, de Staël began composing with torn or cut out shapes of coloured paper around 1953, in what was a late phase of his own particular development. Clearly, paper collage of this sort (as opposed to the Cubist and Surrealist variants) was widely regarded as a legitimate

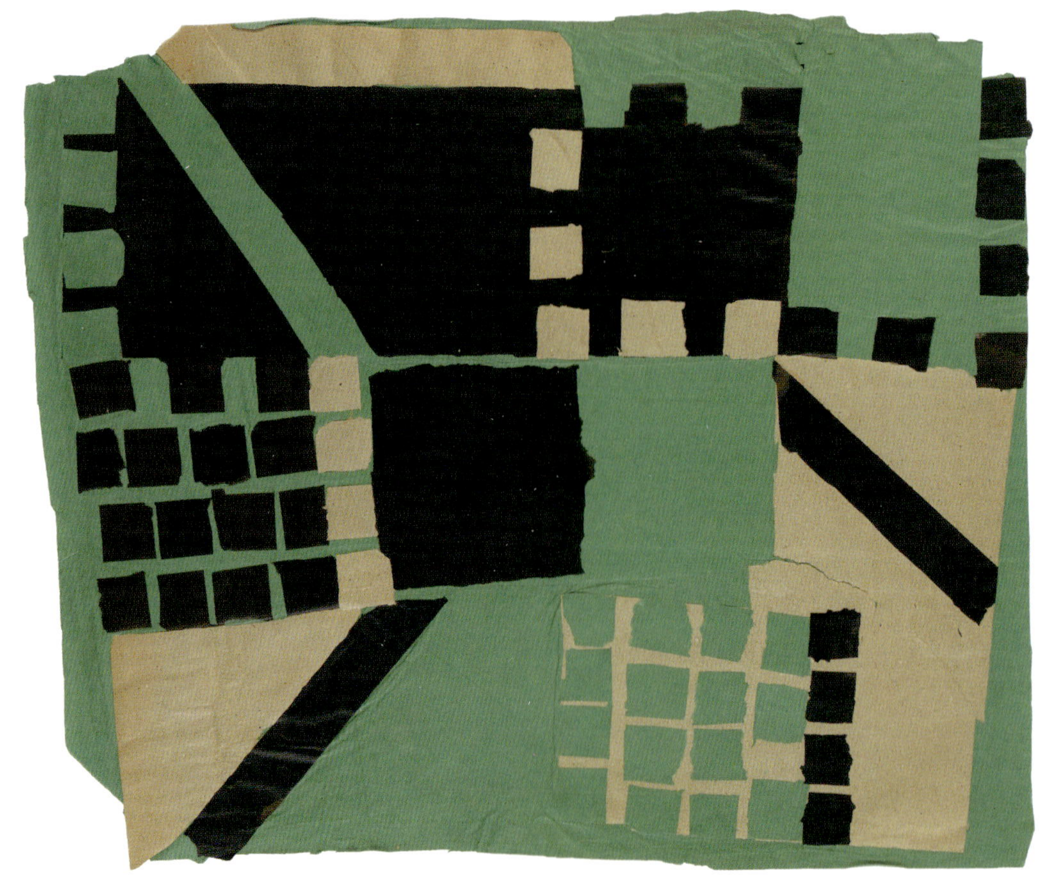

C-55   1965–71   Collage   82 × 97 cm (32.3 × 38.2")

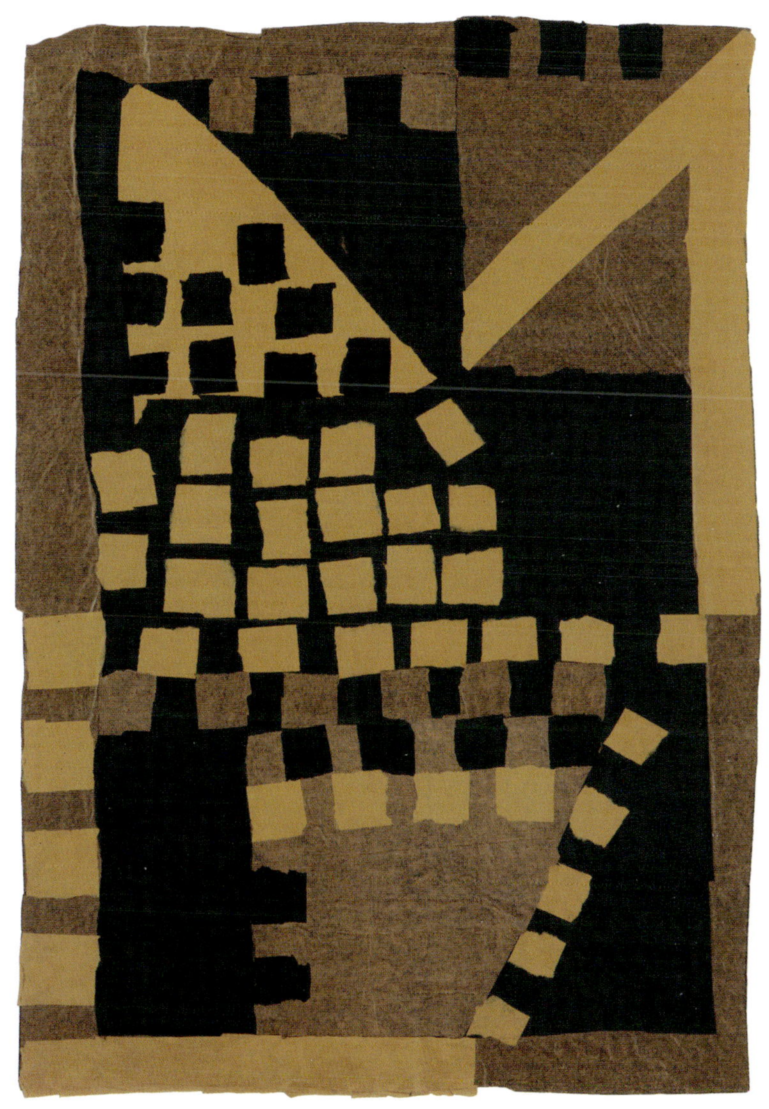

C-58 1965–71 Collage 100 × 69 cm (39.4 × 27.2")

strategy to investigate an idea or solve a problem. But no one used it exclusively in the way that Francis Davison did.

I would not want to over-emphasize any of these comparisons, but they do help to establish the international context in which Davison's work should be viewed. Generally his collages are unsigned, undated and untitled. (Interestingly, the majority of works that Davison sold to public collections *are* signed, with initials in the lower righthand corner; as are some of the collages that were shown in his Hayward Gallery solo exhibition in 1983.) The general lack of dates indicates an unwillingness to be categorised in terms of stylistic development, and underlines Davison's habit of re-working (if not actually cannibalising) earlier collages to make a new statement. The determination not to date or title the work also bespeaks a brave attempt to focus the viewer on the collage without any distractions.

There is no narrative or symbolic meaning to these works. According to his wife, the process of making a collage for Davison was one of distilling the experience of shapes and colours, and making those experiences visible. But also, Mellis thought, suggesting the *feeling* of landscapes or forests or water or mountains. There was no direct reference, but something less tangible – an emanation of a subject, such as the way Suffolk houses join onto each other or sink into the ground. Mellis believed that in a very real sense Davison's inner experiences *became* the material of his collages. As she wrote: 'The great thing about a medium like collage is that you don't have to have an *idea* in your mind consciously. You work with the paper in your hands, feeling it out without any preconceived "ideas". It is the *ultimate* immediate medium particularly as paper is so malleable.'

Also the scale of the marks could reduce the referential content of the work. Although strips of paper may be read as paths or roadways through a wild or semi-industrialized landscape, the painterly 'blobs' of colour (actually roughly torn small square-ish rectangles of paper) that often punctuate the surface are either too big or too small to be read as (for instance) buildings. The blobs are there for their own sake, as part of Davison's potent abstract design, for which they are neither too big nor too small, being perfectly judged for their purpose.

Of course, these collages are not just a play of shapes, however unorthodox the symmetries, euphonies and discords. There is here something of the electric pulse of Mondrian's New York paintings, all dance steps and syncopated beat. In relation to his late work, Mondrian spoke of the destruction of natural appearances and 'construction through continuous opposition of pure means—dynamic rhythm'. This is what Davison was doing with his dislocations of scale and changes of pace: he was dealing imaginatively with the material world in order to liberate it. His collages are about a journey through a changing world, about flux and transition. Each collage was a unique statement rather than part of a series or sequence, and each could be challenged and found wanting (and subsequently re-cycled), if it didn't reach his exacting standards of honesty and originality.

Davison drew by tearing, and thus brought variation to the predominantly flat frontal effects of glued paper. This kind of collage constructs its images in planes in a shallow space, but Davison evoked a deeper space by the apertures in his structures, and the suggestion of an endless recession beyond or behind the overlaps of torn paper. Texture and edge are crucial elements in this language. Tearing implies

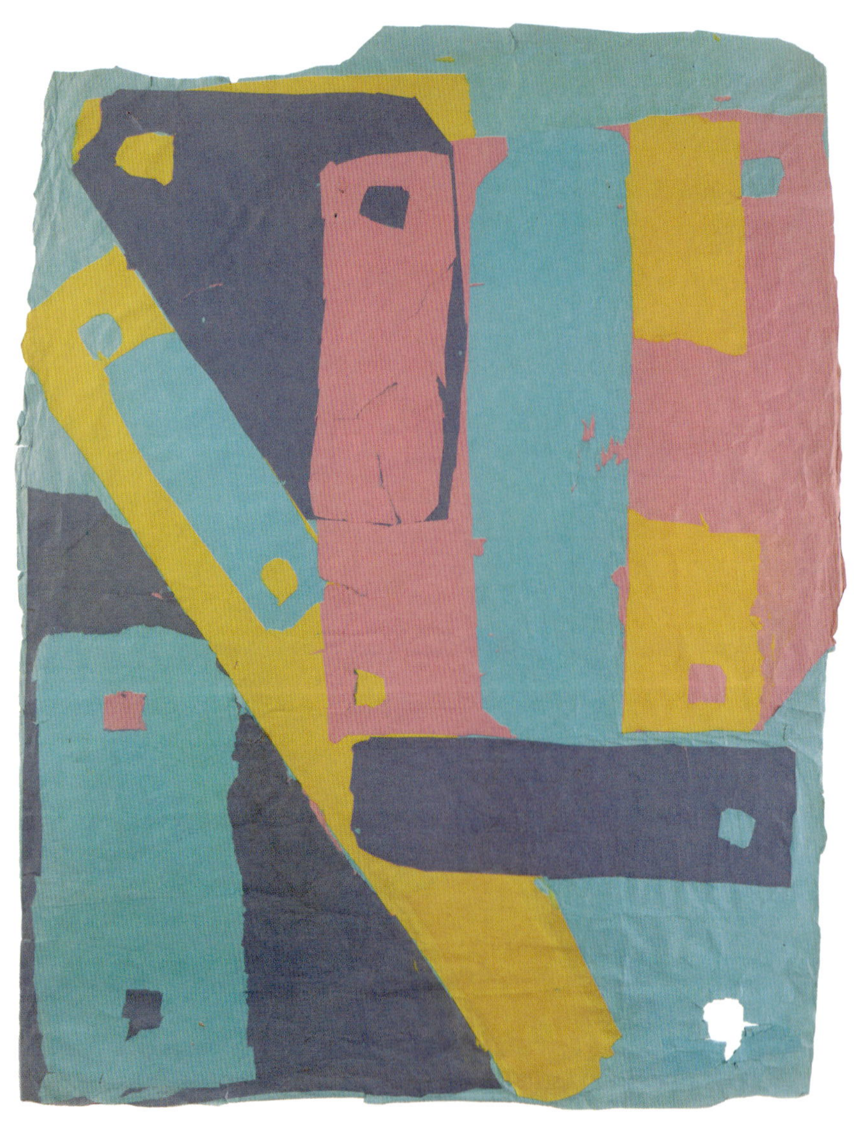

C-149   1970   Collage   147 × 112 cm (57.9 × 44.1")

violence, and can be likened to a hefty splat of paint in its declarative insistence. The repeated adding and removing of paper elements, each leaving a trace of glue or paper behind, are further articulations in the often complex web of imagery each collage creates. Layers proliferate, also contributing to a sense of depth. The patina of age and experience emerges from these formal dispositions – the *used* look of these surfaces – linking us back to the common experience of daily life, in which wrapping paper plays its multifarious roles. These large collages jump the gap between art and life: abstraction touches base once more in reality.

As he gathered confidence in his ability to structure his collage, and to tear precisely the shapes he wanted, Davison began to glue his paper elements more selectively, or even randomly. Often he wanted the 'ripped off' look, so this became the primary aim, rather than the placement of chiming or contrasting pieces. Then in time the 'ripped off' surface clearly began to seem too deliberate an effect. A development from there was to place the elements with greater assurance and less chopping and changing. A by-product of this (or was it intentional?) was that some areas of paper stood out more, sculpturally, from the picture plane. Meanwhile the negative spaces, the apertures or gaps of stillness between the visible bouts of activity, became increasingly charged and dominant, adding to the spatial complexity of the images.

Collage is a highly sophisticated art form, despite (in Davison's case) its often slightly rumpled appearance. It draws upon both thought and feeling, rationality and intuition. It can also engage with extremes of melancholy and joy, emotions which Francis Davison experienced

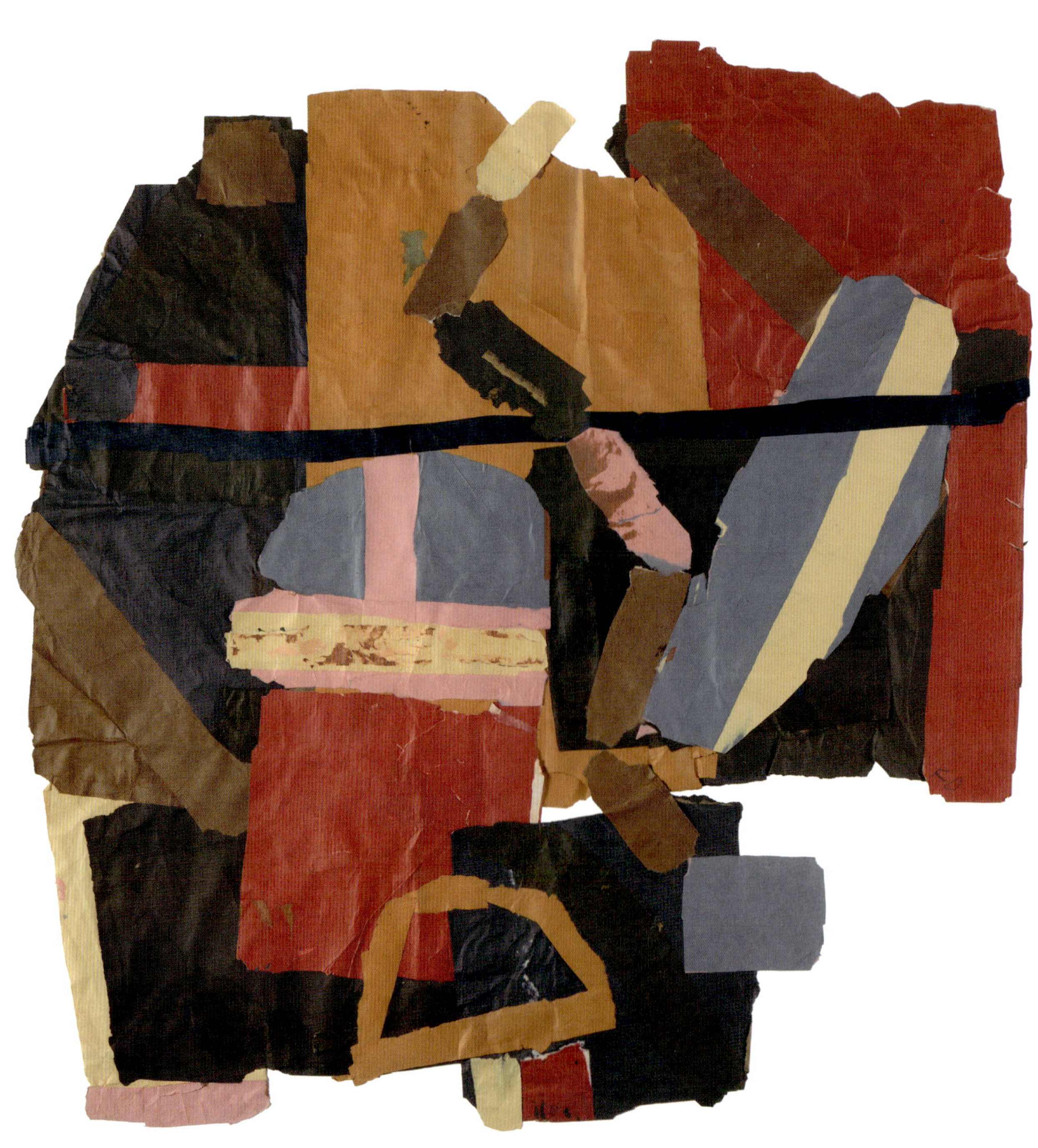

G-609   1978–83   Collage   117 × 110 cm (46.1 × 43.3")

in nature, art and poetry, but which he best communicated through collage.

In Davison's fast-flowing or more deliberately paced linearity, often discontinuous but still strongly assertive, and in his canny interstitial inventiveness, there is a distinctly tactile quality and a rootedness that is essential to the raw elegance and poetic insight of his imagery.

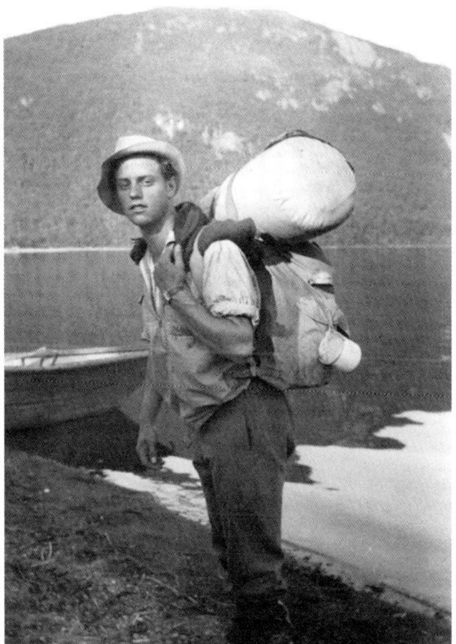

There's fierce wit too in these damaged shapes, that don't pretend to be perfect squares or rectangles. Davison's directness is challenging to our preconceptions of what art is and what it can do. He created a new and unexpected harmony of relational structures from apparent disunion, with colour relationships echoing the interlocking shapes. These crenellated, cogged and toothed shapes – which Mellis called 'nitched' – have a determined irregularity, admirably suited to such a difficult, tough-minded and independent individual.

Introduction

Francis Davison was one of the most innovative and inventive artists to work in post-war England, and yet he remains largely unknown to the general public, and even unfamiliar to the artistic community. He began as a poet but turned to painting in the 1940s before finding his true *métier* as a collagist in 1952. Self-taught but encouraged and nurtured by his second wife, the painter and sculptor Margaret Mellis, Davison invented a brand of paper collage using only found colour. Although he cut some of his materials to begin with, his speciality was to tear the paper and orchestrate the pieces in rhythmic abstract arrangements of shapes and divisions, which sometimes recall the turning and coiling of the human internal organs or the maze of the brain. The improvisatory nature of the work was important, but even more so the manner in which it transfigured its raw materials.

Although he has had influential supporters over the years, Davison's work is little publicized. There is no entry for him in the *Dictionary of National Biography*, nor does he appear in such standard texts on the subject as *Collage: The Making of Modern Art* by Brandon Taylor (2004). Many surveys of Modern British art have ignored or sidelined him. Yet Davison fits comfortably within the great tradition of British art, the linear drive of Celtic manuscript illumination, the national gifts of abstract design and ornament which make the Book of Kells and the Lindisfarne Gospels such masterpieces. British drawing and illumination were of European stature in the Middle Ages, and the great highpoints of British art in the following centuries have most often been involved with the power of draughtsmanship. In one way, Davison's work can be seen as interlocking patterns in space, the artist taking a line for a meander, using colour and tone to emphasize and illuminate his pattern-making. And it should be noted at once how unliterary and formally potent his work was for a man whose first choice of career was poetry.

During his lifetime, there was only one really substantial Davison exhibition – at the Hayward Gallery, 10 February– 17 April 1983. The effort of putting it on was a severe strain on the artist, particularly as it made public an art which he considered to be essentially private. The catalogue is wonderfully discreet. Square in format, it measures 10" by 10". A plain warm grey cover carries the artist's name on the outside, with no other information at all. A flap inside contains an absolute minimum of information: the names of artist, exhibition ('Paper Collages') and venue, the dates of the show, and the Arts Council's suzerainty. Inside are 10 full-page colour illustrations of the collages showing their edges and looking colourful and dramatic, presented on a greener grey art paper. They have no titles, dates or dimensions. At the centre of the stapled publication is a page of text by Julian Spalding, the show's begetter, which limits itself to a formal consideration of the work on show. On the last page there's a paragraph of Acknowledgements thanking artist and writer and stating the following: 'Davison's work was first purchased for the Council's collection in 1962 but exhibitions have been few and far between until the shows in Sheffield, Oxford and Durham last year. We are delighted to add the Hayward and London to that list.' Aside from that, there is absolutely no information about the artist.

Prunella Clough was famous for requesting that only
a minimum of biographical data be published in her
catalogues, and she continued to be successfully self-
effacing throughout her career, but Davison's bid for
anonymity went much further. He didn't even allow a date
of birth in the Hayward catalogue. The work was there to
speak for itself, and the usual human context was largely
denied. This was the way Davison wanted to play it, and had
he still been alive today, he would doubtless have tried to
ensure that this book also was permitted to contain only a
bare minimum of biographical background. Whilst respecting
his wishes that the work should be paramount and be the
real reason for any study of his life and career, I think it
important to establish a framework, however meagre, within
which to present the art. I never met Francis Davison, but I
did meet his widow Margaret Mellis, and recently published
a monograph about her painting and sculpture. A slightly
more detailed account of their life together will be found
in that volume, but a modicum of biographical detail will
feature here in order to adumbrate the human element of
the equation. Whatever Davison himself may have thought
or desired, the kind of man he was and how he lived to some
extent dictated the work he made.

What was he like? His *Carte de Séjour de Résident Ordinaire*
from Antibes in 1947, his residency card, contains a small
black-and-white photo of him in profile. The 28-year-
old Davison had strong features with a prominent nose,
thick hair and his head stuck out at the back – a sure sign,
according to Bertie Wooster describing Jeeves, of uncommon
intelligence. The museum director Julian Spalding described
meeting Davison for the first time: 'He was lean and
intelligent; his actions and his eyes had the alertness of a

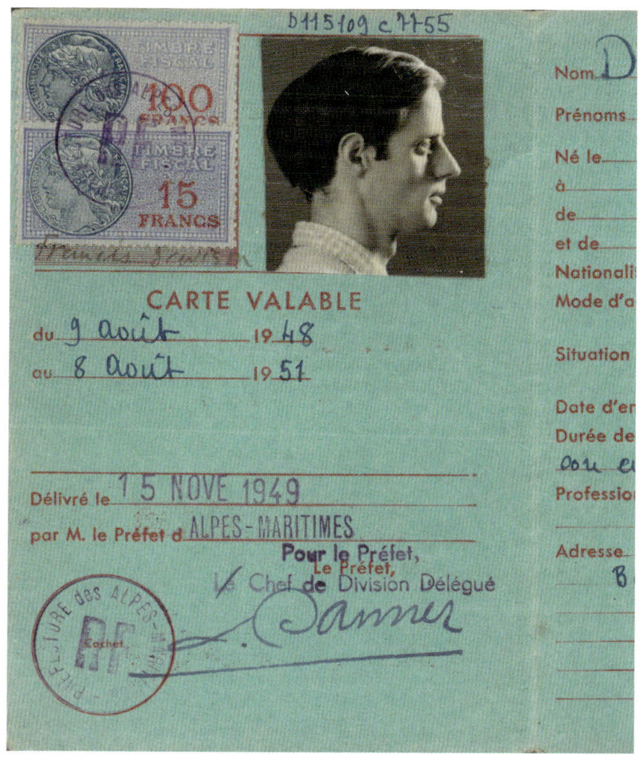

Portrait of the artist as a young man: Francis Davison's Carte de Séjour.

wild bird. I felt at times that I was being watched, but from a great distance.' Davison's step-son, Telfer Stokes, recalls his languid manner (which belied a frighteningly volatile temper) and habit of taking slow bicycle rides, observing the world, occasionally stopping to make a drawing on the back of an envelope.

Davison's oldest friend was the painter Patrick Heron who wrote of him primarily as a poet and wordsmith. In the memoir he composed for the catalogue of the 1986 Davison retrospective at the Redfern Gallery, Heron remembers him writing 'incessantly, filling small notebooks that he carried about with him, and exercise books, day by day, wherever he was. From these it was revealed that he wrote and re-wrote, with extraordinary application and concentration, producing version after version of a line, or a verse, or a theme. When he came with me on a two-week holiday to St Ives in 1943 (when we stayed with Bernard Leach), in addition to the poetry notebooks he was also carrying a small sketchbook – and it's from this trip that I first remember him drawing the landscape (with indelible purple pencil or pen and ink, smudged with thumb and spit).'

Heron recalls that Davison's letters and conversations were intensely memorable. 'And his *talk*, whether spoken or written, was, all his friends would agree, one of his most fascinating gifts. It was *how* he said what he said that was always so funny, so sharp, so original in its perceptiveness, and so quirkily profound.' And Heron concludes that Davison was 'one of the most remarkable friends I ever had.'

By contrast, Wilhelmina Barns-Graham wrote extensively (in a letter of May 1986 to her old friend and contemporary Margaret Mellis) about Davison's art and the Hayward show, and was full of praise, quoting Gertrude Stein on Gris: 'He made something that is to be measured and that is something'; and: 'to complicate things in a new way that is easy – but to see things in a new way that is really difficult.' Barns-Graham admitted that she at first wished the collages were paintings, but then realized that this was to miss the point of them, 'because what they *are* is so important'. She praised the lack of written information in the catalogue – 'few artists have this humility' – because then the visitor was confronted directly with the work. She admired the scale of the collages and the unpretentiousness of the medium and ended by saying 'I should think they must be stimulating and energy-giving to live with.'

Interestingly, she also made this observation: 'This work with its inner construction so much more thought-out than at first hits the eye – should do the younger artists a lot of good.' A couple of years after Davison's death, the young Damien Hirst sought him out and discovered instead his widow, Margaret Mellis. Hirst, a student from Leeds, had been seriously struck by Davison's Hayward exhibition and modelled his own work for the next year or two on the collages he so admired. (They 'blew me away', he said later.) Davison rather than Schwitters (as so often reported) is the guiding inspiration behind Hirst's work of this period. So Barns-Graham's prediction came true in at least one instance, though quite what long-term effect Davison's work might be said to have had on Hirst's artistic development is another matter.

Collage is often thought of as a child's amusement or a Victorian parlour game, yet the re-configuration of fragments holds special meaning for Modernism, and collage (in the sense of bits of paper pasted down in a new order) plays a key role in the artistic sensibility of the twentieth century. There is something provisional and contingent about collage which seems to suit our modern mood: as if the work is not really finished in the way a fully-worked-up painting is. Collage transgresses definitions: it's not painting, though it often resembles it, nor is it drawing, though it can perform similar functions. Collage emphasizes the materiality of the picture by attaching real things (rather than just paint) to the surface, and thus brings the work into the realm of sculpture. Collage re-cycles the discarded and overlooked, what's left over after history has rampaged past, after the consumers have consumed. Real objects with their own pre-existing truth are brought to the construction of a picture. In Davison's collages, they are totally transformed and re-shaped. His procedure re-combined actual physical surfaces by means of hand, eye and glue. In the mature work, the paper was always torn, never cut – one of its main distinguishing features.

There is no other artist who made work quite like Davison's. One looks for parallels and finds a few possible comparisons, but they are not close. Among the Russians, the spare coloured paper collages of Olga Rozanova come to mind. Matisse was of course a great master of collage, but he cut his paper and became a virtuoso with the scissors. Among the British, Gwyther Irwin (1931–2008), who had been briefly taught at school by Roger Hilton, attempted a form of torn collage in the 1950s and 60s that has something in common with Davison's practice. Irwin claimed he 'wrote' his pictures, making complex abstract weavings like Persian carpets from torn strips of old posters. For a time, Irwin was very popular, and John Russell waxed lyrical in *The Sunday Times* in 1963, writing that Irwin 'cannot put two pieces of torn paper side by side without creating an atmosphere of poetic tenderness'. Irwin's use of his raw material was very different from Davison's and has more in common with the early torn-paper collages of Robyn Denny (born 1930). The shredded posters Irwin used represented the popular life of the street, and the language (or at least the letters) printed on them was often incorporated into his imagery, to good effect. Davison was far more pure in his approach, never allowing writing (or any form of narrative) to enter his resolutely abstract images.

In rubbish-strewn Britain we are surrounded by bits of torn paper littering the streets and hedges, so it takes a very special talent to put waste paper together and create something from it of such dynamic and memorable interest. In these collages, the raw material is completely translated and transformed. As an artist friend of mine said of Davison, he gave great virtue to scraps of paper.

1
Early Life and Writing

Francis Davison was born on 9th June 1919, and adopted as a baby. He was unaware of this until he discovered the fact by accident when he saw his passport in his early teens, but he was never to discover who his real parents were. Adopted by George and Joan Davison, he became one of a family of five children, four of them adopted. (Doreen was the only natural child of the couple.) George Davison was a millionaire who made his money from the Eastman Kodak Company, which specialized in inexpensive cameras and photographic film products, and of which he became managing director in 1900. He commissioned the Glasgow architect George Walton, a contemporary of Charles Rennie Mackintosh, to design shops and display stands for Kodak, as well as houses for himself. When George Davison determined to leave England and settle in France, partly for his health and partly to be near his close friends the Scottish Colourist JD Fergusson and his wife, the avant-garde dancer and teacher Margaret Morris, Walton was part of the team.

Davison bought an unfinished nineteenth-century villa at Cannes with already something of a history. Begun for the financier James Close, of the City firm of Close Brothers, it was still only partially built when acquired by the King of the Belgians, who owned the property before George Davison bought it and commissioned George Walton to re-work it. In honour of its youthful occupants, the house was re-named the Chateau des Enfants, Boulevard du Cap, Antibes. As the architectural historian Alan Powers has noted, Davison employed Walton to install fittings taken

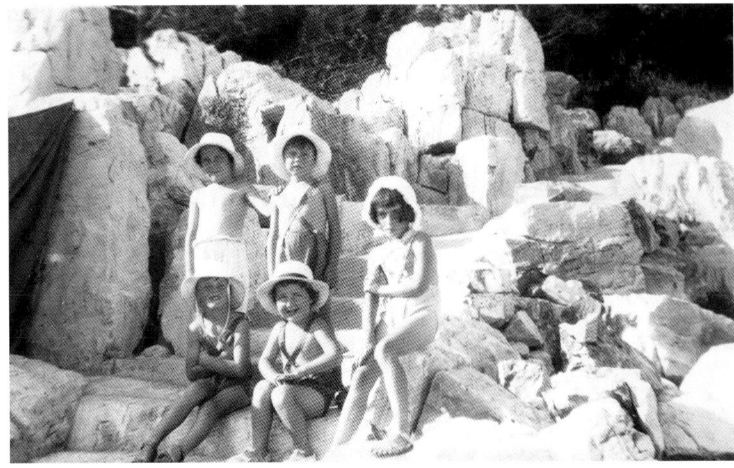

Francis standing in
the middle second row,
at the bathing place,
Chateau des Enfants,
Cap d'Antibes, circa 1927

from his previous house in Harlech, including a pipe organ,
in an attempt to domesticate the massive interior spaces of
the chateau. When George Davison died in 1931, his widow
Joan commissioned Walton to build a memorial chapel in the
grounds even though her husband had been an atheist and
anarchist.

Francis was twelve when his adoptive father died, and the
boy was brought up largely by Mrs Davison and Emily Gerig,
a Swiss governess. Apparently, Joan Davison prided herself
on being modern, and George Walton was instructed to
design appropriately fashionable furniture. Alan Powers, in
a stimulating essay on Davison, points out the similarity
between the layout of carpets at the Chateau and the design
of Davison's collages, citing a photograph in Karen Moon's
monograph on George Walton which shows the nursery at
the Chateau des Enfants with Walton's rugs on the floors.
To Powers this photograph seems to suggest the sense in
Davison's collages of looking down on an abstracted
landscape.

The family entertained a great deal at the Chateau, and among the guests were Oskar Kokoschka and SJ Peploe, together with Fergusson and Morris. The setting was lovely: there were 24 acres of land surrounding the house, a spinney of pine trees, palms, fig groves and fruit trees, and a private bathing beach. Francis went to live there when he was two and received more affection from Emily Gerig, the governess, than from his adoptive mother. (It was Gerig who led Francis away from the prevailing Catholicism of his upbringing towards a lifelong Protestant faith.) In later life, Davison wasn't keen for his friends to meet his family; and as his second wife Margaret Mellis remarked: 'Once I met them, I could see the point.'

Davison was sent to various schools in France and finally in 1932 to St George's co-educational boarding school in Harpenden, Essex, where he met the future painter Patrick Heron, who was to become a lifelong friend. St George's was founded the same year as Bedales, but had a slightly different emphasis – valuing highly rugby football and Chapel. Heron recalled that Davison, who was known to him thereafter as Jacko, was an aggressive rugby player and a 'fiercely devout "warden" or verger of the school chapel'. Davison drew and painted from childhood, but his early passion was for words and his ambition was to be a poet. The friendship between the two boys developed and really took wing after Davison showed Heron his poetry, recalled by Heron as 'a moment of revelation' – perhaps because it demonstrated an equal commitment as his own to painting. Heron wrote many years later: 'I immediately thought of him as a very remarkable poet; and I printed two of his poems, in 1936, in a special "Literary Supplement" of the school magazine which I edited.'

When war was declared Davison's family fled from France to Jersey, and subsequently to St Ives, ironically to the house below Little Parc Owles, the war-time home of Adrian Stokes and Margaret Mellis. At this point there was no social interchange between the two families, though later the alliance would grow intimate. The Chateau des Enfants was occupied by the Italian SS during the Second World War, and the Davisons were never to live in it again, though it did prove to be a useful bolthole for Francis in the immediate post-war period.

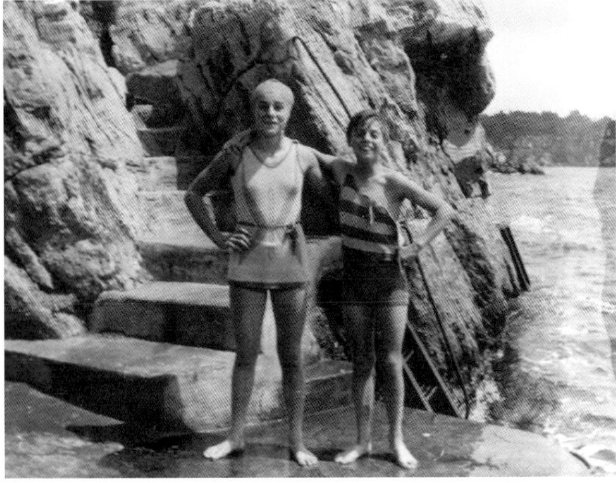

Francis on the right, the bathing place, Chateau des Enfants, Cap d'Antibes, circa 1934

Friendship with Heron also meant acceptance into his family, and Davison often stayed with the Herons at their home in Welwyn Garden City. Tom Heron, Patrick's father, had worked in Cornwall as managing director of Cryséde Silks, subsequently setting up his own firm, Cresta Silks, which eventually bought Cryséde. Both firms specialized in beautiful hand-block-printed pure silk dresses, so for the Heron children (and their friends) there was a background in colour and design right from the start. Patrick knew from an early age that he wanted to be a painter and so elected to study at the Slade while Davison went up to St Catherine's, Cambridge to read English and Anthropology. Both were conscientious objectors in the war, and Davison was involved in social work, for some time living among the Yorkshire mining communities. His life, never well-documented, goes a bit hazy at this point, but it seems clear that he married a girl called Brenda in August 1944, with Heron as best man.

If Davison didn't get on particularly well with his own family, the friendship with Patrick Heron's parents, Tom and Eulalie, lasted for the rest of their respective lives. From time to time, Eulalie wrote Jacko long newsy letters about friends and family, and they visited each other's homes. The Herons came to hear Francis preach a sermon when he lived in Suffolk, and the deep affection between them persisted despite a slackening of visits as age encroached. In fact Eulalie survived Jacko, and wrote in grief to Mellis: 'He was always a special person to me.' She continued: 'I don't know why he has counted for so much in my life – except that everything he said and did was uniquely "Jacko" and couldn't have been anyone else.'

Davison received a small allowance from his mother, but when he married he had to supplement this income by teaching at St Edward's School in Hampstead. The marriage lasted scarcely much more than a year, and Davison promptly gave up his teaching when he no longer had a wife to support, returning full-time to his literary endeavours. He wrote more poems and drew a little. Some writers have suggested that Davison destroyed most of his poetry. He may well have had a clear out from time to time, but a considerable quantity of typescript poems still exists, mostly dating from the 1930s and 1940s. There are also notebooks and masses of jottings. And a series of French exercise books contains the hand-written parts of a connected narrative of symbolic prose which comprise an unpublished novel called *The Burning Cage*.

Davison was certainly intent on publishing his work, and continued to have ambitions in this direction for the next decade or so. A selection of poems written in 1939–40 was typed and sent to TS Eliot at Faber & Faber, who replied generously at the beginning of February 1941 with detailed comments and encouragement. He praised Davison's skill with words but recommended that he try to move beyond that 'to a greater intensity of simplification'.

At this point, Davison seems to be have been experimenting with identity. One notebook is inscribed Douglas Davison, and at least one early letter from Patrick Heron addressed him as Douglas rather than Francis. He published poetry, and a Joycean/Beckettian monologue called 'Adamanodetoevening', under the name Francis Douglas in a magazine called *Now, A Journal of Good Writing,* No 6, Summer 1941. Other contributors included Julian Symons, Oswell Blakeston and Roy Fuller.

Heron certainly took his friend seriously as a poet, though in a letter of 1943 he suggested he was writing too much. 'I feel that you are *always* making (up to and beyond the limits of your strength) these "raids on the inarticulate" and these excursions beyond the frontiers of consciousness which are certainly the distinct activity of poet and painter, or should be. But do you think that simple force and power might be gained more by seeking a subject matter in home waters so to speak?'

Reading Davison's poetry today reveals a body of largely immature work paradoxically restricted by its evident ambition to succeed. His poems make grandiose attempts at timeless generalities, but too often lack the specific intensity that can carry off such aims. When he tried less, he achieved more, and when he wrote from what he knew he was at his most successful. He was a very literary stylist and echoes of other writers abound. Clearly he was trying to exorcise a degree of distress of the soul, but all too often he had no clear vision of what he was trying to say. (The personal meanings are not lifted to a public level.) His verse lacks the precision of image to carry his general statements; hence the incoherence and the echoes. Too often it's as if he hadn't properly visualized what he was trying to say – quite the opposite, as we shall see, of the straightforward clarity of his early drawings.

For Davison, poetry may well have been an outlet for private misery, but that is not enough to guarantee writing that will speak to others. However, there are good things to be found among the mass of typescript poems that survive. For example, this is no 5 in a sequence of short poems:

Image of my desire, a solid granite mass

reclines beside the sleeping beach;

its careful draperies move but cannot stir

sensation's strings; and wandering through the maze

of senses mind constructs

a shape in space that leaves no room for my regret.

Here is a poem called *Adolescence*:

At first I wandered in a maze

where nothing with dead nothing made

the midnight image of my days

seem living in the dream.

I followed those who went before

where they lay down I put my head

in pillows pressed and ruffled beds

through corridors down which they drooped

I cut the slanting sunlight beams.

All in the hall were strangely moved

in a slow kaleidoscope

I could not fit the heads to necks

there was no socket for each bone

and no connection of the parts.

At first I wandered in a maze

following through that one dark door

where those unknown to me had gone,

until I knew the face and eyes

and could erect the fallen days

and resurrect the golden scene

that seemed but fragments of a dream

when first I wandered in a maze.

And here is a poem about a father:

My father died when I was young
with a severe expression on his face,
under the shadow of a casino
fortified by the usual rites.

Timid and turbulent he stumbled on the shore
a ghostly symbol of his age;
dressed in white suits, immaculately clean,
shaking his fist at the briny rose.

Many years after, now the fortune is spent
with no improvement to the daughter or son,
I see the death-mask like a marble
feigning severity and calm of mind.

I hear new voices that whimper in heaven
(higher now than his six per cents)
speaking the words he could not utter then
with a true movement of angelic bones.

Many moons after, many years
and many faces fallen like coins,
after the shoes with the soles gone out of them
the rain still falling and the three per cents.

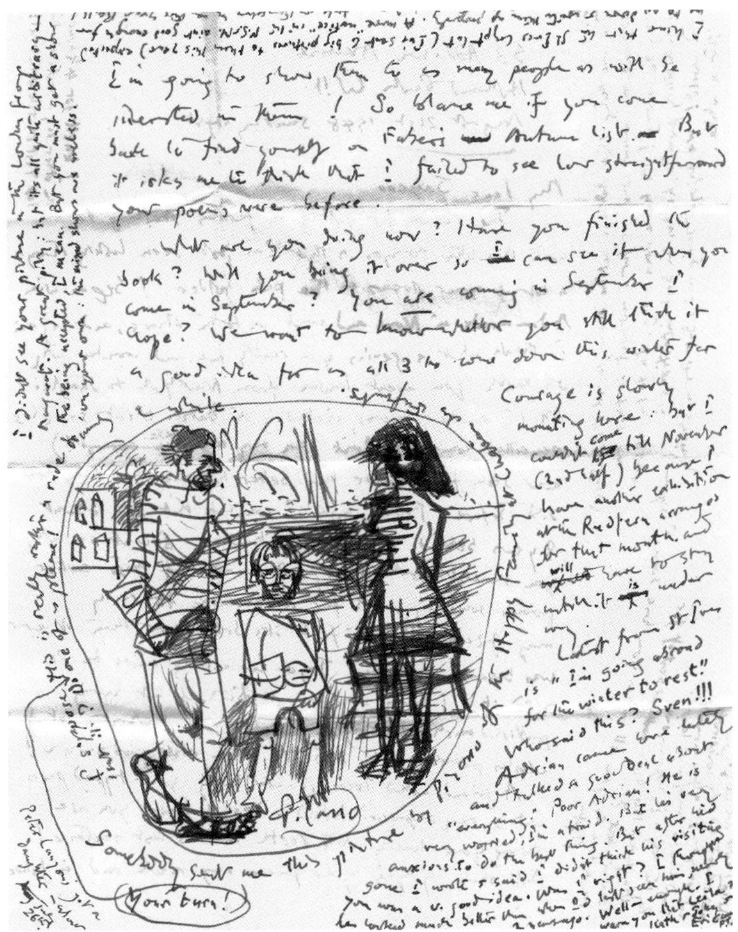

Extract from a letter from Patrick Heron to Francis Davison, 1948.

2

Meeting Margaret Mellis and Painting

Francis Davison's real life as an artist began when he met the painter Margaret Mellis in St Ives in 1946. Davison was staying with Patrick Heron, who now had a home in Cornwall, and Mellis was married to the writer and painter Adrian Stokes, who had just left her. The Stokeses had a young son called Telfer and had been living together in a rather grand house called Little Parc Owles, above Carbis Bay. This was the house to which Adrian and Margaret invited Ben Nicholson and Barbara Hepworth (and their triplets) to sit out the war, and thus inadvertently founded the St Ives school of post-war abstract painting and sculpture.

Mellis was briefly involved with another man, partly on the rebound from her runaway husband, partly obliging Stokes with grounds to sue her for divorce (which was his solution to running off with her sister). Adrian had asked Patrick and Delia Heron to look after Margaret while he was in London, and they introduced her to Francis. They all ended up staying together in Little Parc Owles in pretty good humour considering the various strains upon them. Mellis recalled her first meeting with Davison: 'He just came into the house and I'd forgotten he was coming and we came face to face and I thought "Oh that's someone I can really like", and he thought the same thing.' Both had been hurt by failed marriages and their relationship was at first wary and deliberately restricted to friendship: they treated each other with delicacy and consideration. Mellis in particular was in a state of despair and was amazed in later years that Francis put up with it. Still

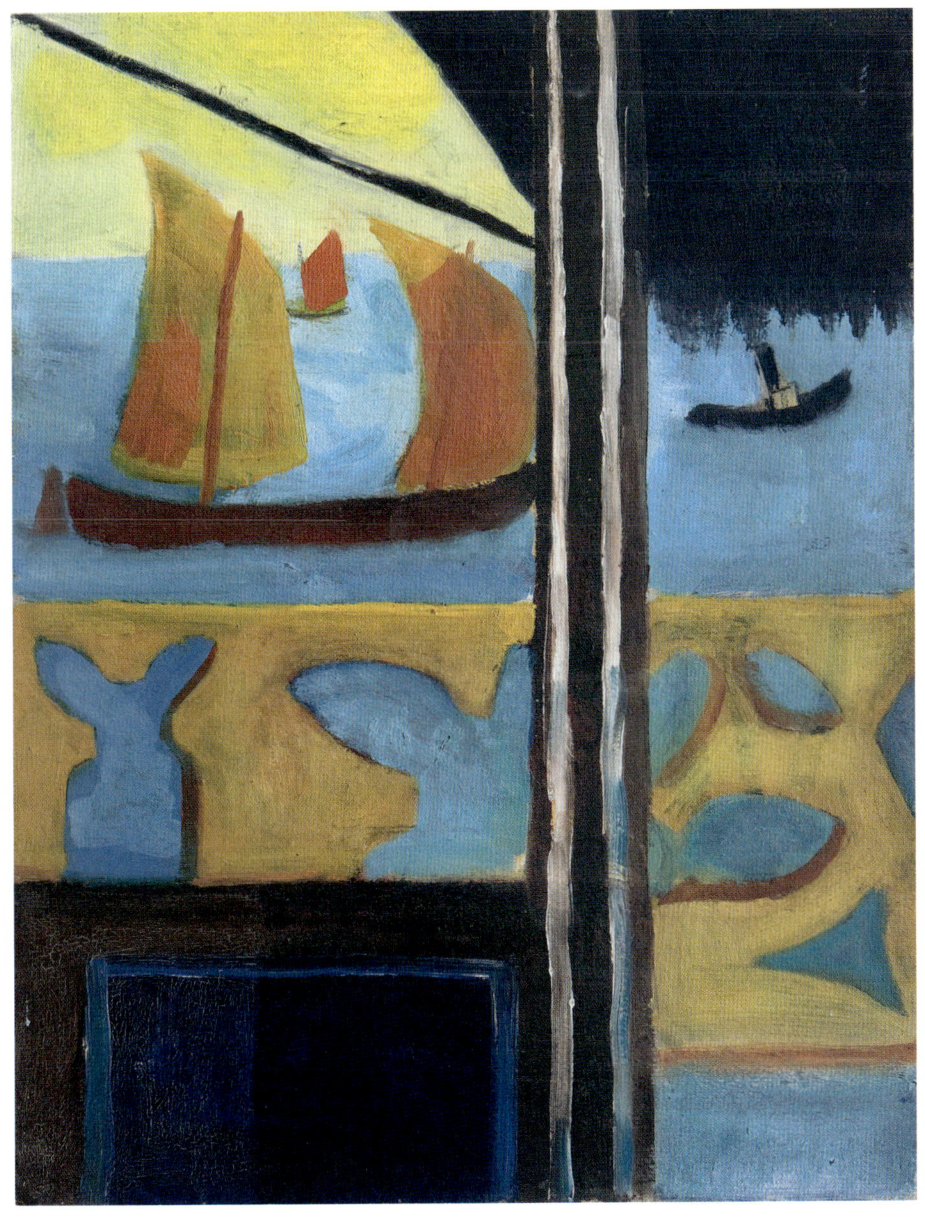

O-11 1948 39.9 × 29.7 cm (15.7 × 11.7") Private collection

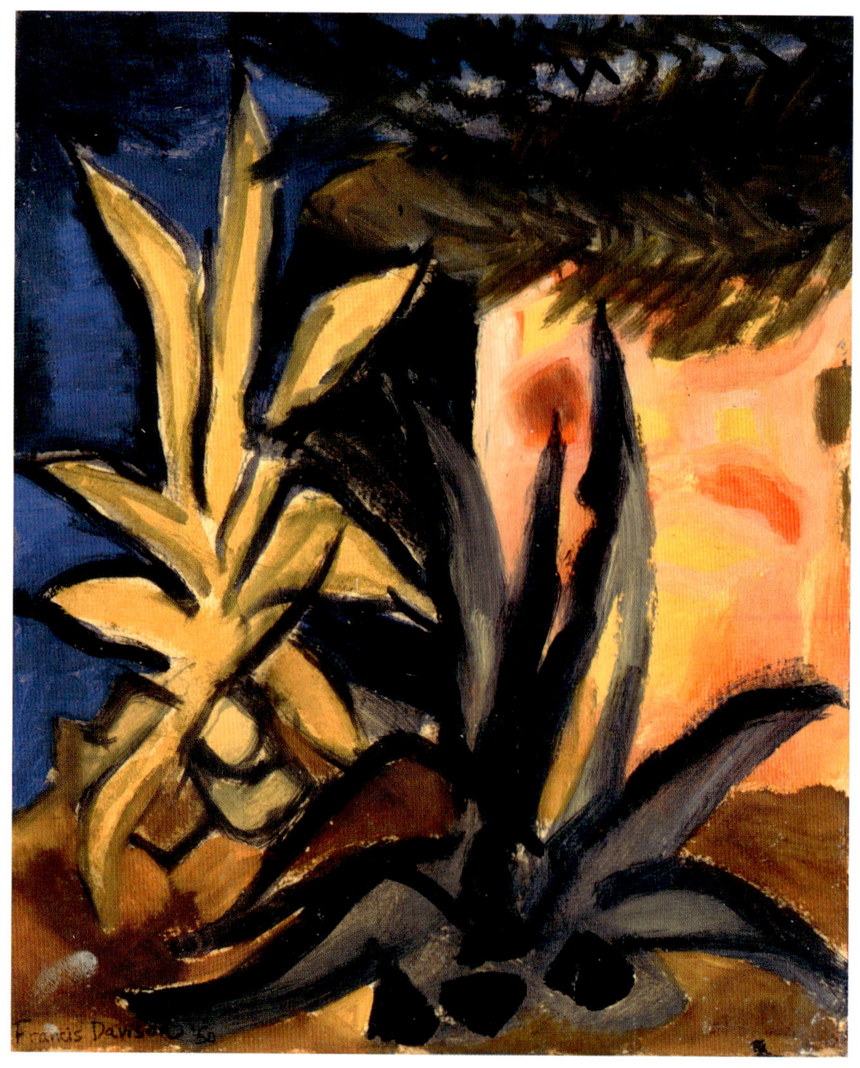

O-64   1948   Oil on board   24.1 × 19.1 cm (9.5 × 7.5")   Private collection

in love with Adrian, she was deeply unhappy. 'I used to wake up crying, go to bed crying and it went on for ages.'

In January 1947 Francis helped Margaret clear out Little Parc Owles and they both moved back to London, Francis to his flat in Shrewsbury House, Cheyne Walk, and Margaret to one room she shared with Telfer, in a flat with her sister's friends. The two sisters remained close, despite Adrian leaving one for the other, and although there were complications of every sort in the years to come, the principal parties all stayed on remarkably good terms.

In the summer of 1947, Davison and Mellis left England and moved into the Davison chateau in Cap d'Antibes. Although this sounds very grand, the reality was rather different. The building had been occupied and considerably knocked about as the local Fascist HQ, there was no electricity or water, and the pre-war staff was reduced to a single gardener and the concierge who, thankfully, was a superb cook. Living was however cheap, and Mellis and Davison subsisted largely on the vegetables they grew and milk from goats they kept. Their friendship and mutual support gradually developed into more intimate relations, but not until quite some time had elapsed after they moved to Antibes. They had a small income: Francis still had his allowance and Adrian paid Margaret maintenance. There was only money for essentials, and when Francis wore a hole in his shoe it had to be filled with a bit of rubber bathmat.

Telfer recalls:

> Chateau des Enfants was like a single-storey castle, there was only a first floor at either end. It had almost square castellations in its four corners, and was long and thin and rectangular. The two squares had rooms facing inwards around a central area.

The corner we lived in was half-covered by the roof, overlooking the courtyard, with what would have been a fountain in the middle paved in white marble slabs. A long lofty passage ran between the squares at either end. It was a derelict building when we got there, and it also had the feeling of being incomplete. The Chateau had many bathrooms but no running water, no phone and no electricity. We camped in one corner of a large building whose vast cellar was over-run by rats, cooked with fir cones in a fire place, had oil lamps for light, and water had to be fetched.

It had stood empty since the Italian SS had occupied it during the war, and there had been some rather strange damage done. In the main drawing room which led out onto a terrace exactly in the middle of the building (off the lofty passage) was an organ built into the side wall, with a room behind it to house all the pipes. Someone had been in there and it looked as if they'd gone berserk: the pipes had been attacked with a sharp instrument and most of them had been decapitated...

The garden that led down to the rocks and the Med was enormous. Here and there among the pine trees there were clearings, orchards of fig and mulberry, a walled garden to the left hand side that had an orchard of orange and lemon trees. The garden was overgrown and thick with pine trees, Ali Baba pots at the ends of gravel walkways which were empty and big enough to hide a person, connecting to paths leading down to the bathing place. It was a lonely and frightening paradise for a seven to nine year old.

In this very different context, Margaret set about rebuilding her shattered psyche by returning to the safe foundations of representational painting, after her recent (and more radical) experiments with abstract collage and sculpture. She picked up the traces of her Francophile Scottish training and took this further in School of Paris paintings of rhythmic toughness and bold colour. Clearly interested in pattern, she painted the subjects around her and re-made them with structural inventiveness. Francis followed suit, drawing constantly. He also began to paint seriously for the first time.

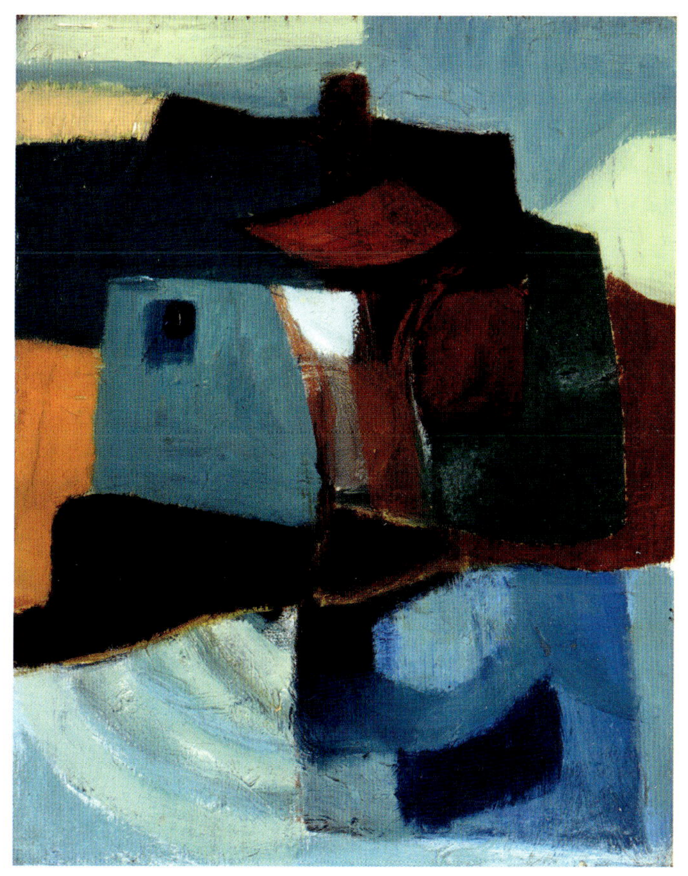

O-181 1950 Oil on board 12.7 × 9.9 cm (5 × 3.9") Private collection

Undoubtedly as an artist Mellis led the way. She was an enabler by nature, and gave both her first husband Adrian Stokes and her second Francis Davison the confidence also to become painters. Of course both were talented, but it was her ability to form and give direction to these inchoate artistic personalities which made their lives as artists possible. This great generosity of spirit in Mellis was not particularly well-repaid by either man. Stokes left her and although Davison stayed, he was very demanding and tended to be jealous of her art. On the other hand, his own work did take off in an extraordinarily significant manner. Looking back on her life from the vantage point of 1997, when I asked her if Francis had influenced her work, Mellis commented: 'He only started painting because I did, I was always painting. I had the influence on *him*. In fact, I brought him up. Then he got frightfully good and went right past.'

Although Davison had been drawing from childhood, it is remarkable how competent and assured was the work he made in the 1940s. On the evidence of his early sketchbooks and the rolls of drawings that have survived the various holocausts to which he subjected his early output, he began very swiftly to look like a fully-fledged artist. Living in France with Mellis he drew a great deal: the landscape, the sea and shore, still-life subjects. He used charcoal, ink, conté – whatever was available, and the paper was also very much what came to hand. There are drawings on scraps of re-used paper, on envelopes or brown wrapping paper, or on the blank verso of the cover of a music score, for example, divided up into several pieces for separate studies. These are strong rhythmic representational drawings, quite similar to what Patrick Heron was doing at the time, though without the art historical consciousness.

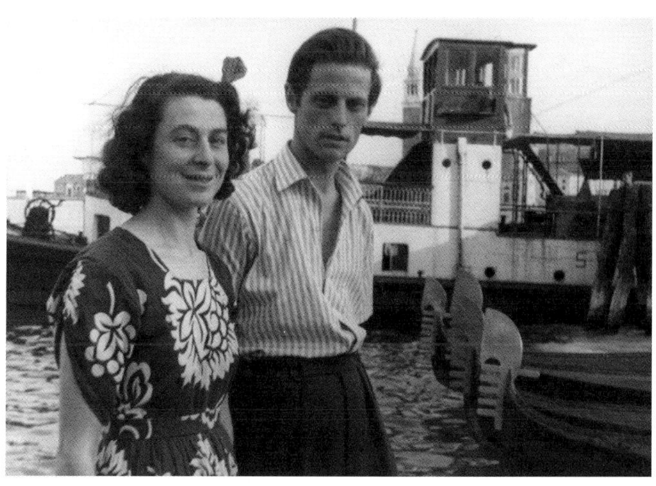

With Margaret Mellis in
Venice, 1948

Among specific subjects there's
a drawing of Cézanne's great
favourite, Mont St Victoire, and
a harbour scene on the back
of an envelope postmarked
June 1948. Trees and woodland
are favourite subjects, and no
doubt the wooded garden of the
Chateau offered a rich range of
motifs. Finally, their relationship
blossoming, Margaret and
Francis decided to get married
at Nice in January 1948, and
honeymooned in Venice. In 1949 the couple went back to
Venice and stayed at the Hotel Gabrieli (according to a card
from Patrick Heron addressed to them there in June). Venice
was plainly a huge inspiration to both artists, but particularly
to Francis. There are several of his sketchbooks filled with
busy, energetic studies of the canals and gondolas, the lagoon
and the vaporettos, and especially the towers and domes of
the churches looming everywhere. A series of drawings of the
canals seen through a pierced foliate stone balcony led to
paintings of the same subject. In all, it was a fruitful time.

The style of these practised-looking drawings is the reverse
of tentative, they are determined and vehement and say what
they want to say with a skilled economy of means and notable
inventiveness. There is a bold simplification of image often in
evidence and a remarkable sophistication of means and visual
perception for a man who had up until now considered himself
a poet rather than a painter. Davison's earliest paintings are
dated to 1947/9, such as *Plants on a Beach* (see O-128, page
46), which seems to summon up the half-wild existence at

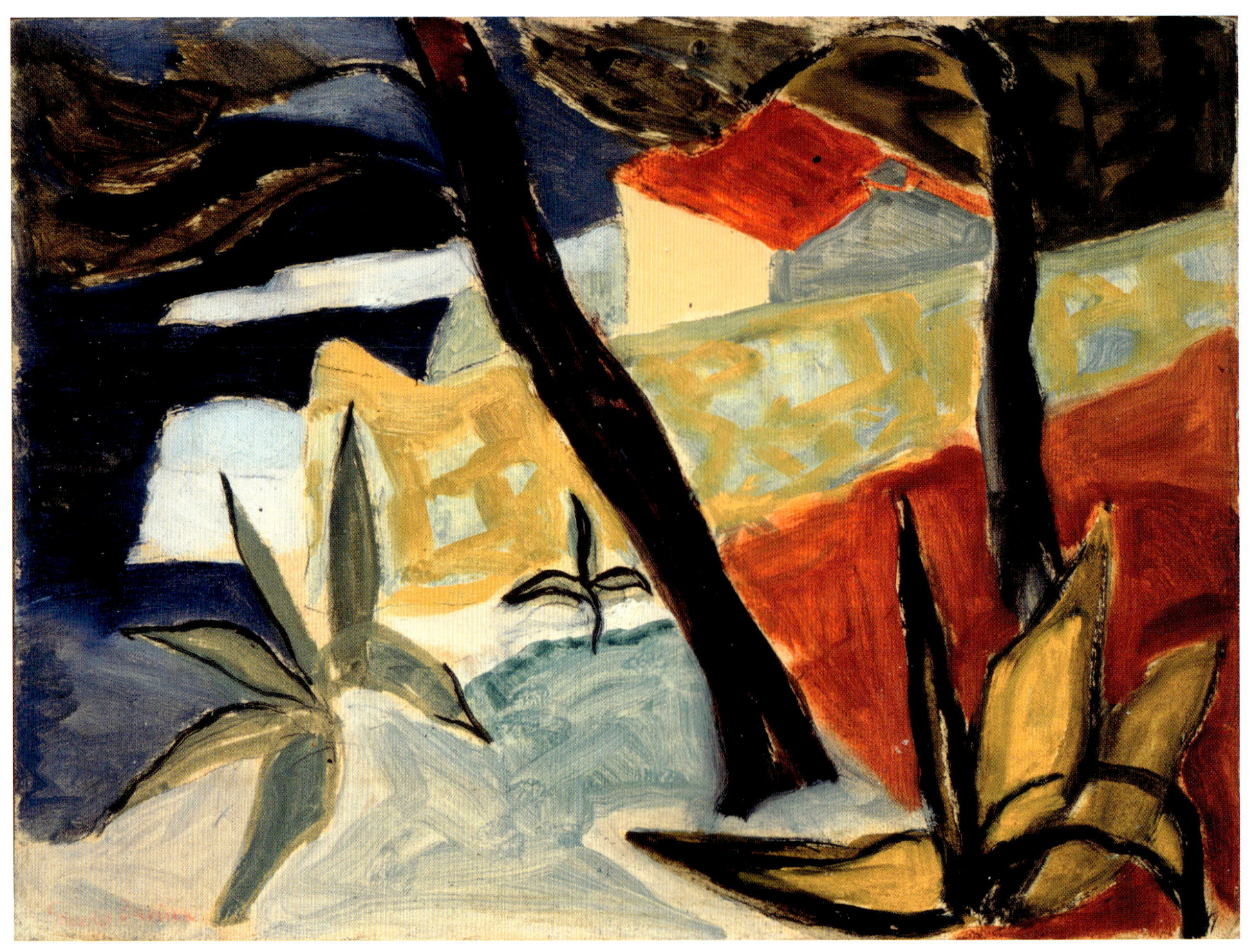

O-128   1948   Oil on board   29 × 41 cm (11.4 × 16.2")   Private collection

the Chateau des Enfants. The rules of spatial recession are sacrificed in the interests of visual excitement, and dynamic pattern is given the lead. Painted in oil on card, it's a strong and lively arrangement, a direct response to the perceived world rather than an abstraction from it, or a carefully composed ordering of appearances. It's vivid and dramatic.

Three Venice paintings give a flavour of the subjects Davison was attempting and the kind of treatment and approach he was able to achieve. The hotel balcony features in one bright blue and yellow painting which is more about pattern and structure – the dominance of shapes in our lives – than about the pleasures of sitting in the sun. A painting of gondolas is again an exercise in pattern: the two contiguous boats slapping up against one another like a couple of kippers, bright-eyed and richly painted. The third picture, entitled *Canal in Venice* (see O-110, page 49), perhaps dates from 1949 and is more complex in shape-arrangement, juxtaposing waterside facades with boat and sail shapes in a fractured and overlapping way. (The emphasis on house fronts seems to foreshadow Davison's interest in cottages which would reach fruition in the first years back in England.) Generally, the paintings are dark and rich and continental-looking. They belong more to the School of Paris than to contemporary British painting, and they conform closely to the type of picture that Margaret Mellis was currently producing.

At the same time, Davison was clearly pursuing his activities as a man of letters, and attempting to earn some money in the process. He continued to write poems and also tried his hand at short stories. He was also making translations of modern French writers, some of which were published under his own name in such periodicals as the *New English Weekly*, to which he also contributed other articles. Valéry and Sartre were amongst the authors he translated, sometimes on spec, not

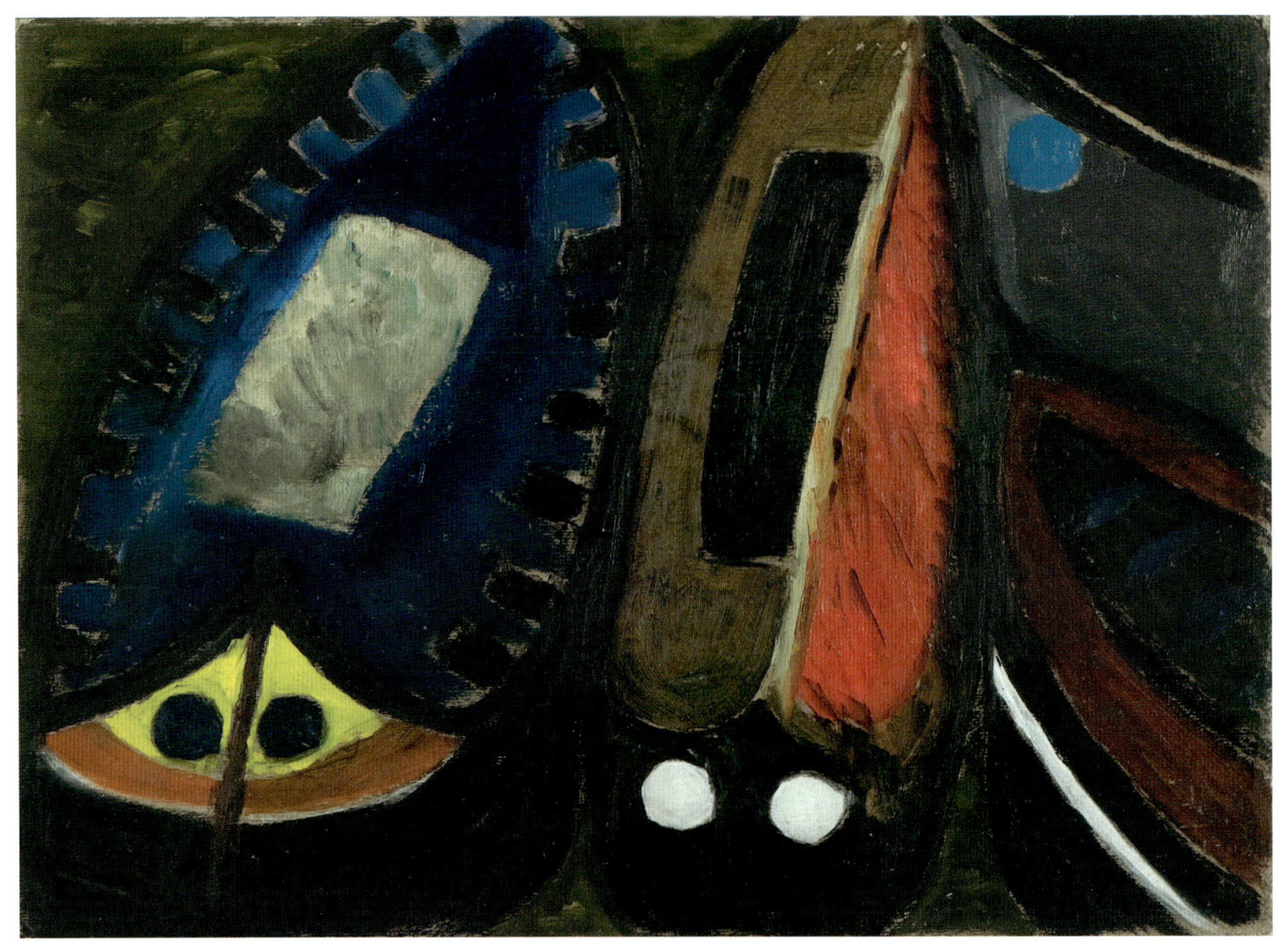

O-112   1948   Oil on card   28.4 × 39.4 cm (11.2 × 15.5")   Private collection

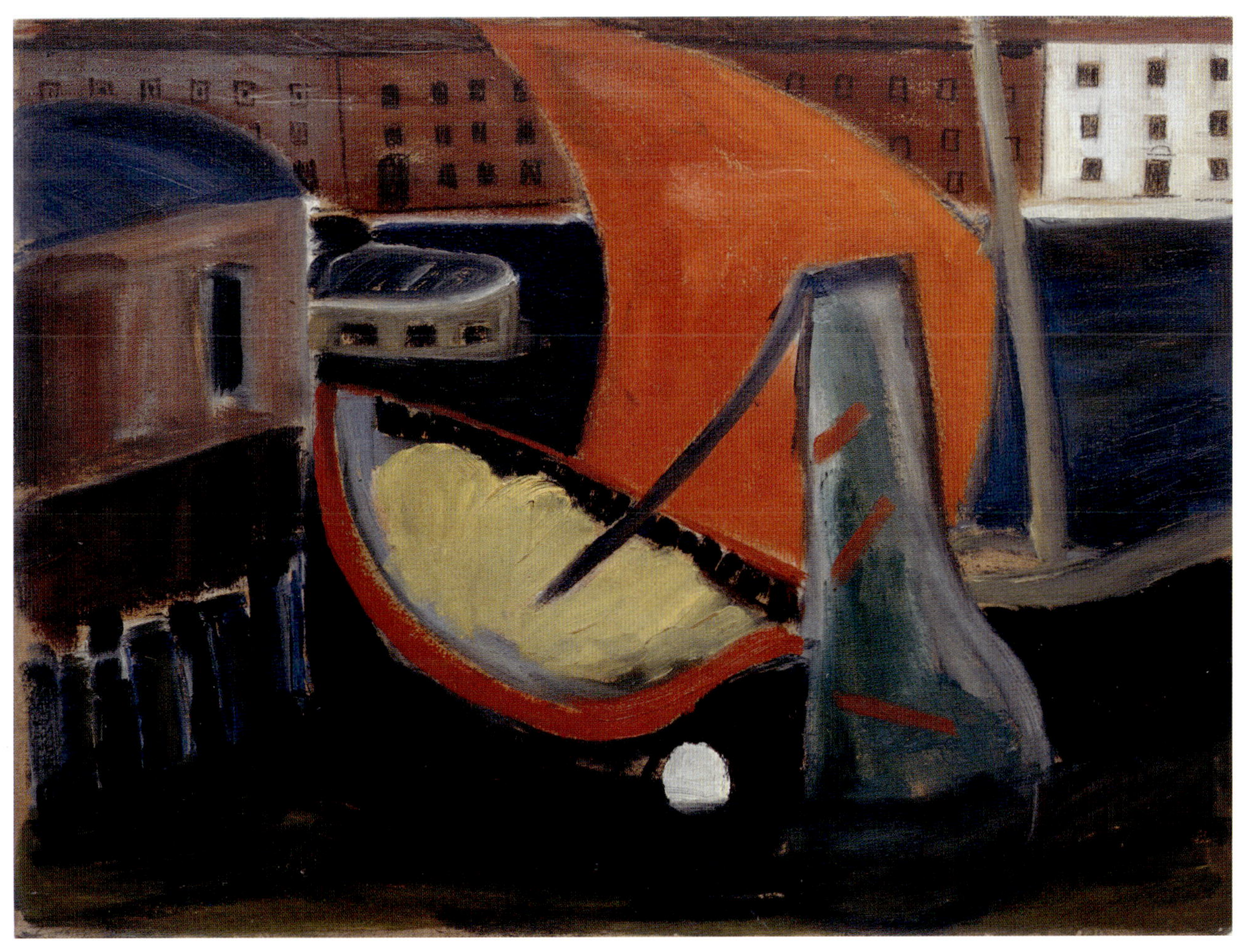

O-110   1948   Oil on board   29.7 × 39.9 cm (11.7 × 15.7")   Private collection

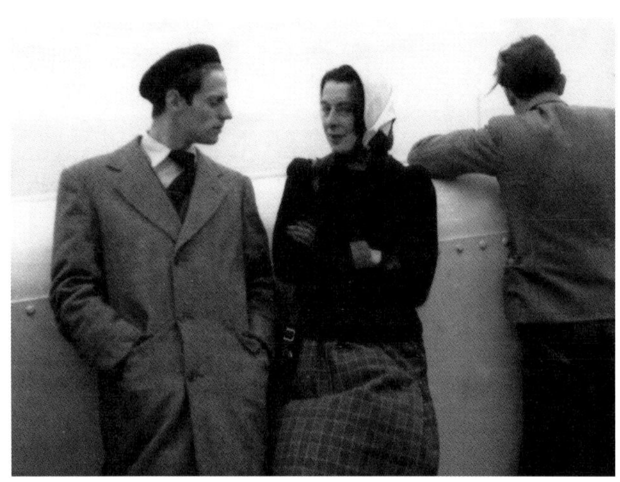

On the Dover–Calais Ferry, 1948/9

always commissioned or accepted. For instance, James Laughlin's American publishing company New Directions turned down Davison's translations of Sartre in 1947 as being too English in tone. But there were also successes. The following comes from a corrected proof of one of his articles in the *New English Weekly*: 'A life in which there is no straining, in which the personality is rounded off, as it were, developed and living what it is and not striving beyond its limitations into artificiality is a rare thing.' And: 'Everywhere the word is used we find a substitute for living …' It seems as if Davison was experiencing a growing dissatisfaction with the literary life, and preparing himself for a life-change.

By 1949 Patrick Heron was acting as Davison's unofficial agent in England, forwarding a manuscript to *Horizon* (who returned it) and reporting on Davison's contribution to *L'Age Nouveau*, a recently-founded French monthly arts review. In August that year Heron also took some of Davison's paintings along to the Redfern Gallery in London's Cork Street, where he himself was showing, in the hope that they would respond to his friend's work. The two were very close at this period, with Francis staying at Addison Road (the Herons' London home) in the summer of 1950, and Heron getting Davison's paintings into the summer exhibition at the Penwith Society down in St Ives that June.

On a scrap of paper (dating from Antibes in the late 1940s) Davison had written: 'A human life, I think, should be well

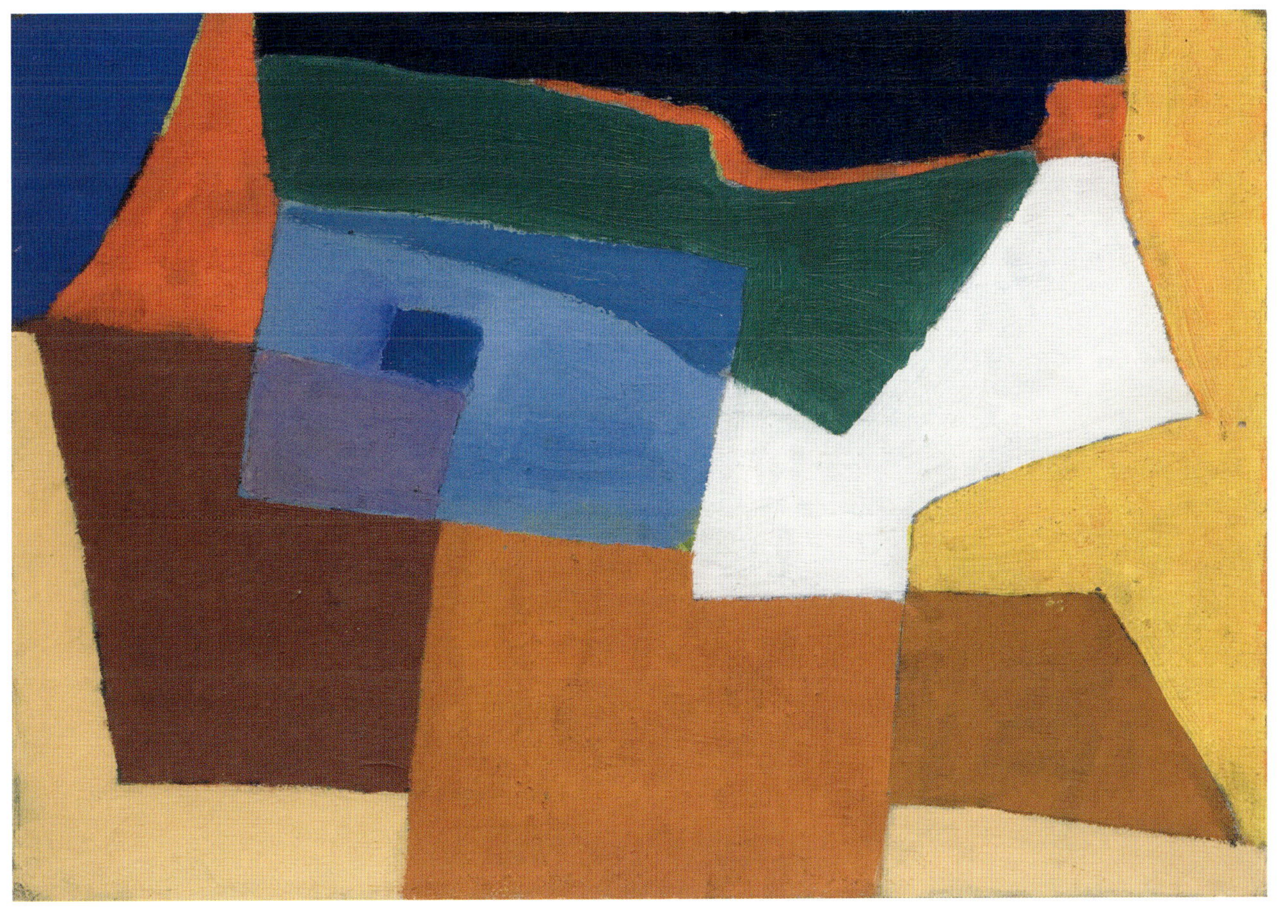

O-185   1950–1   Oil on card   36 × 40.6 cm (14.2 × 16")   Private collection

rooted in some spot of a native land, where it may get the love of tender kinship for the face of earth, for the labours men go forth to, for the sounds and accents that haunt it, for whatever will give that early home a familiar unmistakeable difference amidst the future widening of knowledge.' The paragraph is unattributed, but whether it is a piece of Davison's own writing, or an admired quotation, is not as important as the fact that the sentiment expressed is evidently one endorsed by the writer who has taken the trouble to record it. He was clearly looking to put down roots somewhere he could work undisturbed, and the opportunity to do so soon arose.

In December 1948, the Herons came to stay at the Chateau. Patrick at this point was painting in a Fauve palette – landscapes of hot dark colours – which no doubt proved an inspiration (or a challenge) to Francis. The two couples obviously got on well enough together for the stay to be a lengthy one, and in January, Patrick and Francis set out to visit Matisse, who was living at Vence, just up the road from Antibes. Sadly the master was not well enough to receive them, but on the long walk back Heron decided that he'd identified the bend in the road where Matisse painted *Route du Cap d'Antibes – Le Grand Pin* in 1926. He wrote: 'I manoeuvred myself about until the two pine trees reaching up across the road from the seashore below were exactly where I thought they were in Matisse's landscape and took a photograph. By now my right shoulder was up against a corner in a loose stone wall beside the road, on the right.

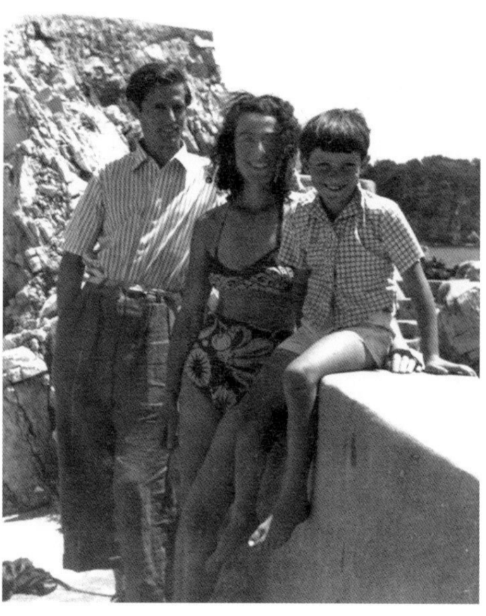

With Margaret Mellis and Telfer Stokes at the bathing place, Chateau des Enfants, Cap d'Antibes, 1948/9

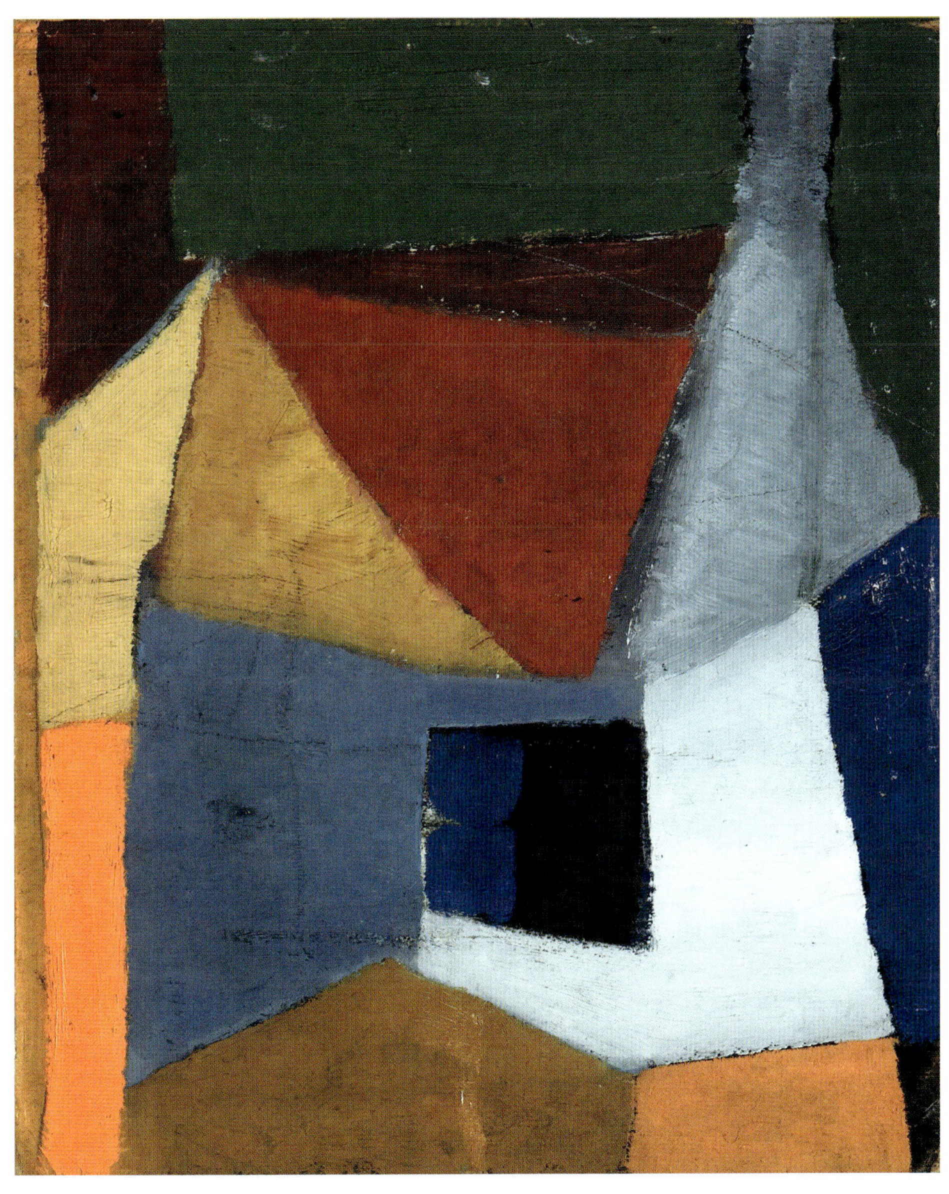

O-57   1950   Oil on card   41.9 x 33 cm (16.5 × 13")   Private collection

Somehow I must have seen a gleam of red among the mosses and lichens on the wall. I peeled them away and, sure enough, there were a lot of oxidizing palette scrapings – ultramarine, violet, emerald green and scarlet, all knifed into a crack between two jagged pieces of that whitish rock of the coast of the Cap. Developed, the photograph exactly corroborates the angle from which Matisse painted that famous landscape …'

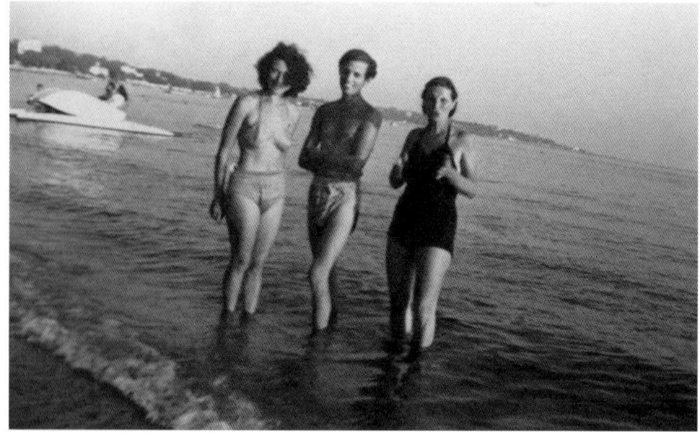

Juan-les-Pins, 1949

Besides being evidence of Heron's obsession, this first-hand encounter with the stuff of paint – the colours of Matisse – was a crucial experience for Davison, and helps to set the scene for the colourful physicality of his later work. Heron was equally struck by their joint experience, and evidently found it a sustaining and enriching one. In a letter dated 16th February 1949 he wrote: 'Antibes is a colossal and permanent acquisition: it goes on erupting inside me: it returns at all times of day and night to be compared with old England, in all its greyness! Now I know where the great painting has its roots.'

In 1949, on a trip back to England, either Francis or Margaret had taken some work to a couple of London galleries in the hope of it being accepted and exhibited. Roland, Browse and Delbanco later included Davison in stock shows and even sold a painting to Peter Pears. (This was *Vase of Flowers in Window*, bought in June 1952 for 12 guineas.) Gimpels took some other paintings and showed them in a mixed exhibition, which Roger Hilton saw and admired. This was followed

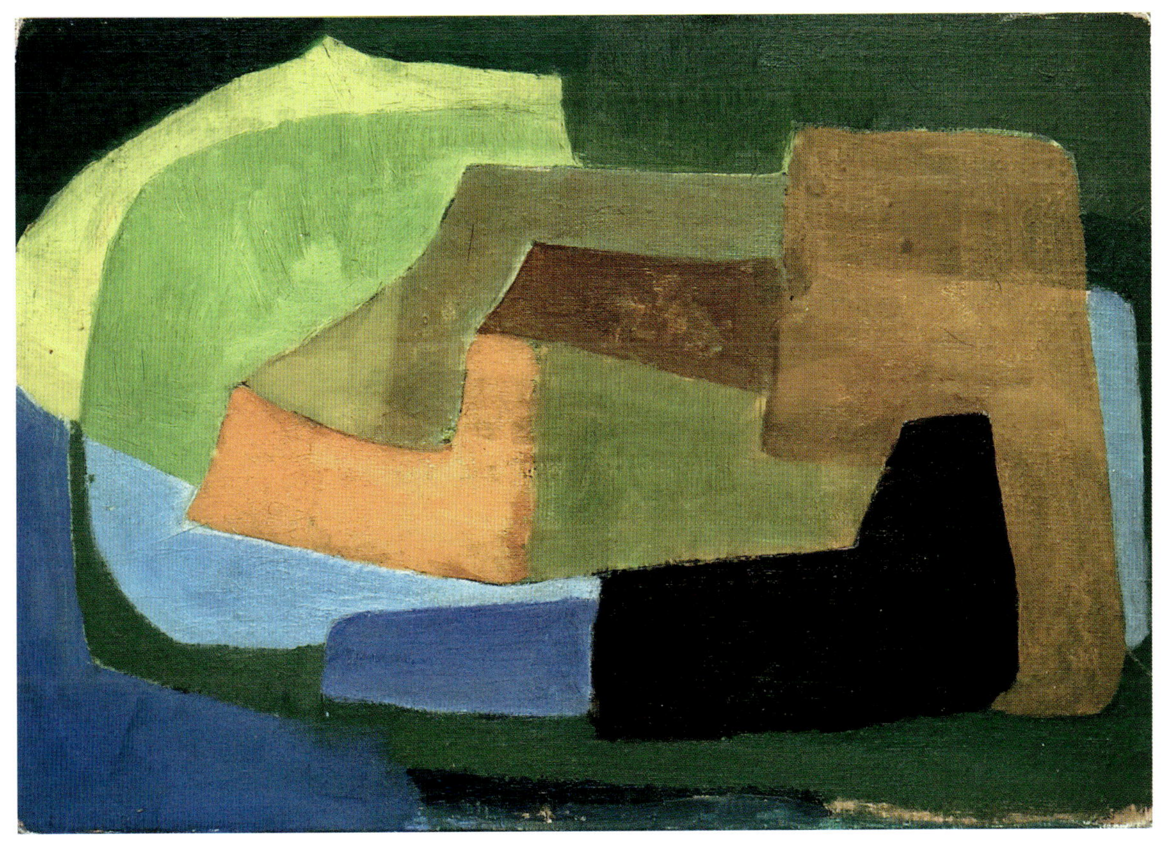

O-213   1950   Oil on card   25.4 × 34.3 cm (10 × 13.5")   Private collection

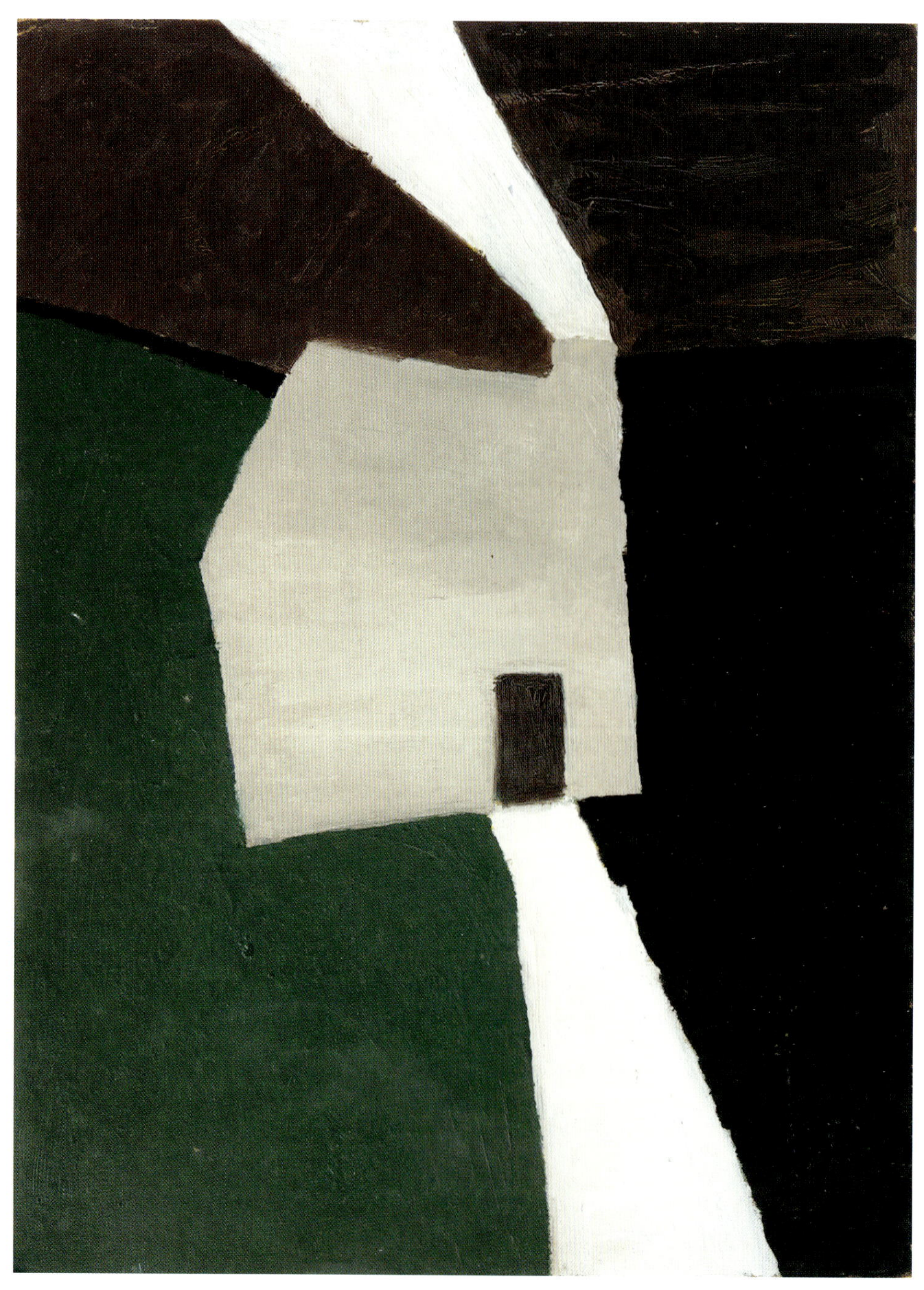

O-40   1950–1   Oil on card   56.4 × 36 cm (20.2 × 14.2")   Private collection

up by the offer of a solo show for 1950, but Davison worked so slowly (and life was much interrupted around that time) that he didn't have enough work until 1952. And by then the moment had passed and Gimpels were no longer interested. It was shortly after this non-event that Davison began to make collages. Was this a direct result of his lack of success as a painter? Perhaps. Certainly collages were cheaper to make and easier to store.

The semi-idyll in Antibes came to an end when Mrs Davison decided to sell the Chateau, and in 1950 Francis and Margaret returned to England. They arrived on 1st May from a scorching south of France to find England covered in snow. They stayed in a borrowed fishermen's hut in Walberswick, the Suffolk fishing village famous for its painters, and shivered. But they liked Suffolk and soon found a 200-year-old house they could just about afford. With a small inheritance they bought Church Farm Cottage at Syleham, near Diss in Suffolk, with four acres of land, and moved in. They kept ducks, geese and a large quantity of hens, sold the eggs and grew barley. However, they were entirely reliant on neighbouring farmers for the loan of harvesting machinery, which proved unsatisfactory. As a direct result, they gave up trying to run the farm as a small holding after about four years of hard and increasingly frustrating labour. The egg market was their main source of income in the following years, eked out by the infrequent sale of a painting or collage.

Each had a separate studio, where as many hours as possible were spent, but the farm demanded attention and the chickens had to be tended. There was no chance to go on holiday and leave everything, but Mellis (the more sociable of the two) used to visit the Herons in London periodically to see what was going on in the art world and try to place some work by herself

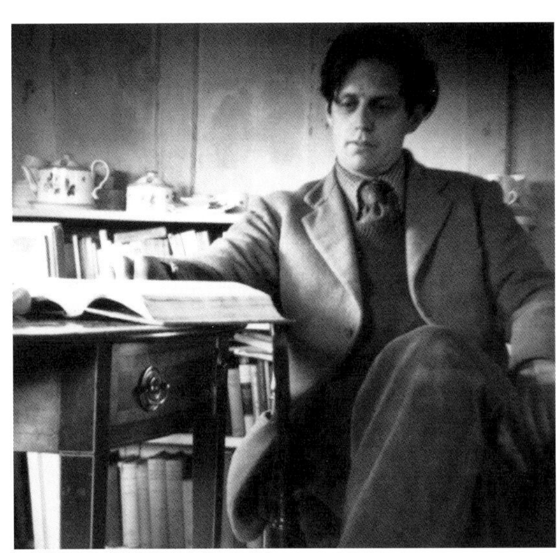

Church Farm Cottage,
Syleham, Suffolk, circa 1952

or Francis. There were other occasional excitements. For instance, in May 1950 Davison was included in the Spring Exhibition at St George's Gallery, a venue of some distinction where he was showing in very good company: Oskar Kokoschka, Prunella Clough, Josef Herman and Merlyn Evans were amongst the exhibitors. Davison was represented by an oil called *Flower*. But such events were rare.

After the Ecole de Paris style of his Antibes and Venice pictures, with their fluid brushwork and rich palette, Davison's early 1950s work was very much involved with the landscape he had moved to – a pattern of small fields and scattered farm buildings. The paintings became starker, simpler, and the palette more appropriately austere, in line with the post-war mood of continued rationing. Compositions were distilled to a geometrical essence that was evocative rather than descriptive. 'In reducing vernacular cottages and barns to the simplest flat forms,' writes Alan Powers, 'Davison produced ideograms that are absolutely true to the strange syncopated rhythms of country building, while retaining their essential domesticity. There is a resemblance to the way Ben Nicholson drew houses in landscape, but Davison's are in some ways more serious and less formulaic as paintings.'

The closest comparison is with those abstract paintings of Roger Hilton's which look like stretched and ragged hides, owing something to the sophisticated jigsaw patterns of Serge Poliakoff. But these were painted in 1953–4, by which time Davison had turned to collage. Another artist working in the same area, particularly in the mapping of large near-geometric

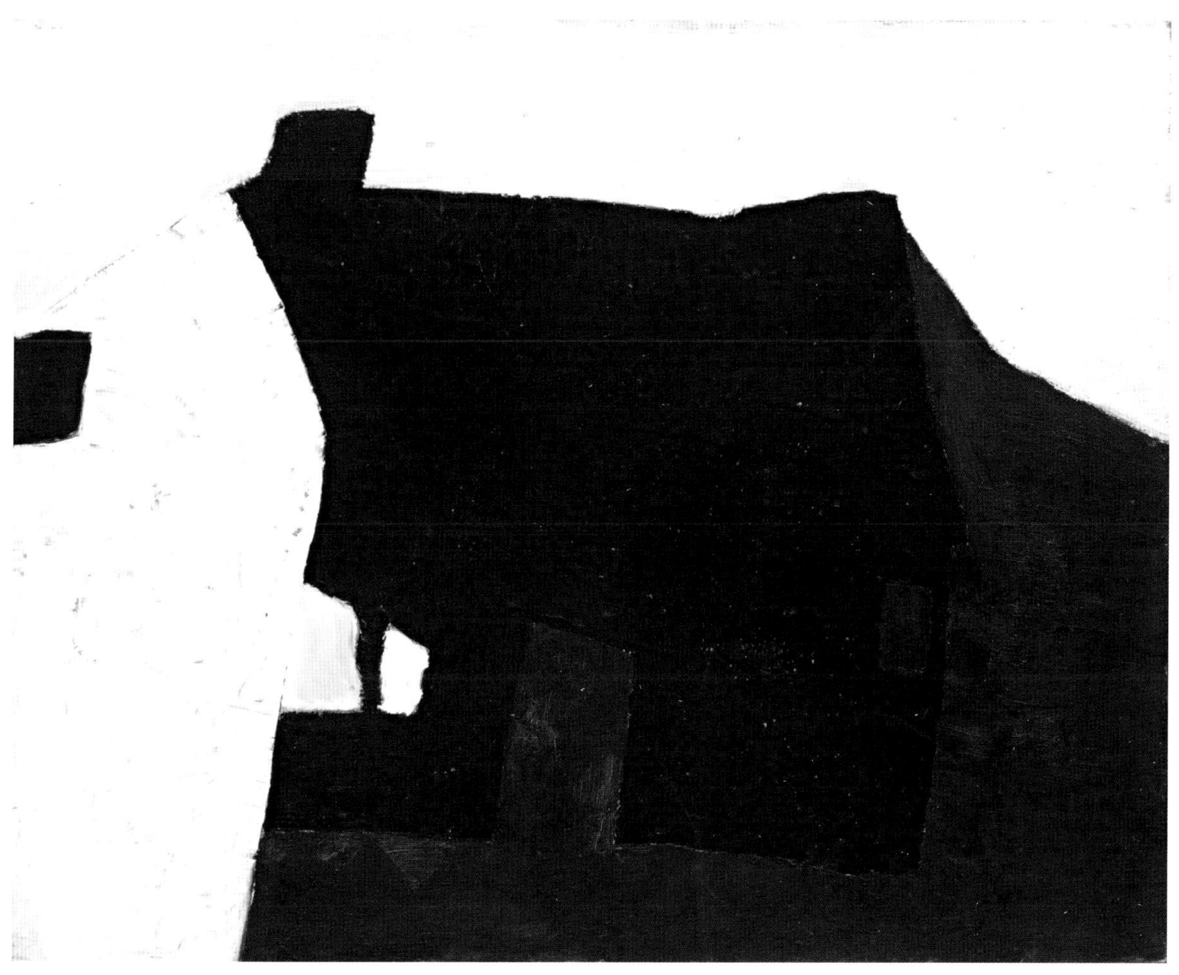

O-51   1951   Oil on board   33 × 40.6 cm (13 × 16")   Private collection

areas with an organic bounding line, is William Scott. Again, the specific comparison is with paintings being made around 1952–3. I am not suggesting that Davison pioneered a movement, or that Hilton and Scott borrowed his ideas, merely indicating that this sort of approach was very much in the air at the time, and that a number of artists were linked in to this particular aspect of the zeitgeist.

The Suffolk paintings and drawings (Davison often used an effective mixture of oil paint and graphite, or thin washes of emulsion and conté drawing on card) play with the negative/positive dichotomy like a checked tablecloth or a chess board stretched out of all recognition, powered by diagonal thrusts and vectors, in a dynamic re-interpretation of the relationship between house and land, road and field. Distortion is both witty and emotionally appropriate to a deeper understanding of the precariousness of life on the land: look at the radical abstractions of *Fields and Road* (c.1950/1) (see O-183), and its exquisitely interlinked and rhythmical wedges, or the sheer inventiveness of shape in *Green Cottage* (see O-160, page 62) of the same date. Compositions in black, brown and white – the colours of demotic rural architecture – are surprisingly daring in their bold simplifications. Already here is an original voice in contemporary art.

Essential shapes were what preoccupied both Mellis and Davison. Francis was inspired by the shapes of the Suffolk houses and the way they met the ground, almost as if growing out of it. Both had been looking a lot at Matisse and Gris and were influenced by their brilliant colours and good shapes, but Davison moved steadily towards a refinement of shape, while Mellis concentrated on colour. Neither was precious in terms of approach to materials or paint application, both deliberately courting imperfection and rough spontaneity in the urge to

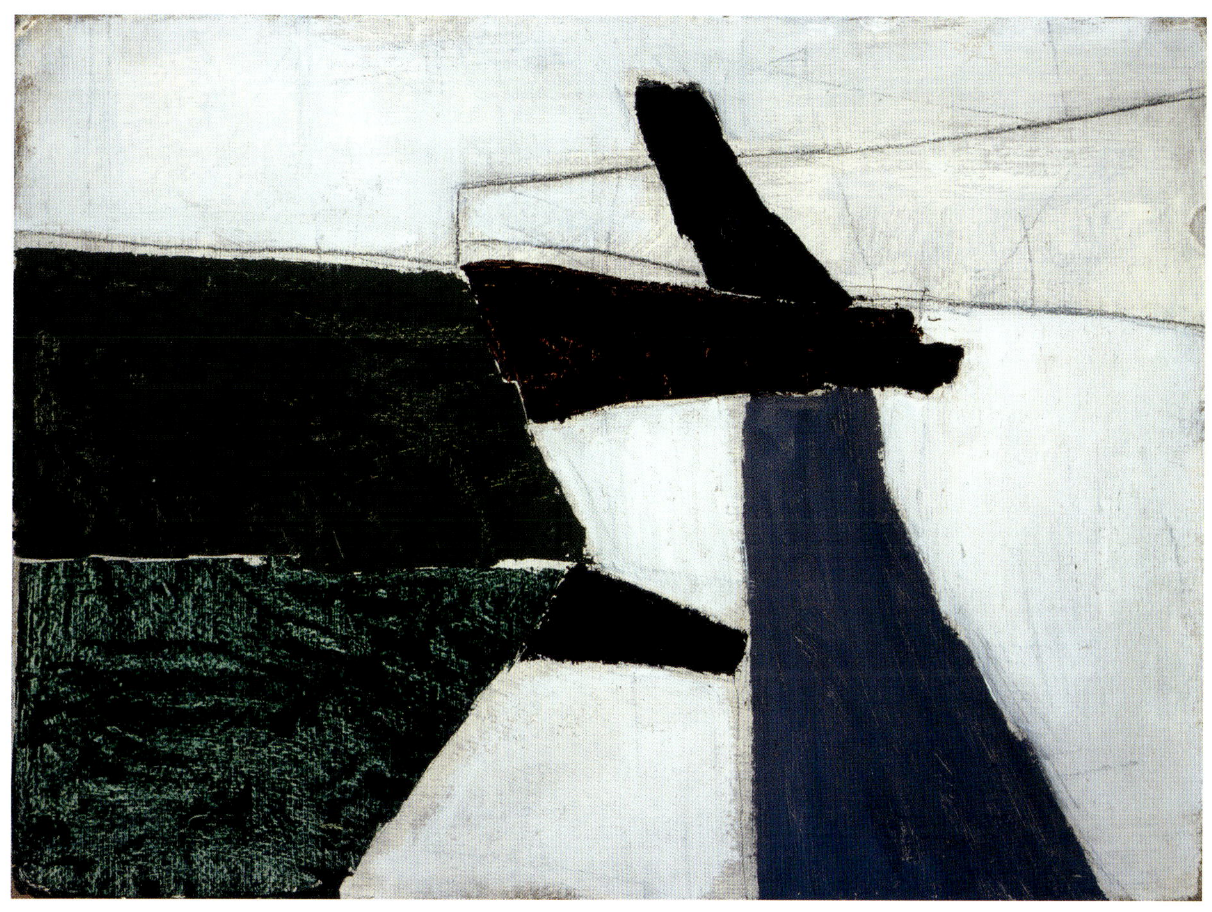

O-183   1950   Oil on board   29.8 × 40 cm (11.8 × 15.7")   Private collection

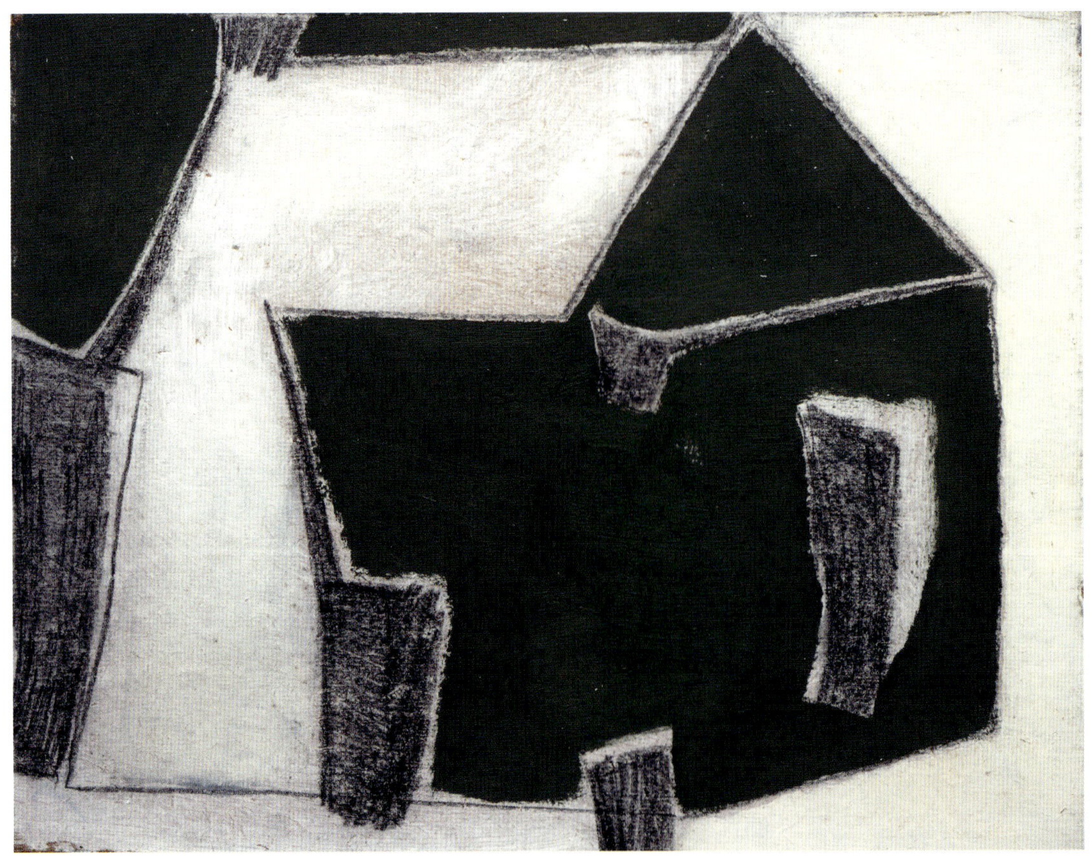

O-160   1950   Oil and graphite on board   24.8 × 30 cm (9.7 × 11.8")   Private collection

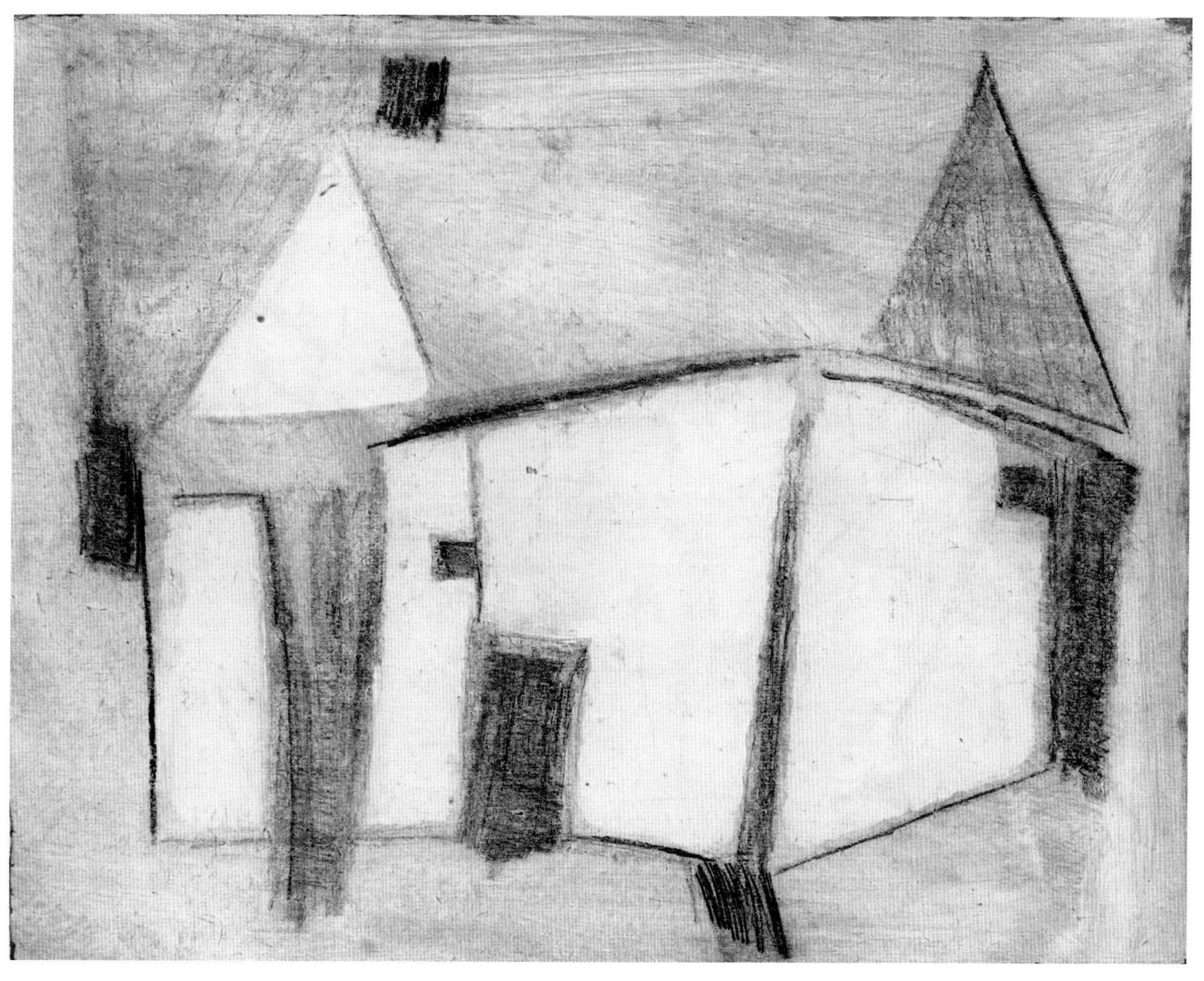

O-24 1950–1 Graphite on card 37.7 × 41.3 cm (13.25 × 16.25") Private collection

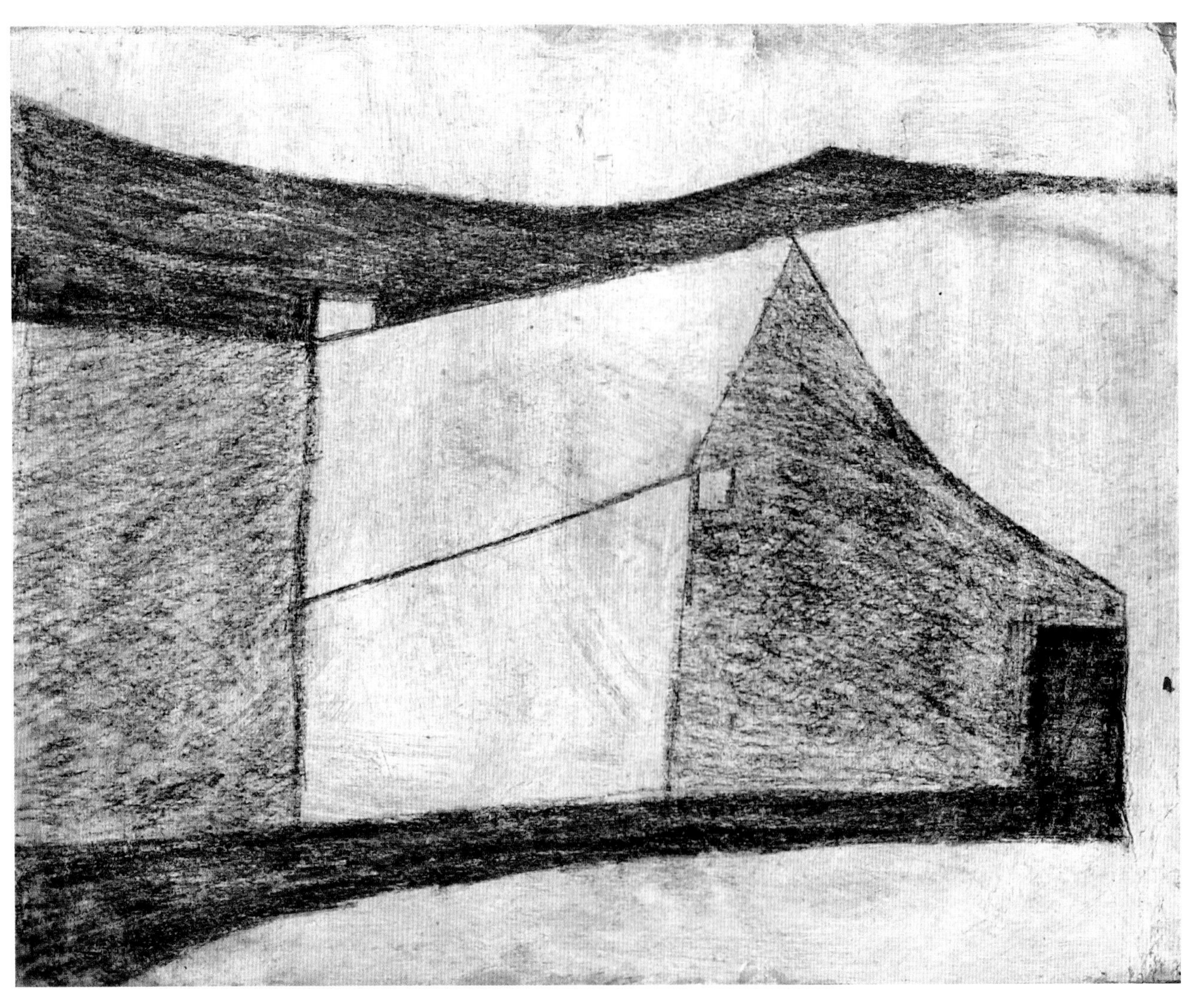

O-53   1950   Graphite on card   33.7 × 40.6 cm (13.25 × 16")   Private collection

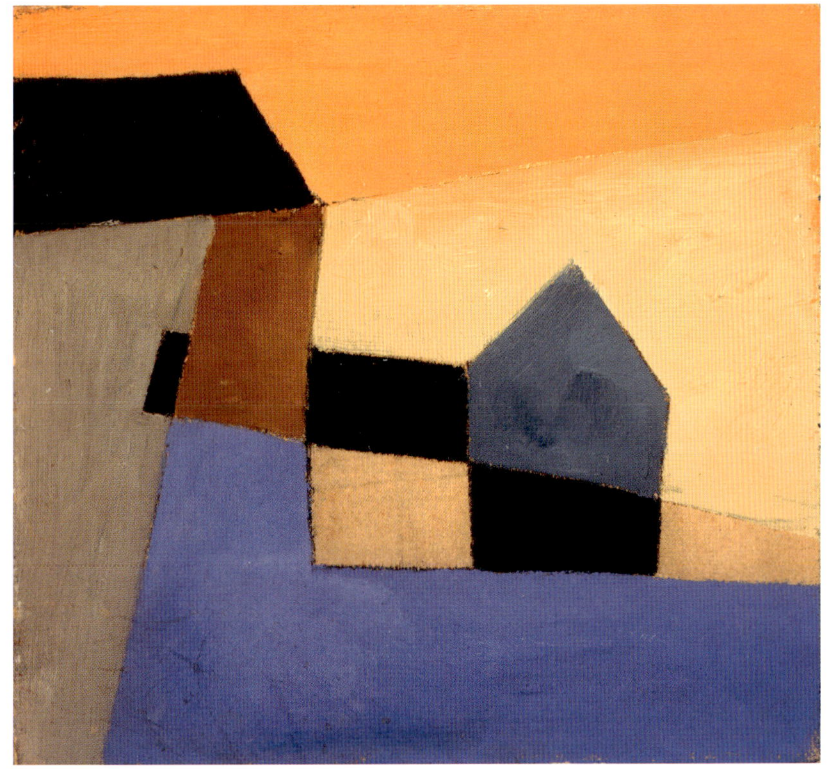

O-214   1950–1   Oil on board   21.6 × 22.2 cm (8.5 × 8.75")   Private collection

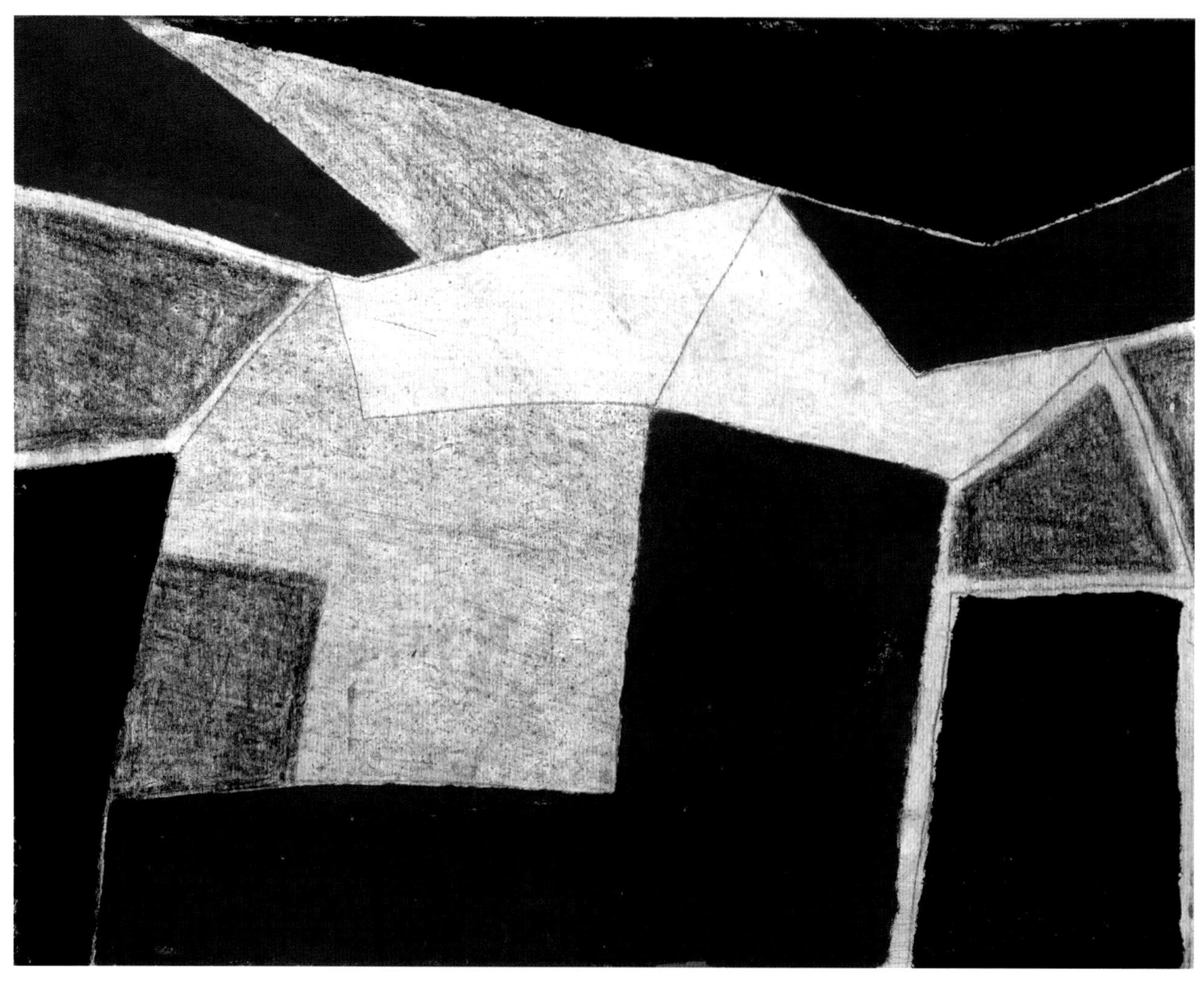

O-193   1950–1   Oil and graphite on board   27.9 × 41.9 cm (11 × 16.5")   Private collection

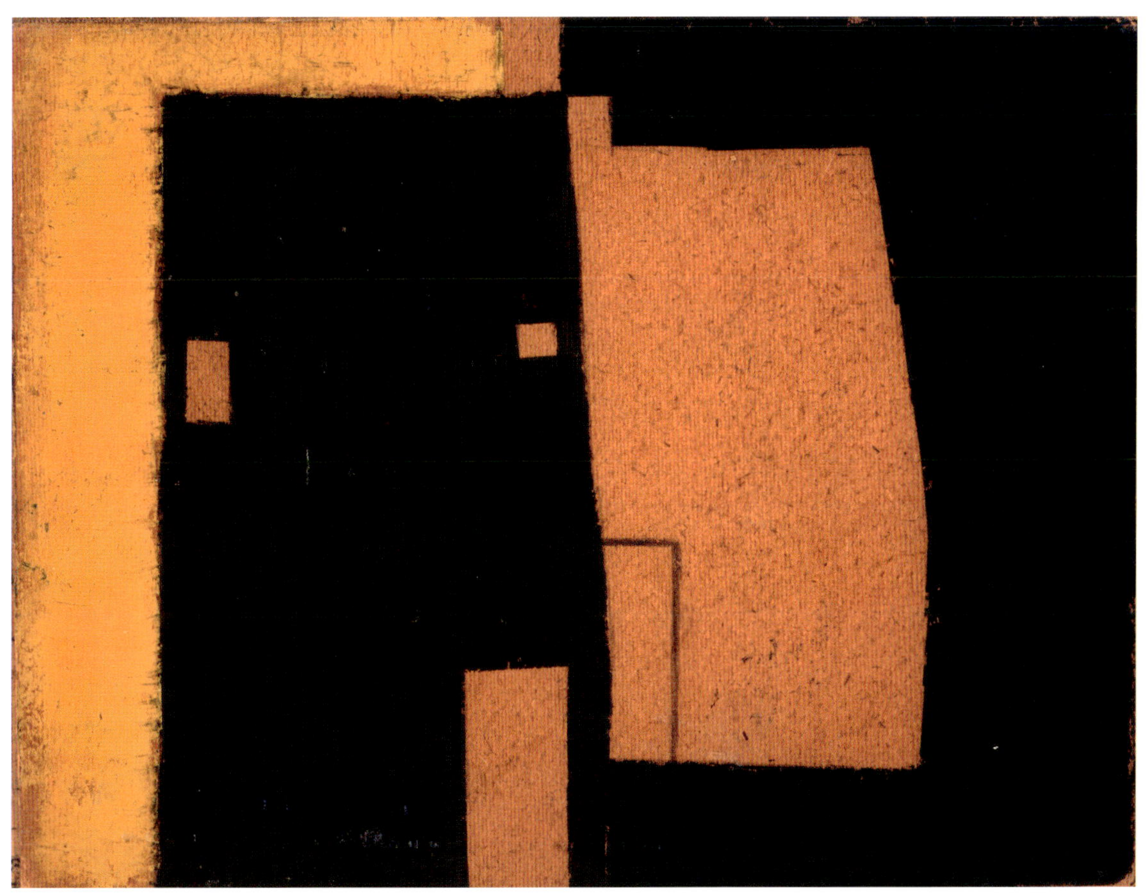

O-143   1950   Oil on board   25.5 × 31.8 cm (10 × 12.5")   Private collection

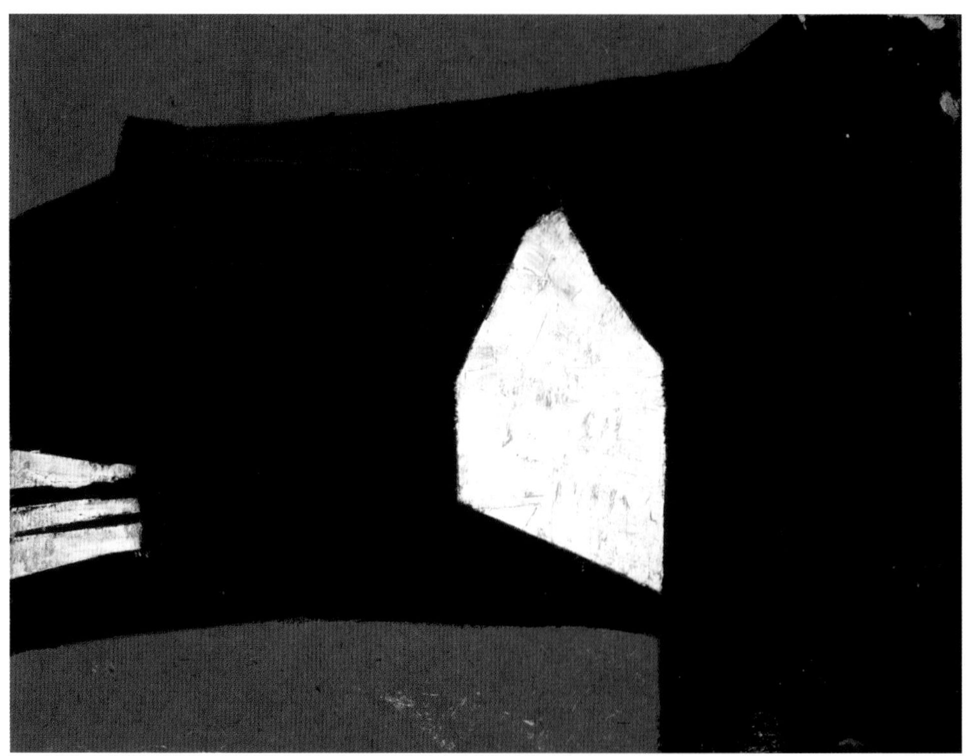

O-158   1950   Oil on board   24.9 × 30.5 cm (9.8 × 12")   Private collection

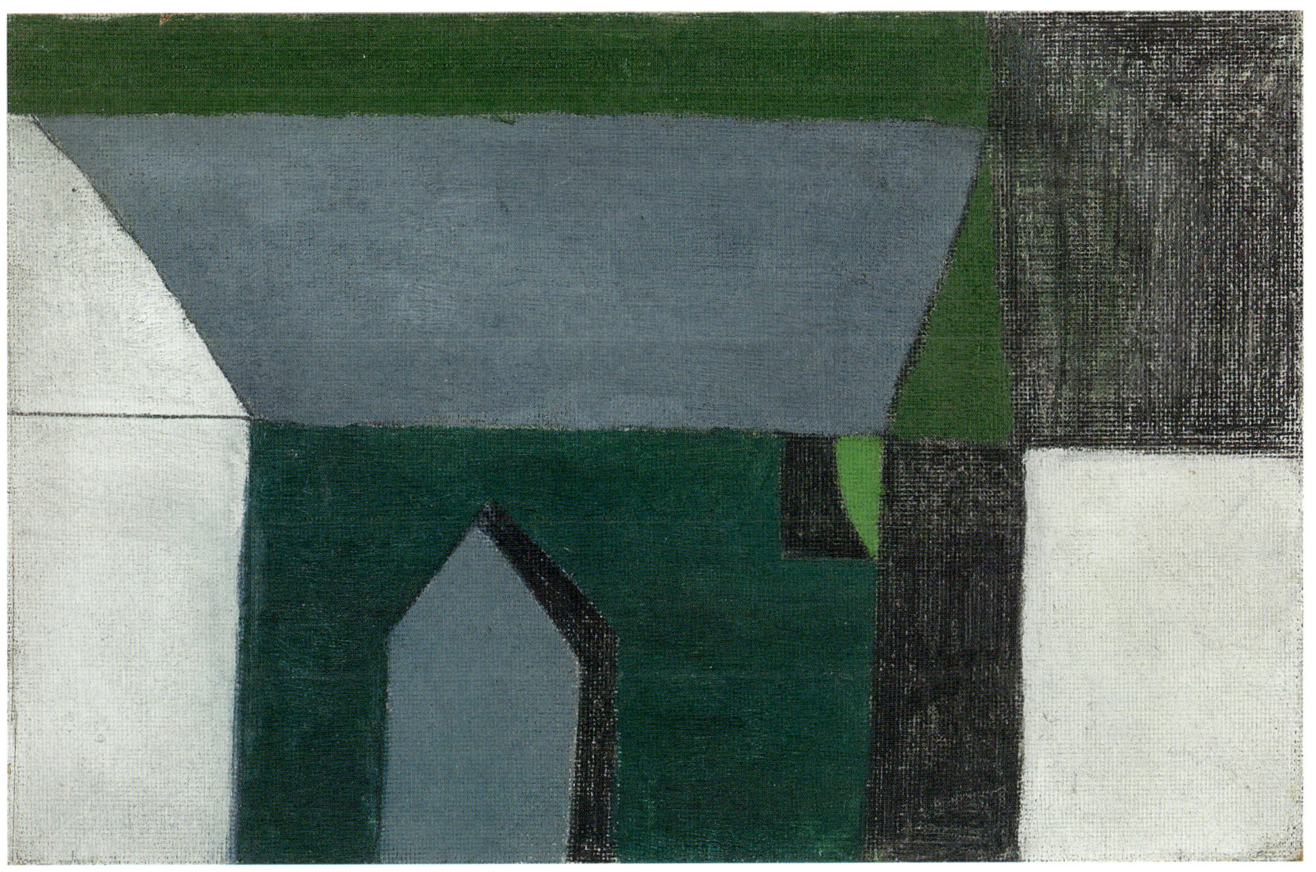

O-186   1950–1   Oil and graphite on board   27.9 × 41.9 cm (11 × 16.5")   Private collection

convey an authentic response to the world. House paint was cheaper than oil, and Essex board less expensive than canvas.

Davison's Suffolk paintings are mostly made on Essex board and small in scale, and began as semi-representational, but became increasingly schematic and symbolic. Forms are flattened to the picture plane, and the sides of dwellings begin to look like field plans from the air. Colour is variable, though mostly drab: ochres, greens, browns, lots of grey and black. Fields and roads alternate with windows and doors or towers and cottages. Essex board was much used by both Davison and Mellis in the early years. A highly compacted light-weight paper-based alternative to plywood or hardboard, it has a smooth surface and is easily cut with a Stanley knife. Alfred Wallis often used cardboard as a support for his paintings which became so important to the English avant-garde painters. And of course Davison would have been aware of Wallis at first hand because Margaret owned a number of paintings by the old sea dog, some of which she'd bought from him directly, and others she had saved from being burnt.

The Herons came to stay for short visits in both 1951 and 1952, and their presence was undoubtedly a spur. By the winter of 1951–2 the interlocking rectangles of Davison's imagery had been further simplified to white abstracted areas, or flat low-keyed colour patches, divided by black lines. His Suffolk paintings were never really about paint – about paint's specific properties or what it could do, and were not deeply involved in colour. (Unlike his earlier Mediterranean works.) His chief preoccupations were with shape and line and tone. It was therefore not a great upheaval for him to move across from painting to collage. In many ways it was a distinct advantage – he discovered he could work faster and in new ways. He had in fact at last found his medium, and he was to run with it.

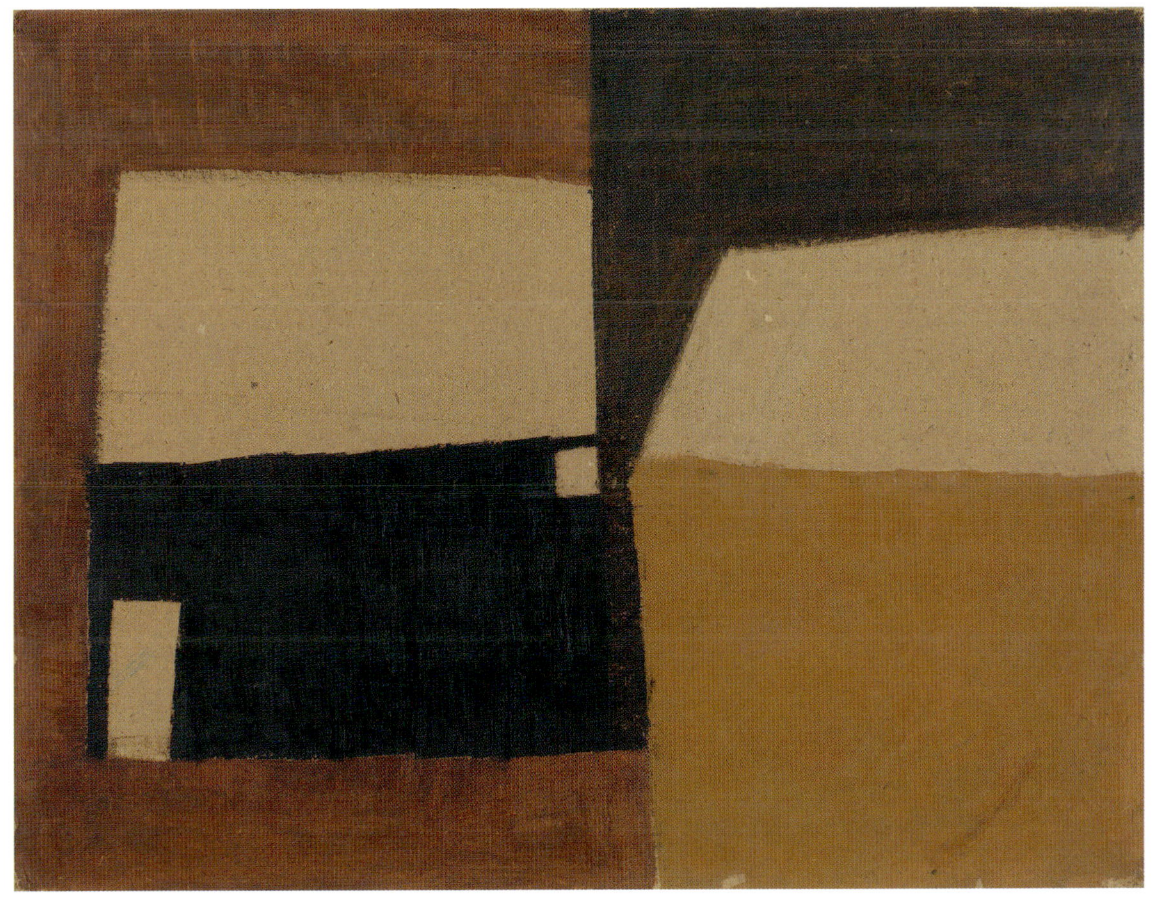

O-55   1950–1   Oil on card   43.2 × 55.9 cm (17 × 22")   Private collection

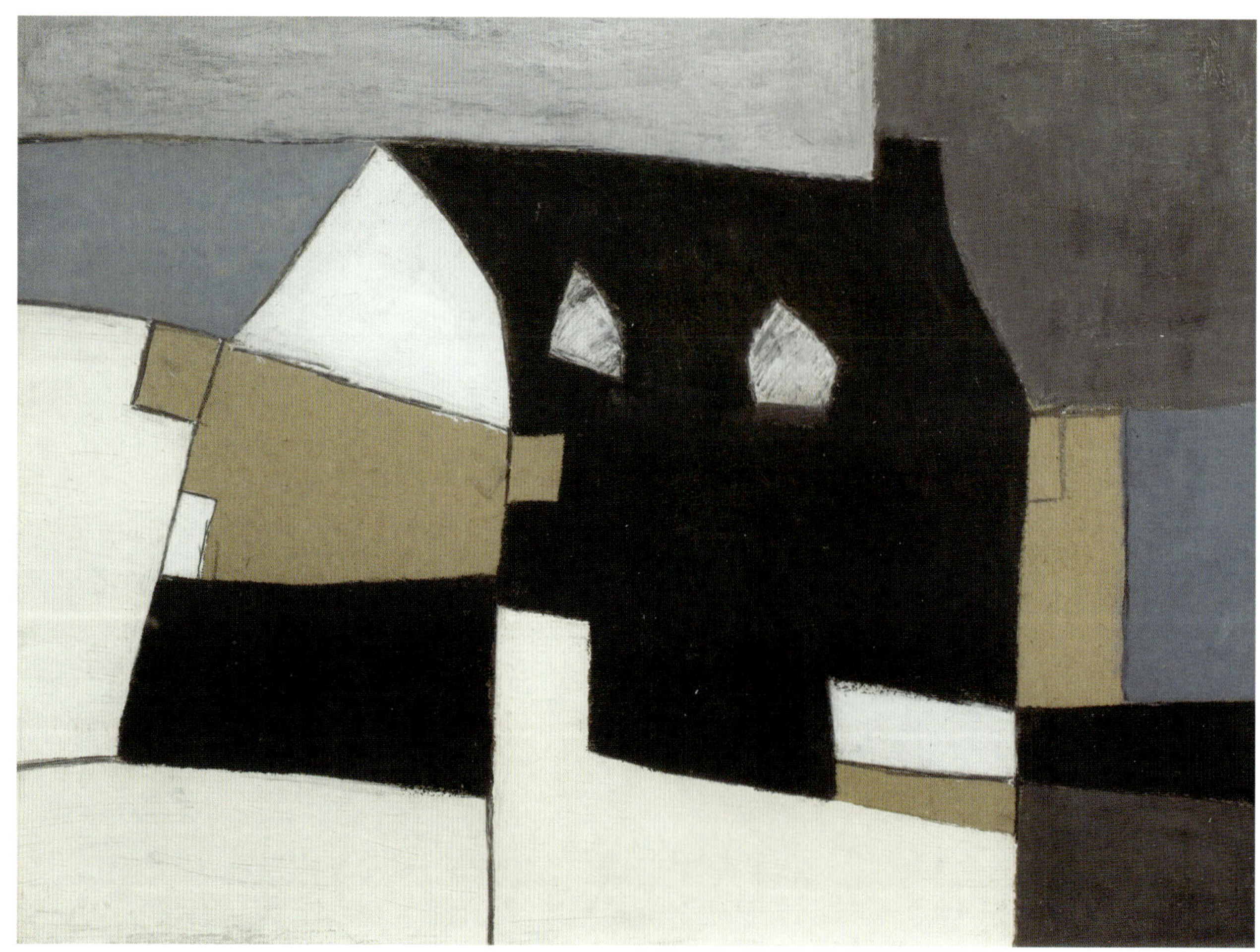

O-215   1951   Oil on board   46.4 × 61 cm (18.25 × 24")   Private collection

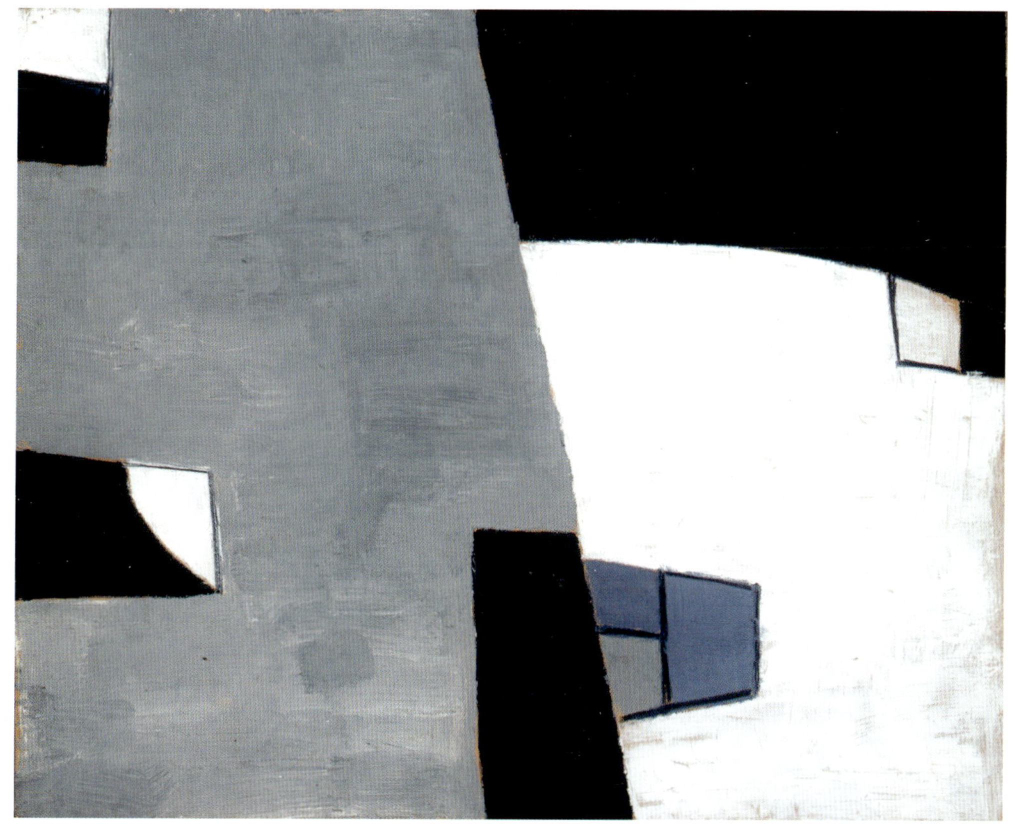

O-34   1950   Oil on board   25.4 × 31.8 cm (10 × 12.5")   Private collection

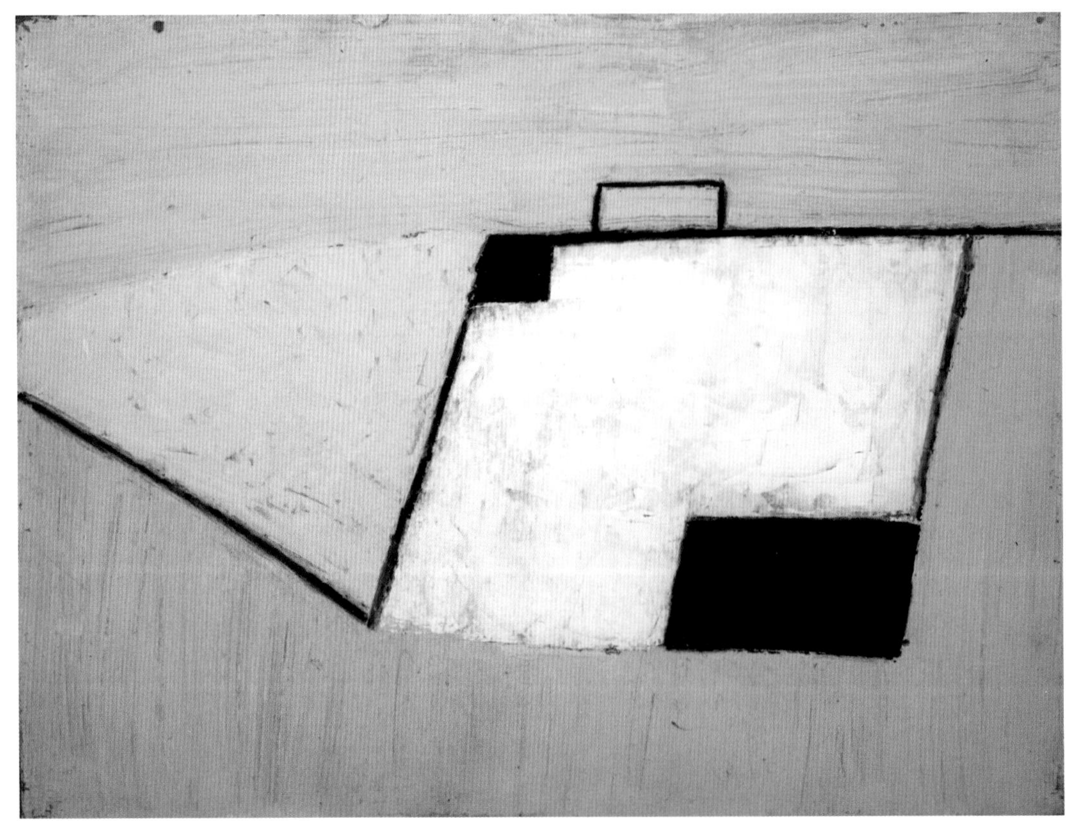

O-145   1950–1   Oil on board   25.4 × 31.8 cm (10 × 12.5")   Private collection

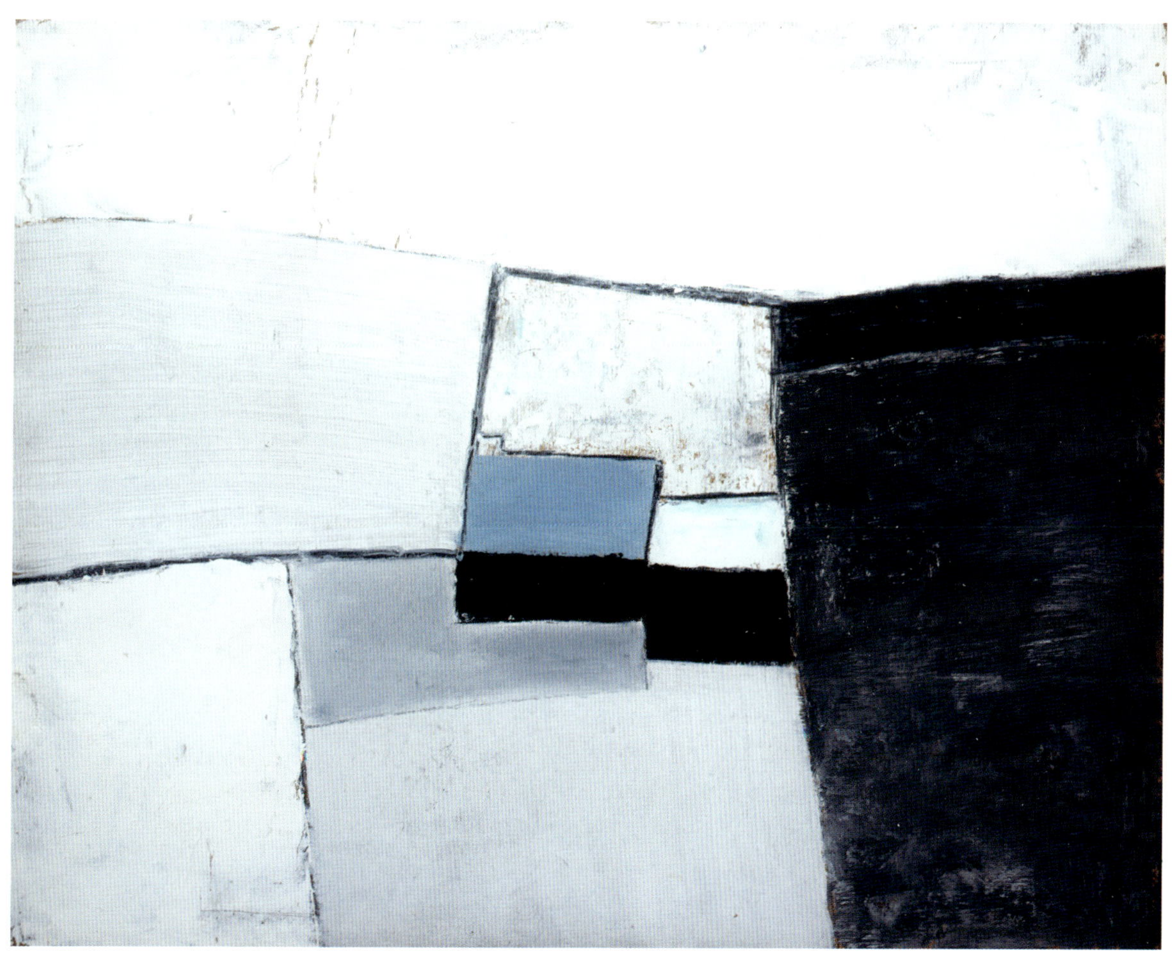

O-35   1950   Oil on board   33 × 39.9 cm (13 × 15.7")   Private collection

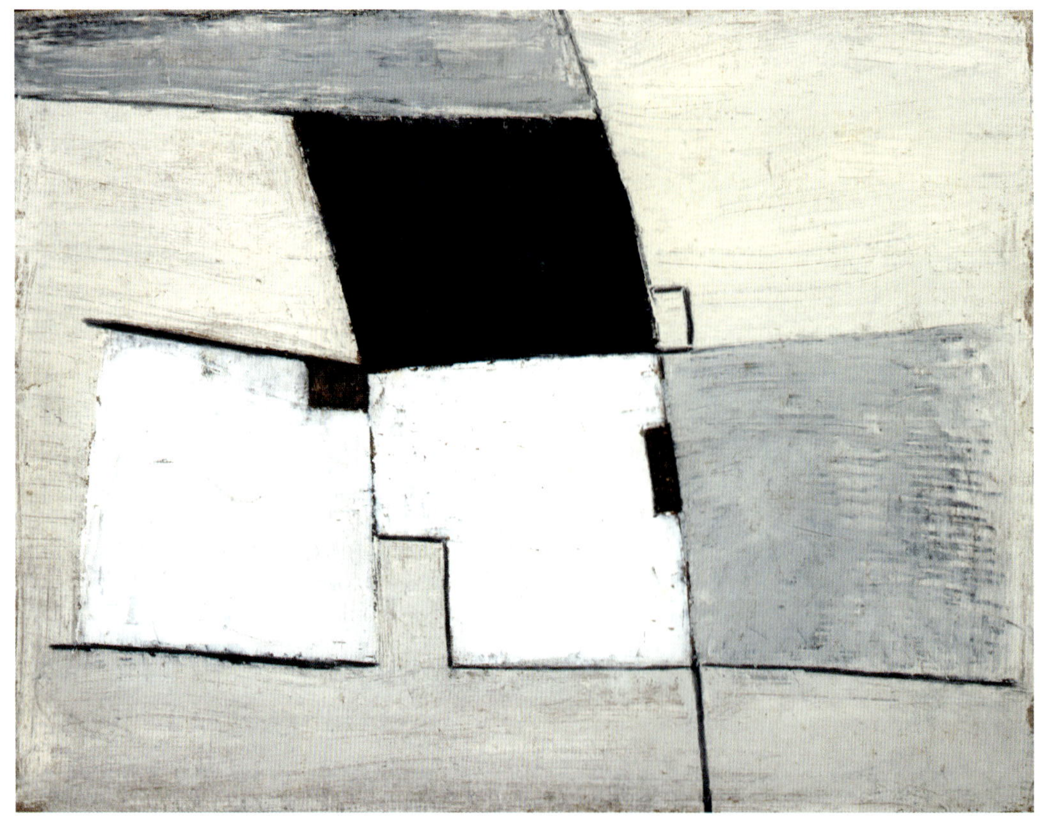

O-141   1950   Oil on board   25.4 × 31.8 cm (10 × 12.5")   Private collection

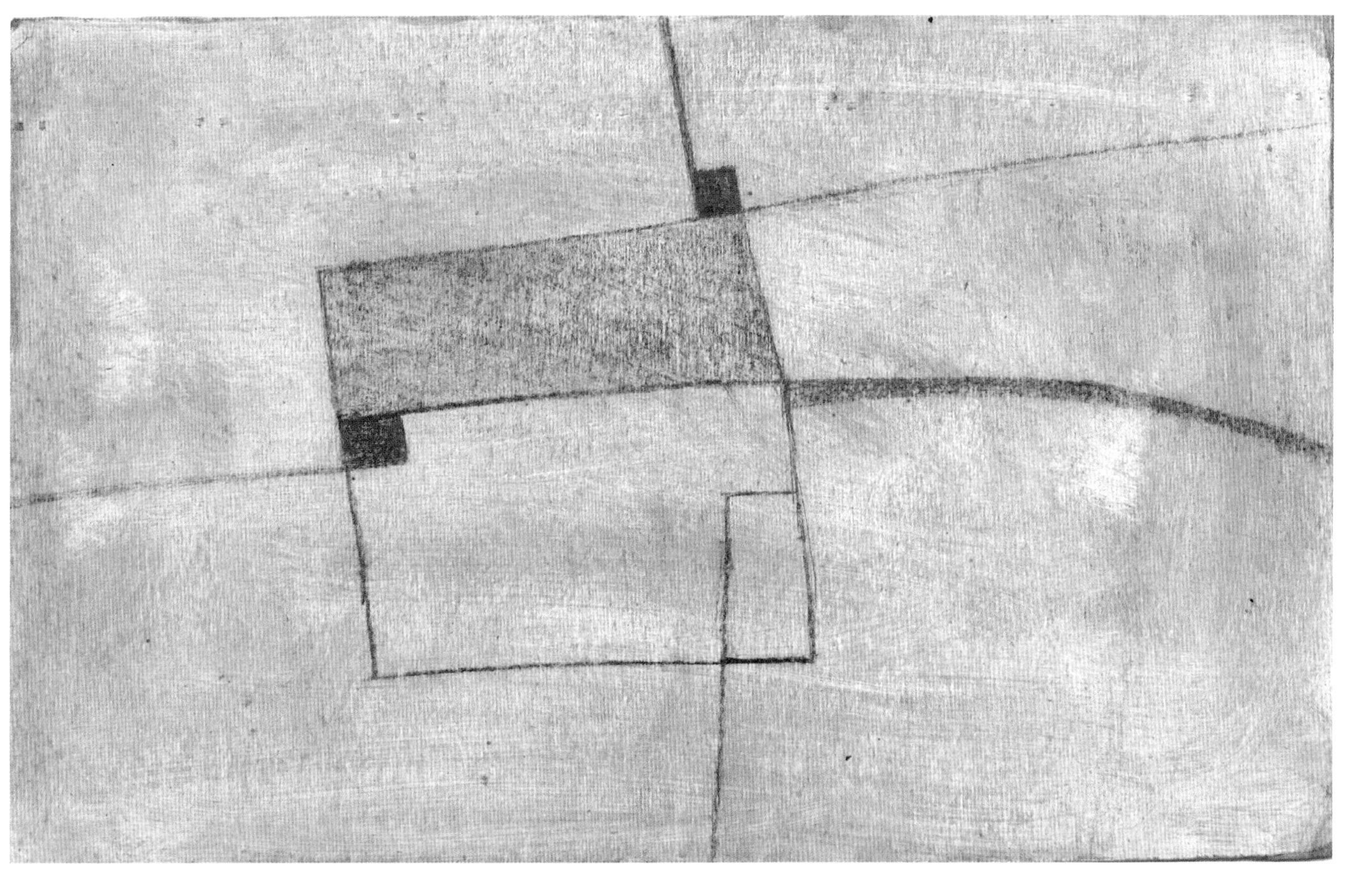

O-31   1950–1   Graphite on card   27.2 × 41 cm (10.7 × 16.2")   Private collection

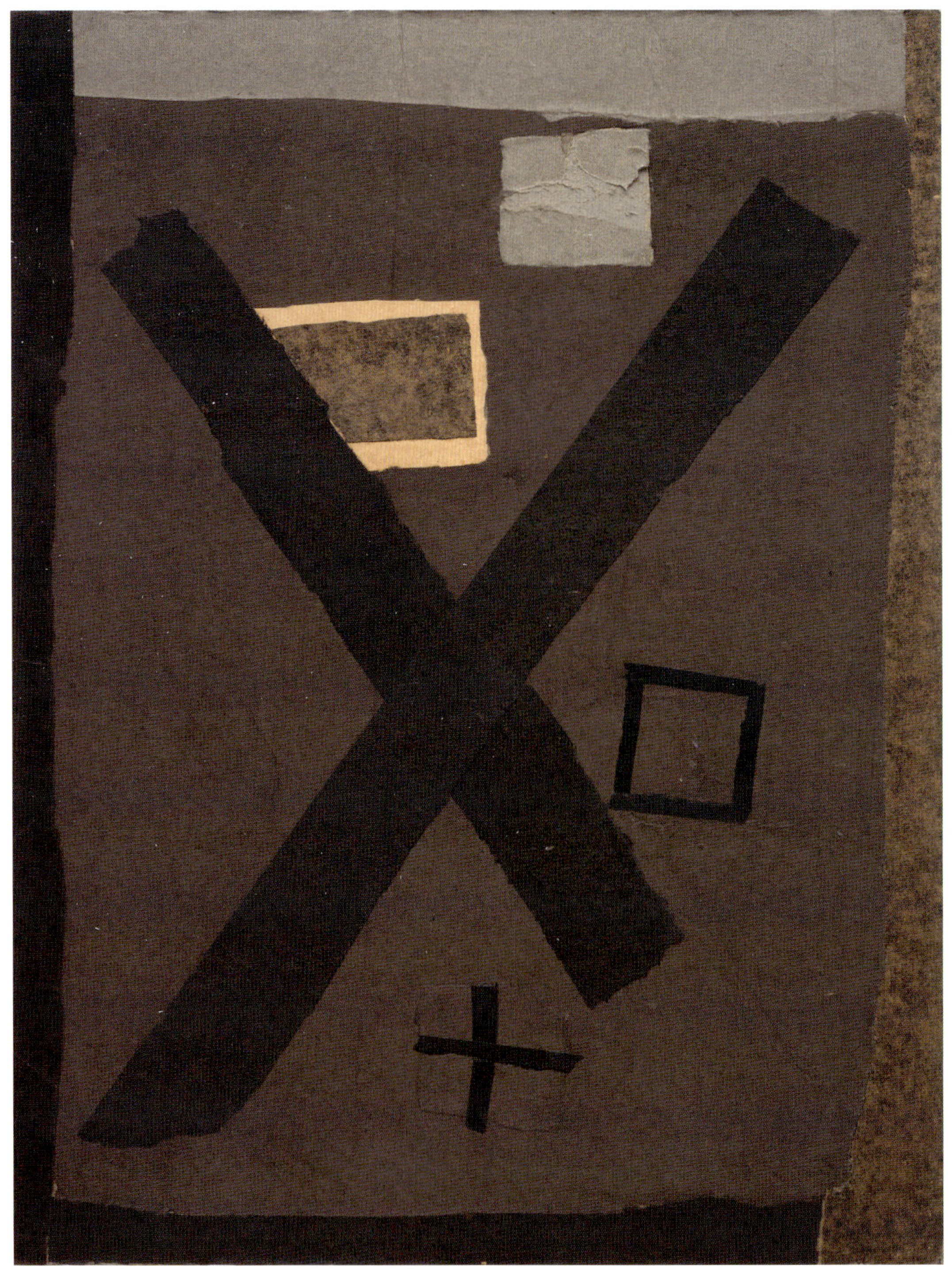

A-51　1952–63　Collage　65 × 45.7 cm (24 × 18")　Private collection

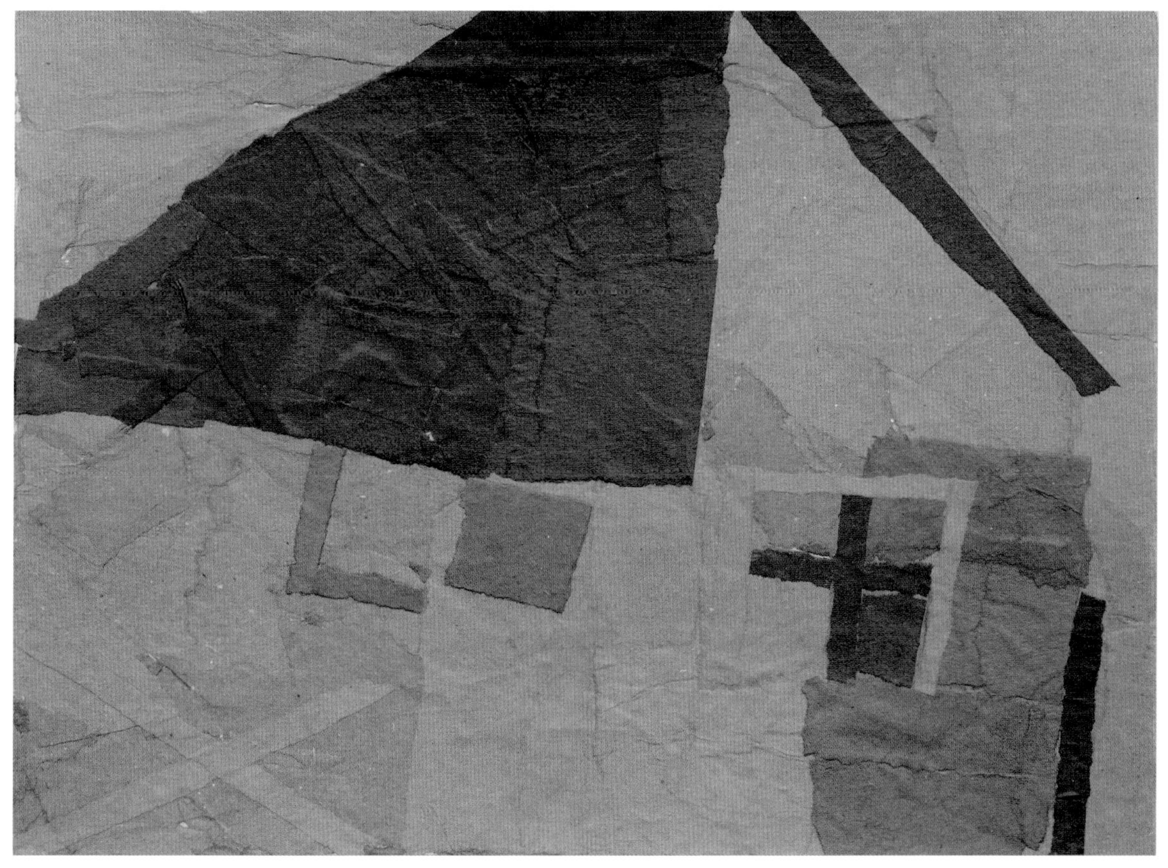

A-52   1952   Collage   29.7 × 45 cm (11.7 × 17.7")   Private collection

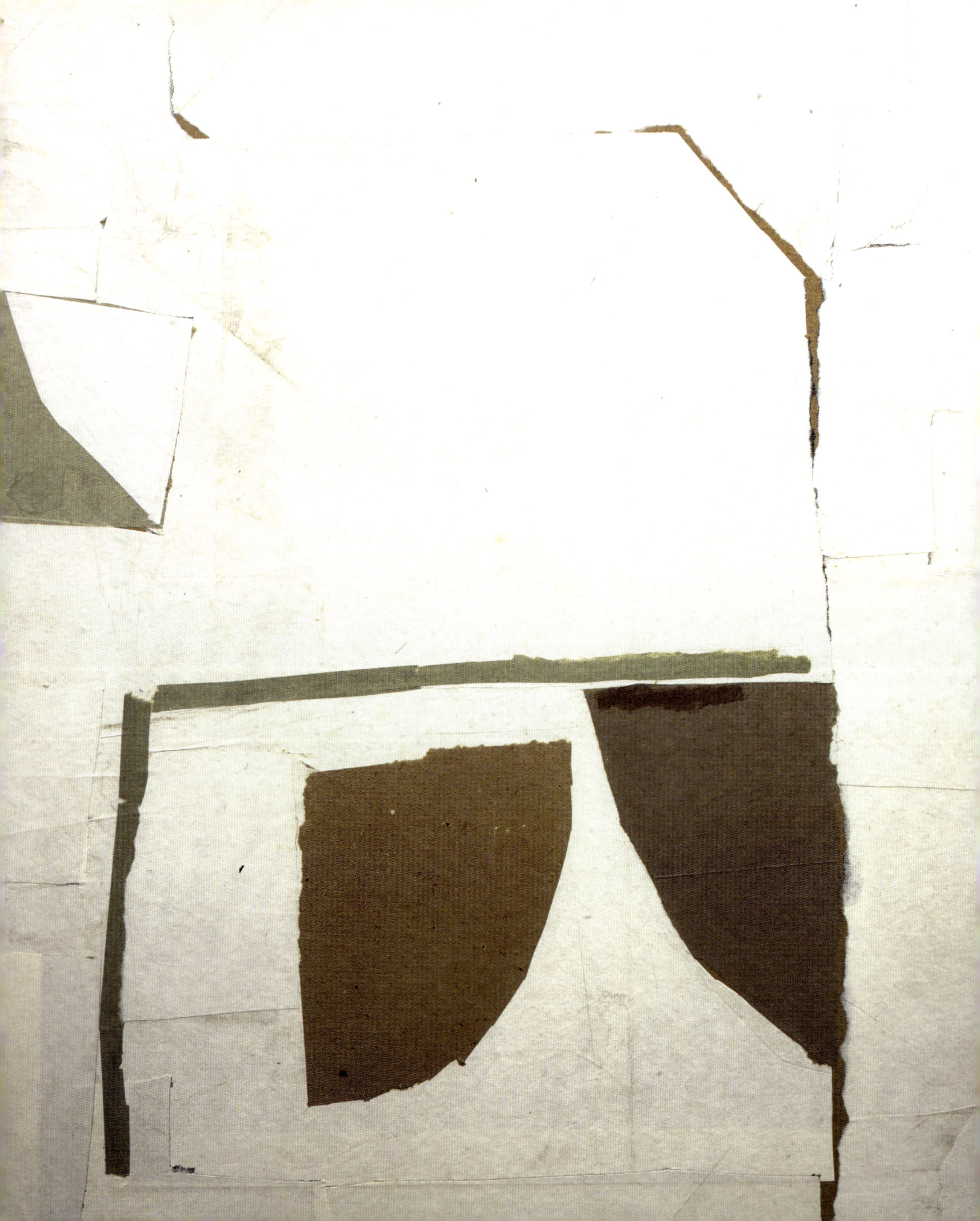

3
Collage

So in 1952 Davison started to make collages and gave up painting, partly in response to his disappointment when Gimpel Fils reneged on their promise of an exhibition. In protest he transferred his language to a new medium, perhaps because scavenged paper was cheaper than oil paint, and all economies made a difference to the impoverished pair. But the principal reason must have been because he loved paper and recognized its potential. To begin with, he used it in a similar disposition of forms – the interlocking of simplified areas or blocks of colour. Then he developed a language of found paper. He didn't paint it different colours, nor did he refer directly to its previous use in any way. The paper, unlike so much Surrealist or Pop collage, remained anonymous, without any narrative implications.

Davison's early collage work tends to be subdued in colour, simply because the paper that was available did not come in striking colours. Later this changed. He also tended at this point to fill his compositions to the edge of the given rectangle (a section of Essex board), and used the edge significantly. Later he created a much more open-weave approach with no backboard and an edge that meandered independently. Then his collages found their own shape and boundaries, but it's revealing how little they still strayed

A-75   1960–3   Collage   61 × 45.7 cm (24 × 20")   Private collection

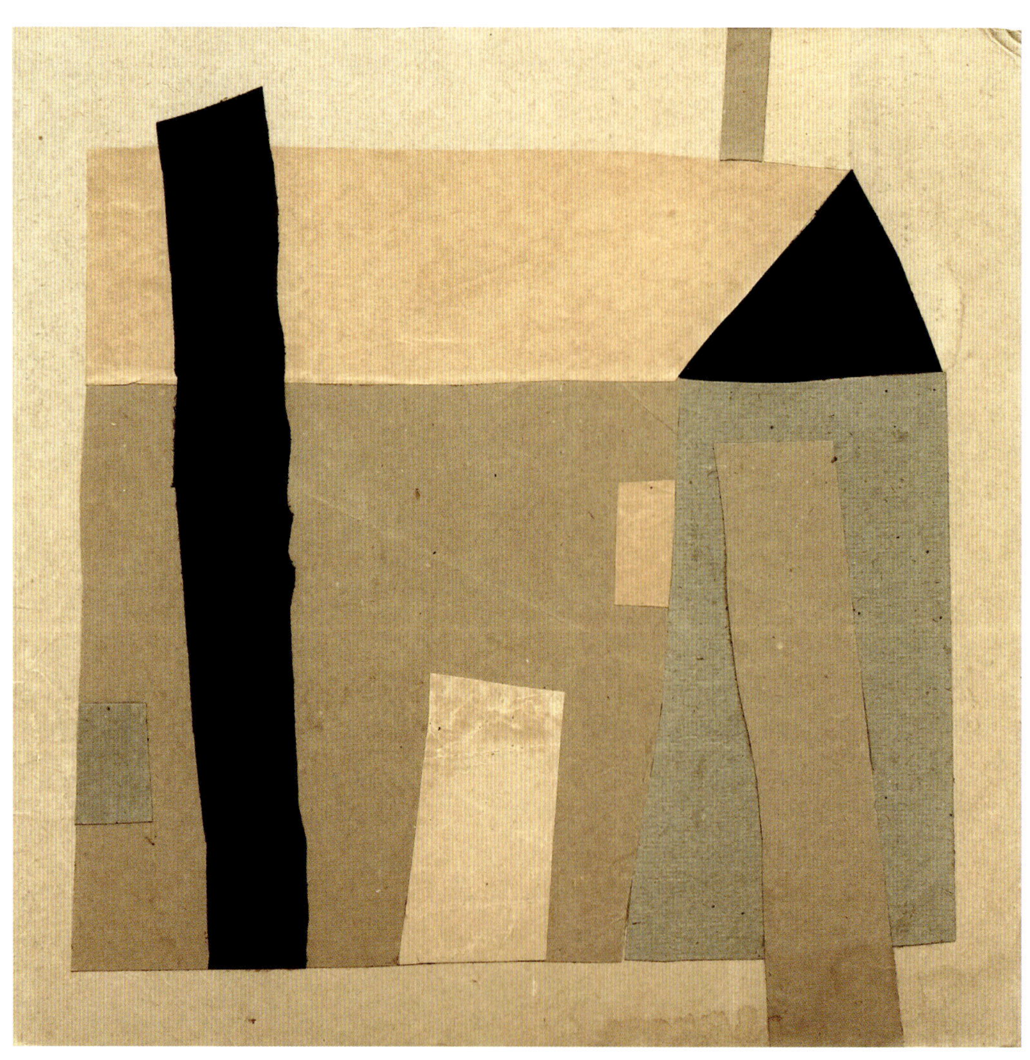

A-15   1952   Collage   40 × 40 cm (15.75 × 15.75")   Private collection

from the traditional rectangle or near-square. Not for Davison the shaped picture that became fashionable in the 70s and 80s: the diamond or oval. His quadrilaterals simply became a bit more ragged.

Although by 1949 painting had become Davison's chief occupation, to be supplanted in 1952 by collage, he still remained a man of words: a great letter-writer and conversationalist. He was still sending out manuscripts in an optimistic way – to Lund Humphries, for instance, in May 1952, a long poem in four parts called *Persephone*. There is, however, no response from the publishers among his papers. Meanwhile his religious beliefs found more prominent enactment in lay preaching and parish visiting when the resident vicar left Syleham. Whether this was the best possible expression of Davison's faith, or indeed the best use of his abilities, he certainly gave a great deal of his time to it. Telfer recalls the power of Davison's convictions: 'One Christmas I was given a passage to read from the bible as part of the service. We went down to Syleham Church prior to the service and practised reading for about half an hour. When it came to the actual bible reading I felt the whole process had been taken out of my hands and intuited by him. The only conscious thing I remember was turning the page on the lectern.'

When he first started making collages, there was a distinct advantage to making art from materials that were effectively scrap or junk. Initially, Davison was restricted in colour by the paper available to him, so he concentrated on tone. The first simple geometric arrangements grew more complicated. The ragged shapes in Hilton's mid-50s paintings may have been a continuing influence, but Davison took the implication of these further by forming and tearing and

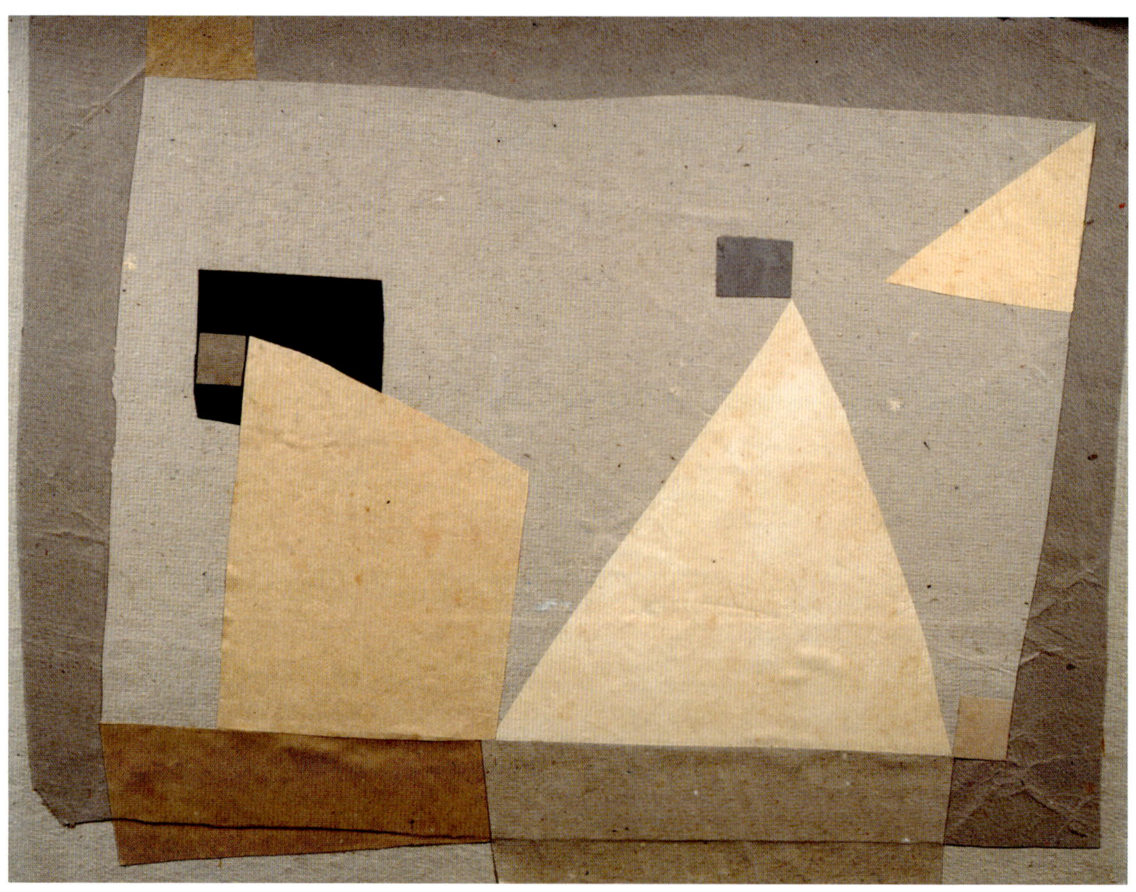

A-22 1952–3 Collage 43.2 × 58.4 cm (17 × 23") Private collection

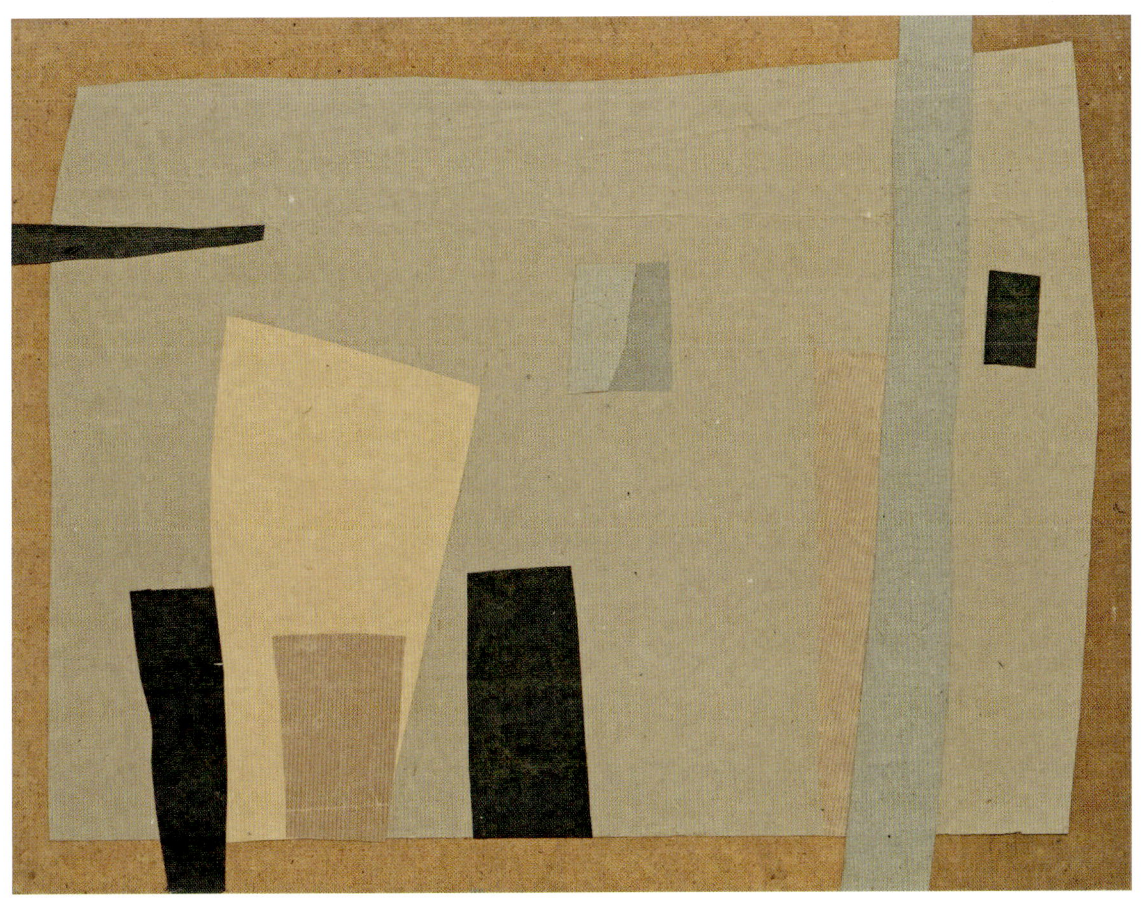

A-31   1952   Collage   43.2 × 55.9 cm (17 × 22")   Private collection

layering the paper in a multiplicity of ways to make much more complex arrays of shape. Alan Powers describes the work up to the mid-1960s as having 'an austere grandeur, more architectural perhaps, but also quite domestic and intimate. The range of browns suggests Vuillard, or some of the posters of Ben Nicholson's father, William, working with James Pryde as the Beggarstaff Brothers in the 1890s. These posters were composed at full size on the floor using cut paper, so the resemblance is not surprising.'

The problem of identifying these collages was partially solved by Mellis after Davison's death by giving them descriptive titles rather than simply numbers, and very approximate dates. For instance, the collage now known as *Condemned House* (c.1952–63) (see A-51, page 78) has a great X over it, like a cancelled photograph on a contact sheet – implying not suitable for use. What better way to condemn a building? There is wit here and economy of means. It's quite a dark piece but is poignantly lit up by a yellow-edged rectangle towards the centre top. Three squares (one with a cross through it) and various rectangles make up the composition. The Greek cross recurs through these early collages and could refer to the leading in a window, or be a basic symbol for a church.

Black Landscape (c.1952–63) (see A-4) is not nearly as dark as it sounds, being composed of three darkish squares (containing other squares or rectangles) and various lighter paths, on a light greyish ground. The pale stone colour of the underlying Essex board appears through the grey at intervals and lights the picture, and the central curved band of board has deliciously ragged edges where the grey paper has been roughly torn. Here is an early example of Davison's painterly approach to collage: this band looks more like a brushstroke

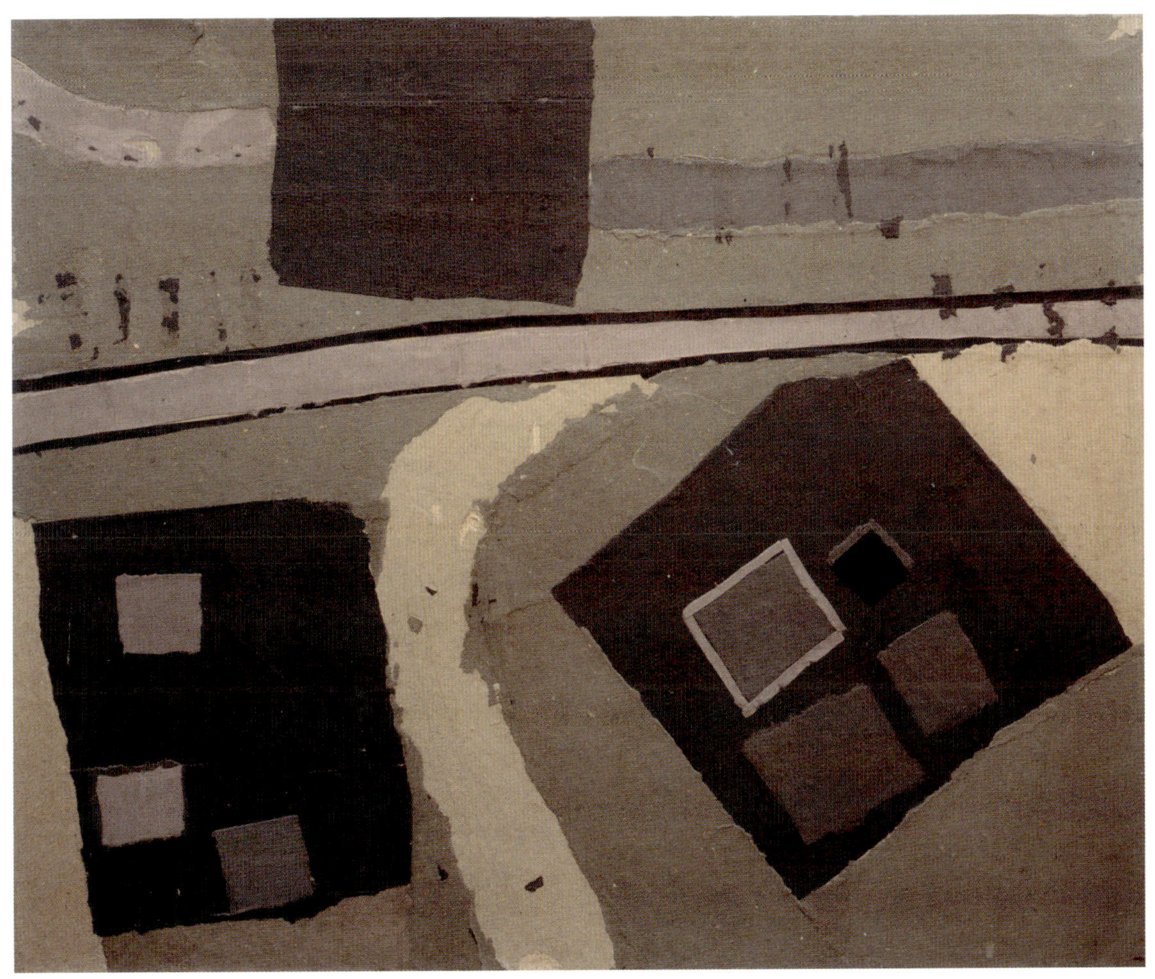

A-4   1952–63   Collage   63 × 75.9 cm (24.8 × 29.9")   Private collection

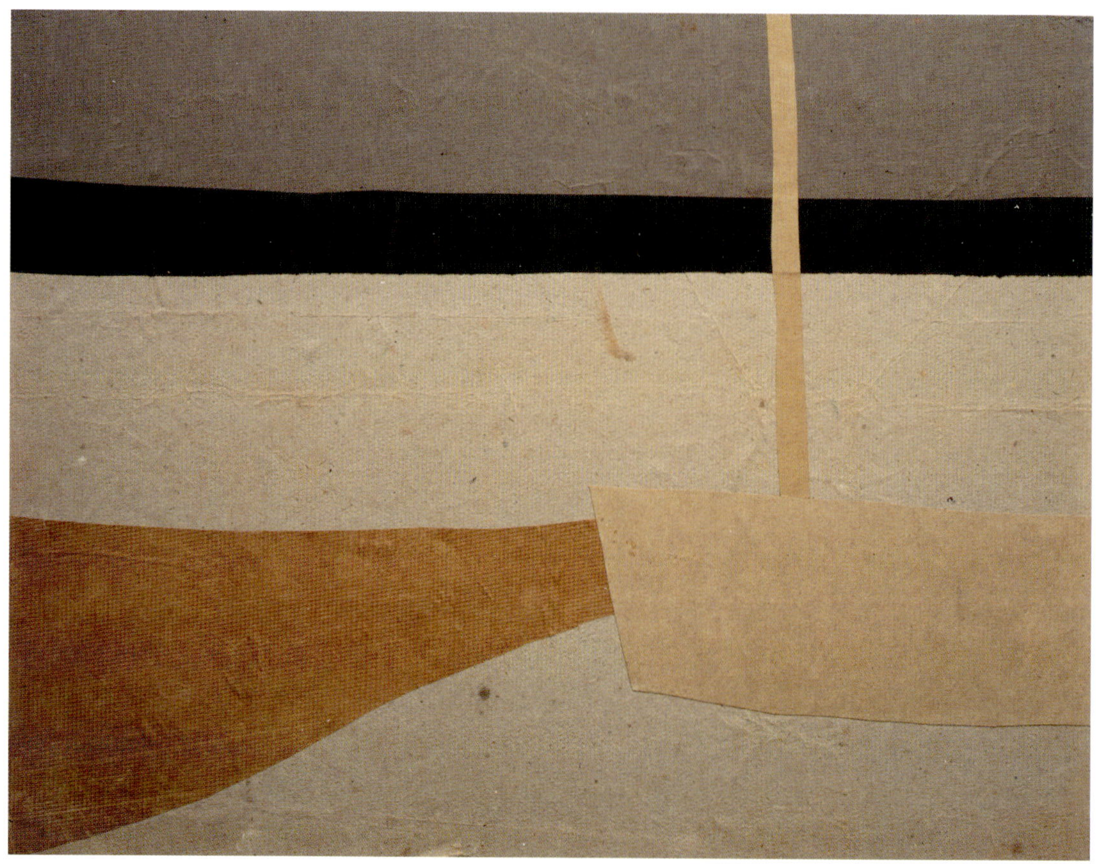

A-236 1952–63 Collage 43.2 × 55.9 cm (17 × 22") Private collection

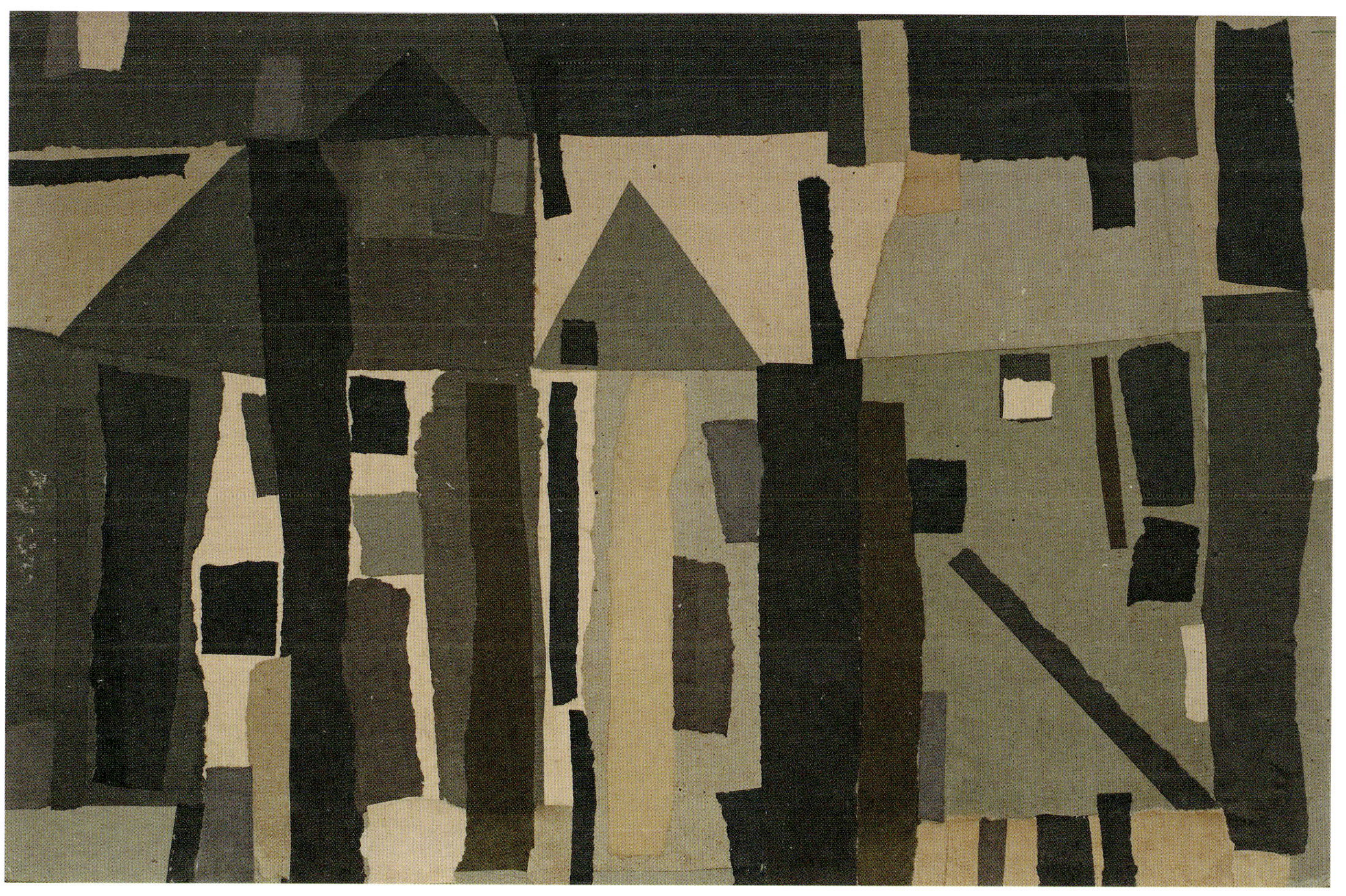

A-76   1960–3   Collage   45.7 × 76.2 cm (18 × 30")   Private collection

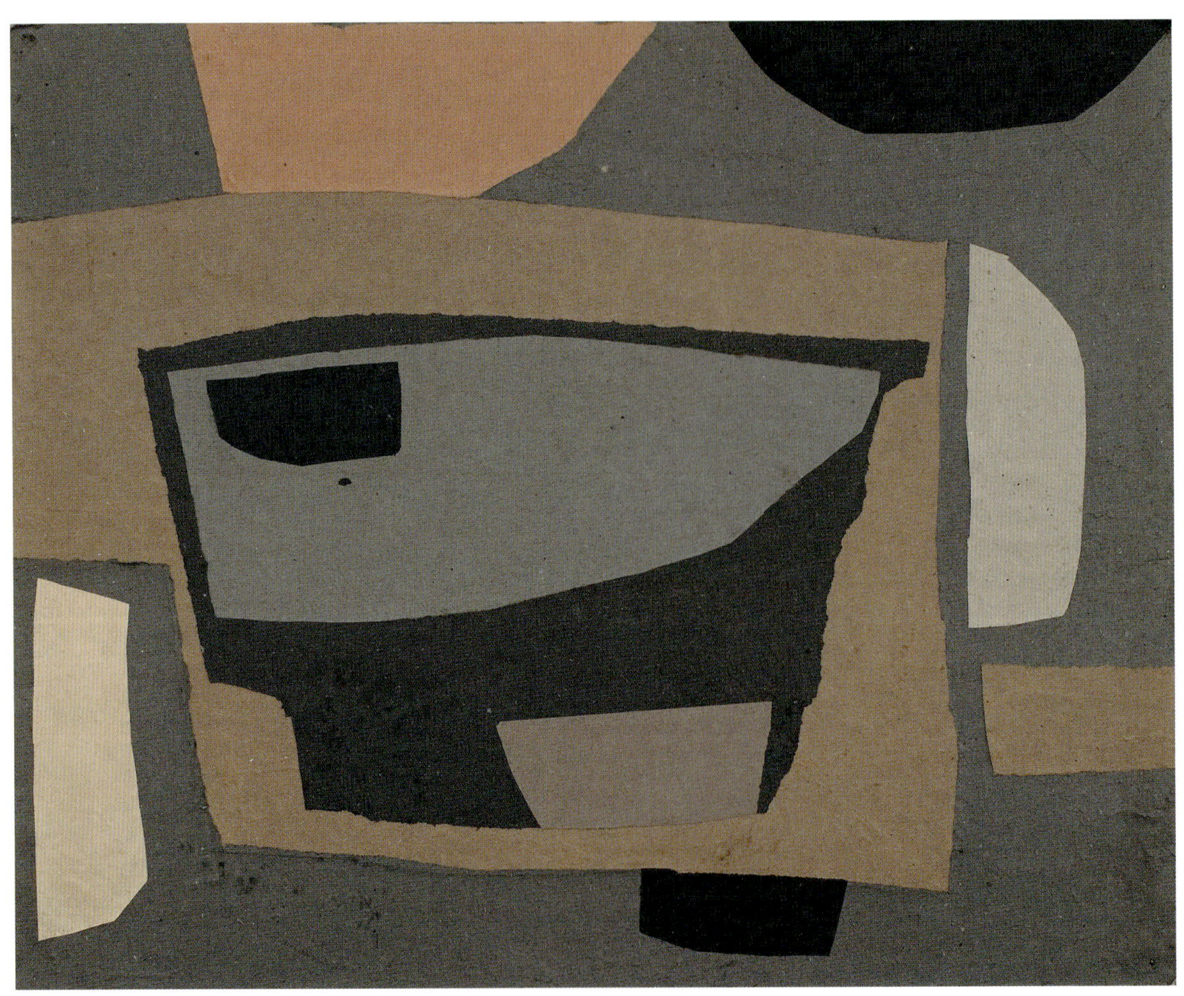

A-42   1952–63   Collage   45.9 × 58.4 cm (19.5 × 23")

than torn paper – a characteristic that was to preoccupy him increasingly throughout the 1960s and 70s. By contrast, *Beach and Boat* (c.1952–63) (see A-236, page 88) is a deceptively simple composition, sharply outlined, spare and flat, but with an unexpected sense of spatial recession and a very complete and satisfying design. The shapes of the paper in this work do not look torn, and it is hard not to conclude that they were cut with knife or scissors.

Although they had chosen to isolate themselves in East Anglia, there was still some communication between the Davisons and the London art world, though it tended to be sporadic. Sometimes Mellis would stay in London with Roger Hilton and his first wife Ruth in St Anne's Road, not far from Patrick Heron in Addison Avenue. Although Hilton had been initially drawn to Francis's work, friendship with the prickly Davison was no easy task, and it was Mellis and Hilton who became close. Hilton actually came to stay at Church Farm Cottage in the autumn of 1955, but the visit was not a success. Despite Hilton's enthusiasm for his work, Davison grew convinced that Hilton wanted to steal his ideas and he hid his collages away. The argumentative and rapier-tongued Hilton could alienate most people, but Davison withdrew before he had even tried.

In 1955 Roland Browse & Delbanco showed a group of collages of which one was reserved but none eventually sold. After that, Davison worked in isolation and remained largely unknown except to a handful of friends and supporters. Occasionally something would be included in a local Suffolk mixed exhibition, and it seems that both the painter Mary Potter (who bought a fine collage) and the sculptor Robert Adams were first acquainted with his work in this way, and then became enthusiastic advocates. Potter's endorsement was especially useful as it was her collage that Julian Spalding saw as his first example of Davison's work, thus triggering an important relationship which led to several exhibitions. But at this point in his career, when he might be thought to be most in need of encouragement and income, Davison didn't exhibit anywhere in London. Around 1962/3 Adrian Stokes took some examples of Francis's collages to Victor Waddington, but the timing was unfortunate as Margaret's own short-lived relationship with the gallery was at that moment coming to an end, and nothing came of this generous gesture.

Although it is often difficult to date the collages, they can be divided into two basic periods: those early ones mounted on Essex board, in restrained colours with much tonal manipulation, and the post-1963 ones. In 1963, the Davisons went to stay with the Herons at Eagle's Nest in Zennor, near St Ives. Francis had brought no backboards with him but he wanted to work, stimulated no doubt by Heron's studio activity. So he was forced to work without, and this liberated his approach to space and shape. Now his collages could find their own edges without being constrained within a rectangle. It is revealing, however, how few really unusual shapes he employed – Davison's collages tend to remain largely rectangular, with a tendency towards the off-square. And yet even within this basic conformity, he was able to create an unlimited variation of edge and outline, a rich addition to his invention within the picture limits.

How much did Davison destroy? He later took to cannibalizing his earlier collages, and it's clear that he frequently re-worked current images, so whether he actually destroyed a great deal remains conjecture. We know that in 1959 Mellis had a studio clear-out and it's more than

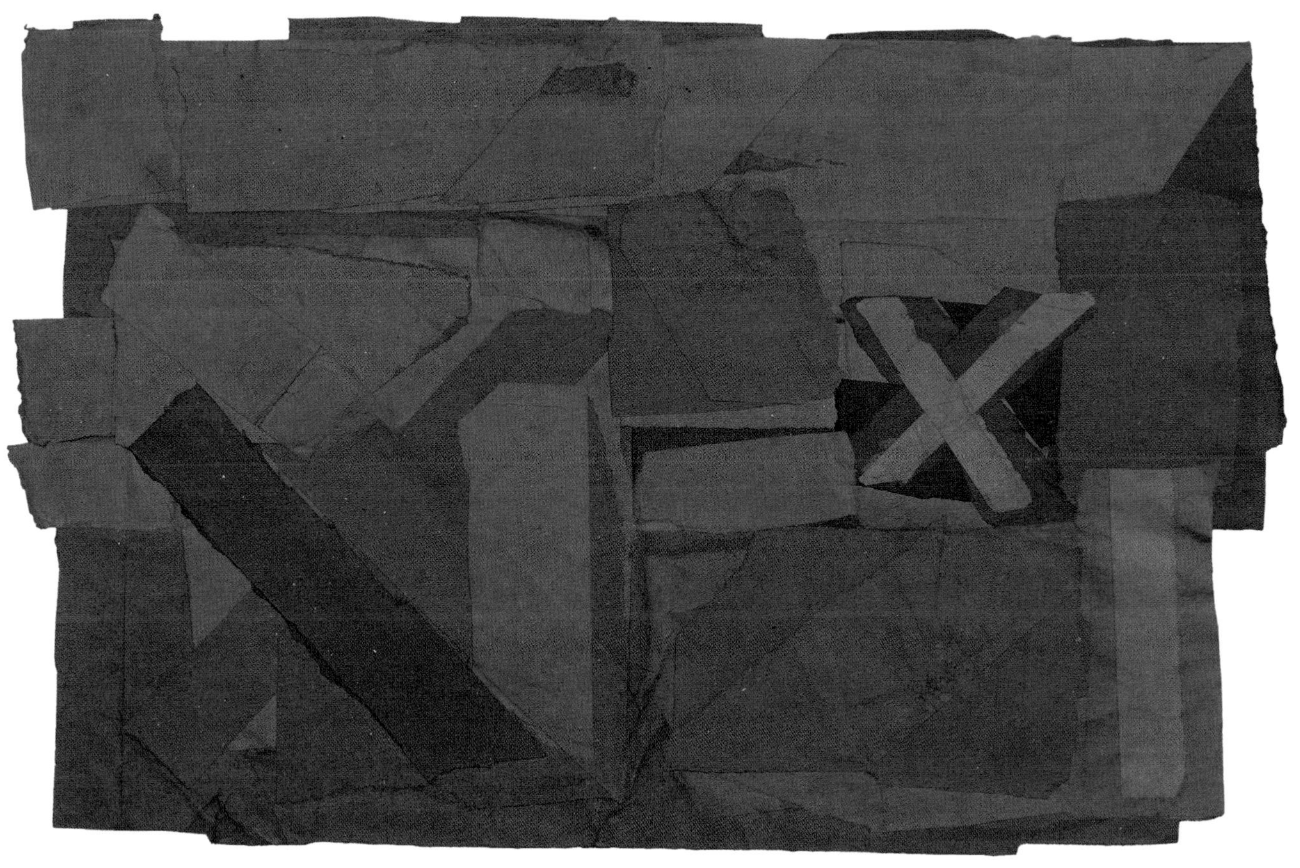

B-3   1963–5   Collage   36.8 × 61 cm (14.5 × 24")   Private collection

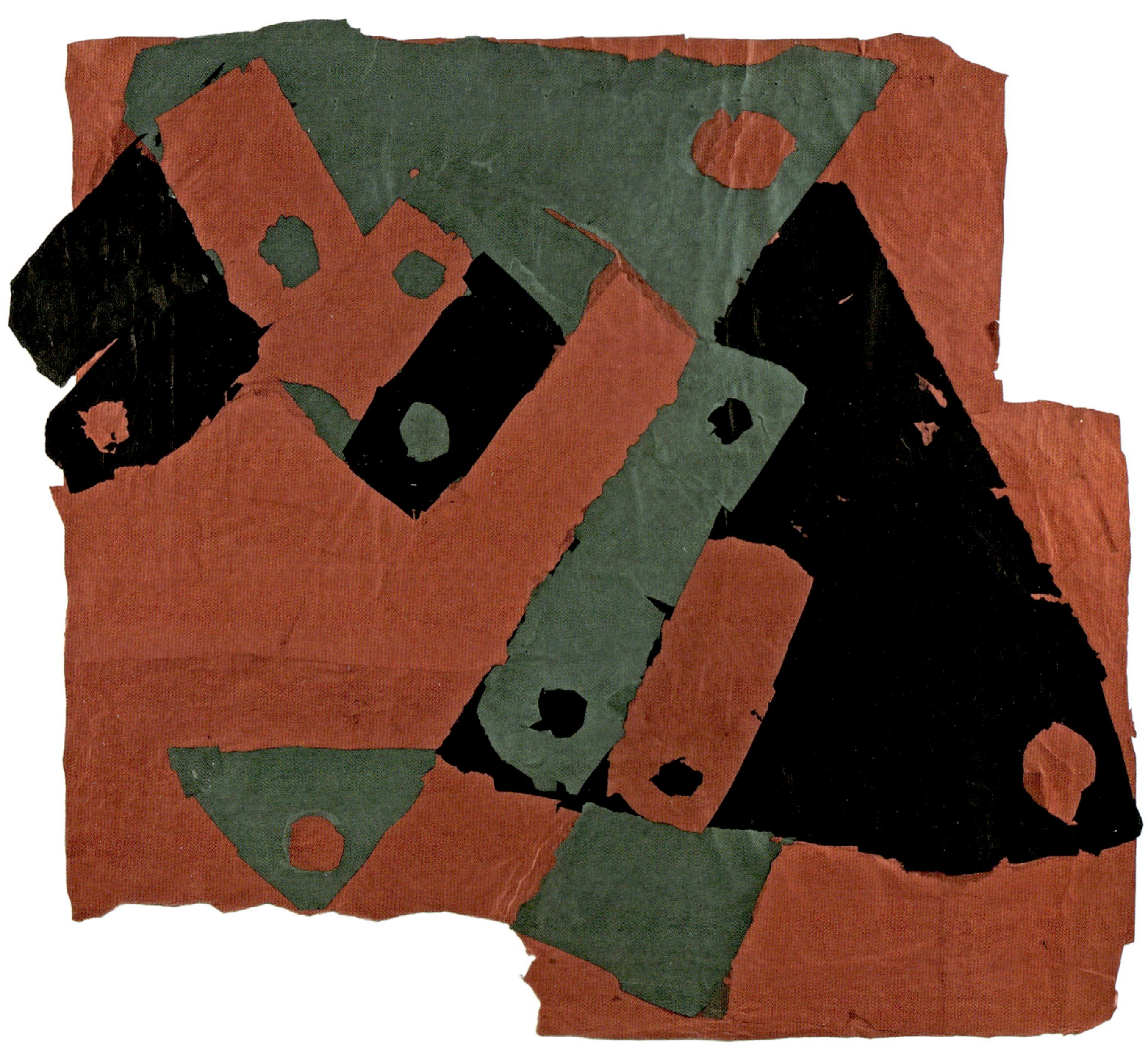

C-145   1970   Collage   100.3 × 114.3 cm (39.5 × 45")

possible that Davison did the same, but perhaps early paintings were then the victims. (Certainly, there aren't many extant Davison paintings.) It's impossible at this remove to ascertain quite how much influence husband and wife exerted on each other's development, but it's clear that they were thinking along the same lines as artists, and no doubt discussed common problems. Revealingly, Mellis often wrote (in letters to her friend, the painter Olga Davenport) about shape and colour – her constant preoccupations.

One of the things that had initially drawn her to Adrian Stokes back in the 1930s was the play of ideas he was to formulate in his book on the subject, *Colour and Form*. She was naturally attracted to painters who shaped colour, like Matisse or Rothko, and commented: 'What one is doing in painting is finding the right place and size for the right amount of colour.' In a draft letter to Davenport, Mellis wrote: 'I was rather surprised to find that the shape of the areas of colour had to be so definite before the colours, which are shapeless and spreading left to themselves, could transform into real solid colour.' Of course, she is talking about painting but these remarks could be very easily applied to collage and in fact are at the root of Davison's mature approach to his art.

Much depended on the density of the colour as well as its shape. For Davison, the colour was always found, never applied. Davison disliked unused paper, and wouldn't incorporate it in his collages, so there was a built-in history to his materials before he started. (Revealingly, he left instructions that all his hoarded paper, his raw material, should be burnt after his death, which perhaps reveals a slight paranoia that his work might be posthumously continued or forged.) His collages have a used look: the paper is often wrinkled and resembles the archaeological strata of old posters on a wall or billboard, or torn layers of wrapping paper in some mad 'pass the parcel' game. As much as anything, these collages are about flux – the experience of walking through constantly changing nature, the experience of living in the modern world.

The 1960s saw him exploring optical relationships as the range of coloured paper available to him opened up with new habits of packaging and eye-catching branding. The earliest collages, with their mixture of torn and cut paper, the straight cut edges alternating with uneven torn ones, and triangular forms proliferating, seem to recall one or two of Mellis's 1940 works: for example, *Construction in Wood* and *Collage with Red Triangle*. But as Davison began to explore his new language, the similarities vanished, and he was out on his own, orchestrating wedges and slabs of black against grey or brown, or adding a segment of dusky pink to a meeting of rough boat shapes in blue-green, brown and black. Forests of verticals read like medieval strip farming, but with the loss of the Essex board backing, an initially denser configuration of elements takes over. The paper is layered and overlapped to keep the collage together, as can be seen in the fine petrol blue and olive composition from 1963–5.

Gradually stronger colour began to appear, and although Davison never lost his skill with tonal juxtaposition, or his enjoyment of it, the manipulation of bright and contrasting colours formed an increasingly dominant part of the work. Look, for instance, at the two collages illustrated here dating from 1965–71. The dense tangle of vertical and horizontal bars is punctuated by 'full-stops' of contrasting colour, which actually look very like dabs of the brush. Davison was beginning to open up space in his collages by cutting holes

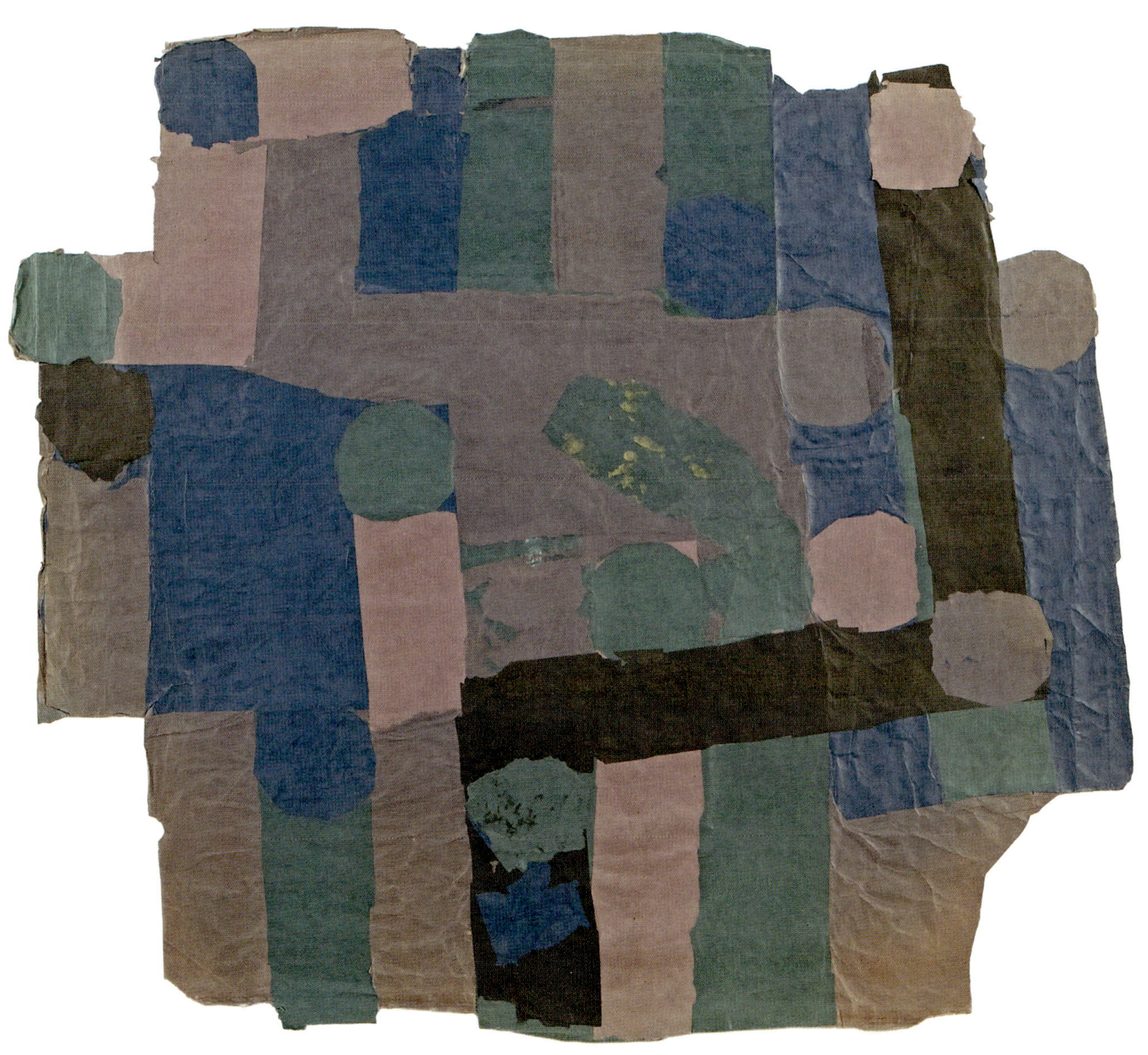

C-46   1965–71   Collage   88.9 × 96.5 cm (35 × 38")

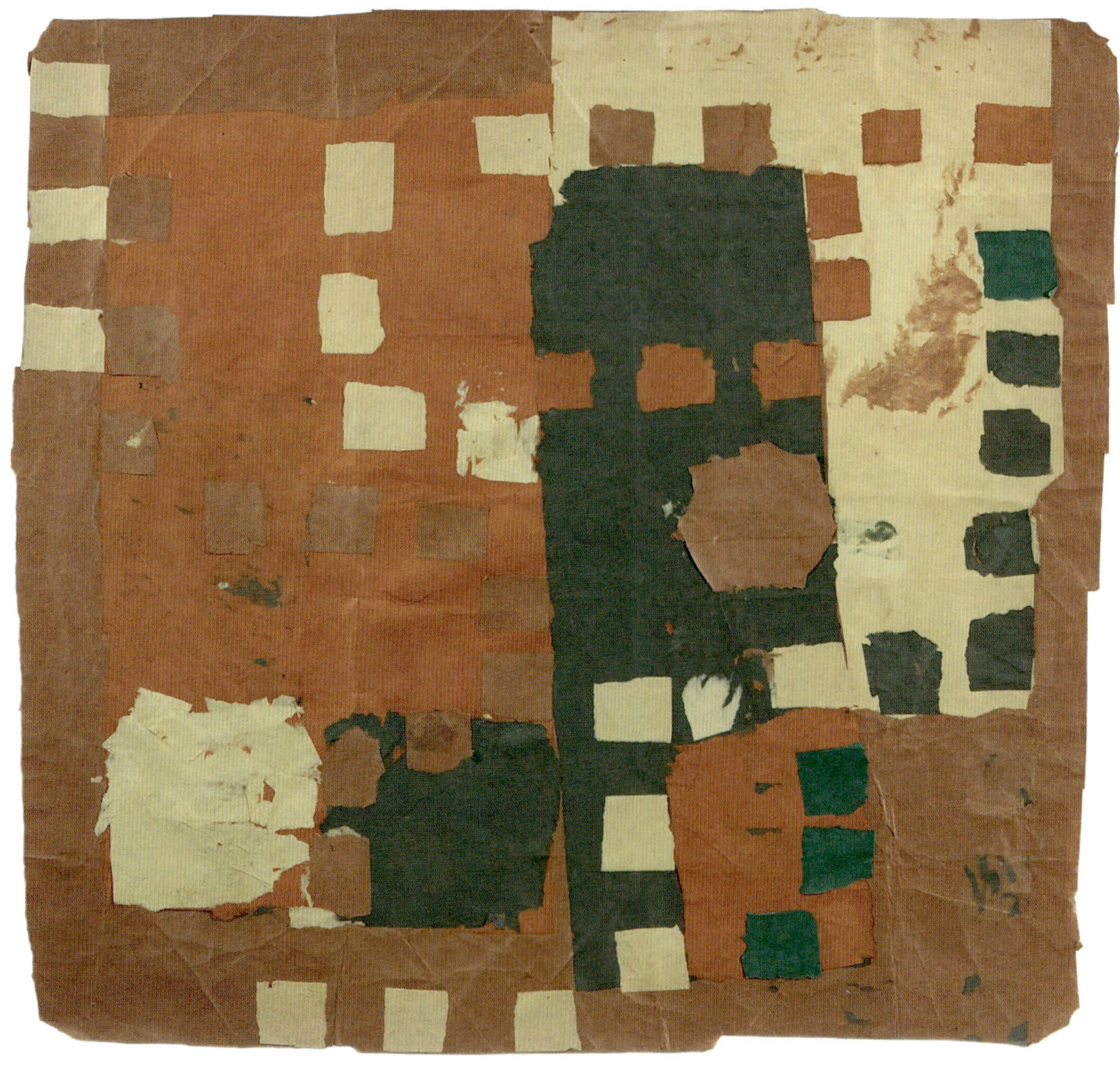

C-77a   1965–71   Collage   67.3 × 69.9 cm (26.5 × 27.5")

through layers – sinking wells, creating observation stations – and at the same time using his horizontal bands like the hoops on a barrel, holding everything together.

The interruption of his lines in this manner creates a different, syncopated rhythm to the works and immediately suggests comparison with Mondrian's late paintings – and particularly *Broadway Boogie Woogie* (1942–3). But against the complete statement of Mondrian, Davison's work looks excitingly provisional and contingent. The dominant themes are rhythm, colour, space relations, and Davison plays interesting variations on them. The poppy red, green and black collage from 1970, with its domino-like dots or eyelets, has an altogether freer, more open-ended feel, and although evidently self-contained could easily be a part of a larger continuum. There is a powerful sense that by looking at these collages we are re-engaging with the fabric of the world: this is a material rather than intellectual exploration, but one which was to become increasingly spiritual. The assurance with which Davison deals with the physical allows the spirit to soar: we are paradoxically grounded to be able to fly.

At this point, it is revealing to compare Davison's work with Arp's *papiers déchirés*. To take two examples of Arp's work: one from the collection of MOMA New York, dating from 1916–17; the second in the Tate Gallery, dating from 1933. Both were created 'according to the laws of chance' and are collages of torn paper, but where they signally differ from Davison's work is the way in which each element of torn paper sits discretely on its backboard, totally separate and distinct. Some are closer than others but there is no overlapping. Davison laps and overlaps and derives much of his richness of effect from layering. In fact, even his less complicated earlier works go in for overlapping papers, and

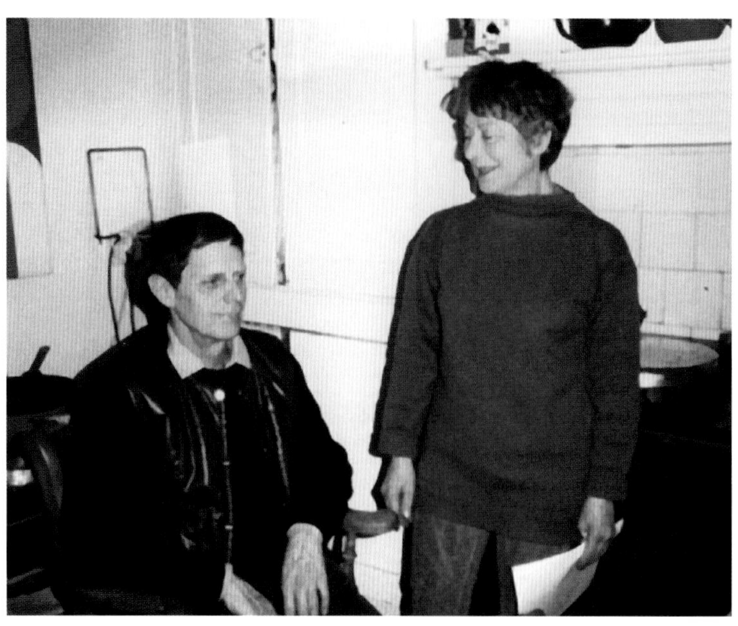

Francis and Margaret,
Southwold, 1980

this became an essential part of his artistic signature. So, the work of these two artists is very far apart in appearance and formal construction, but the drive behind them may not differ quite so much.

In the following extract, Arp describes how his very precise early methods of cut collage gave way to a use of torn paper, after he discovered a batch of early work he'd stored in the attic had been ruined by damp. He felt that by tearing the paper rather than cutting:

> I had accepted the transience, the dribbling away, the brevity, the impermanence, the fading, the withering, the spookishness of our existence. Not only had I accepted it, I had even welcomed transience into my work as it was coming into being. These torn pictures, these *papiers déchirés*, brought me closer to a faith in things other than earthly.

It is that suggestion of a spiritual component that one finds increasingly in Davison's work.

4
Late Work

Life as a Suffolk small-holder was by no means easy. In 1970 the hens got fowl pest and all 500 of them had to be destroyed. A pig farm next door was now discharging its waste into a ditch running in front of the Davisons' home. They were both getting older and a move to a less isolated place seemed sensible. In 1971 Mellis was first laid up with rheumatoid arthritis, confined to bed and unable to paint. An isolated existence in the country no longer seemed feasible or even advisable. The small allowances both Margaret and Francis had relied upon had dwindled under inflation, and they could barely afford to run the car essential to living in the country.

The work that Davison made between 1971 and 1973 has a particular character to it. Lines and blocks of strong colour are combined and overlaid, but air is also allowed in for the first time, and gaps between the elements appear, bringing the concept of blankness, or negative space, into the work. There is, therefore, an unusual degree of transparency to these works. Although they could be hung, without benefit of framing, straight onto a gallery's white walls, presentation becomes an intriguing issue. There had already been experiments in the 1950s with hanging paintings from the ceilings of galleries rather than against walls. Roger Hilton did it in 1955 at the Simon Quinn Gallery in Huddersfield. It was intended to demonstrate the 'space-creating' properties of the paintings, through the organization of a kind of picture-grid. There's no indication that Davison was after a similar effect, so presumably the collages were intended

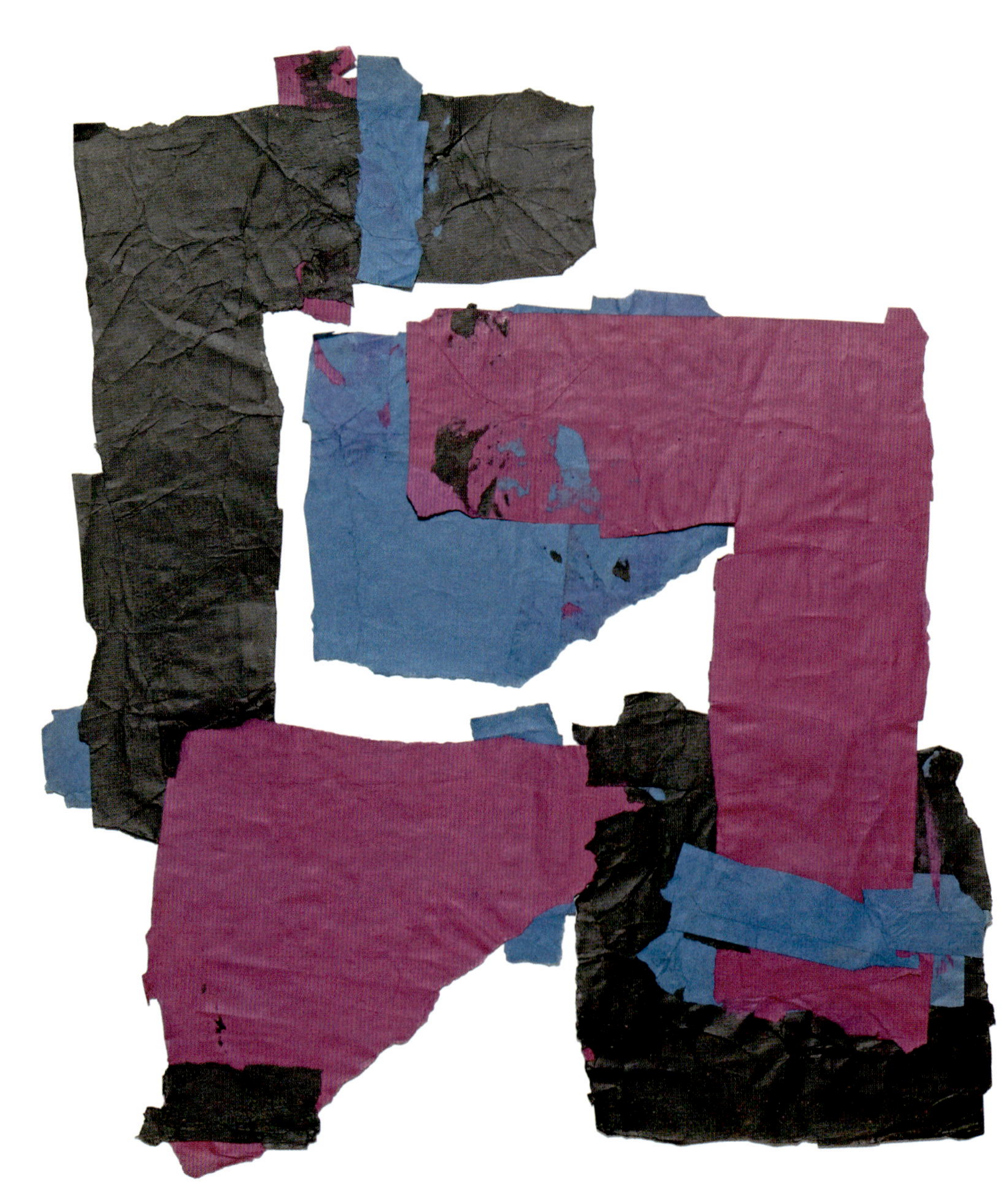

D-317   1972   Collage   92.7 × 77.5 cm (36.5 × 30.5")

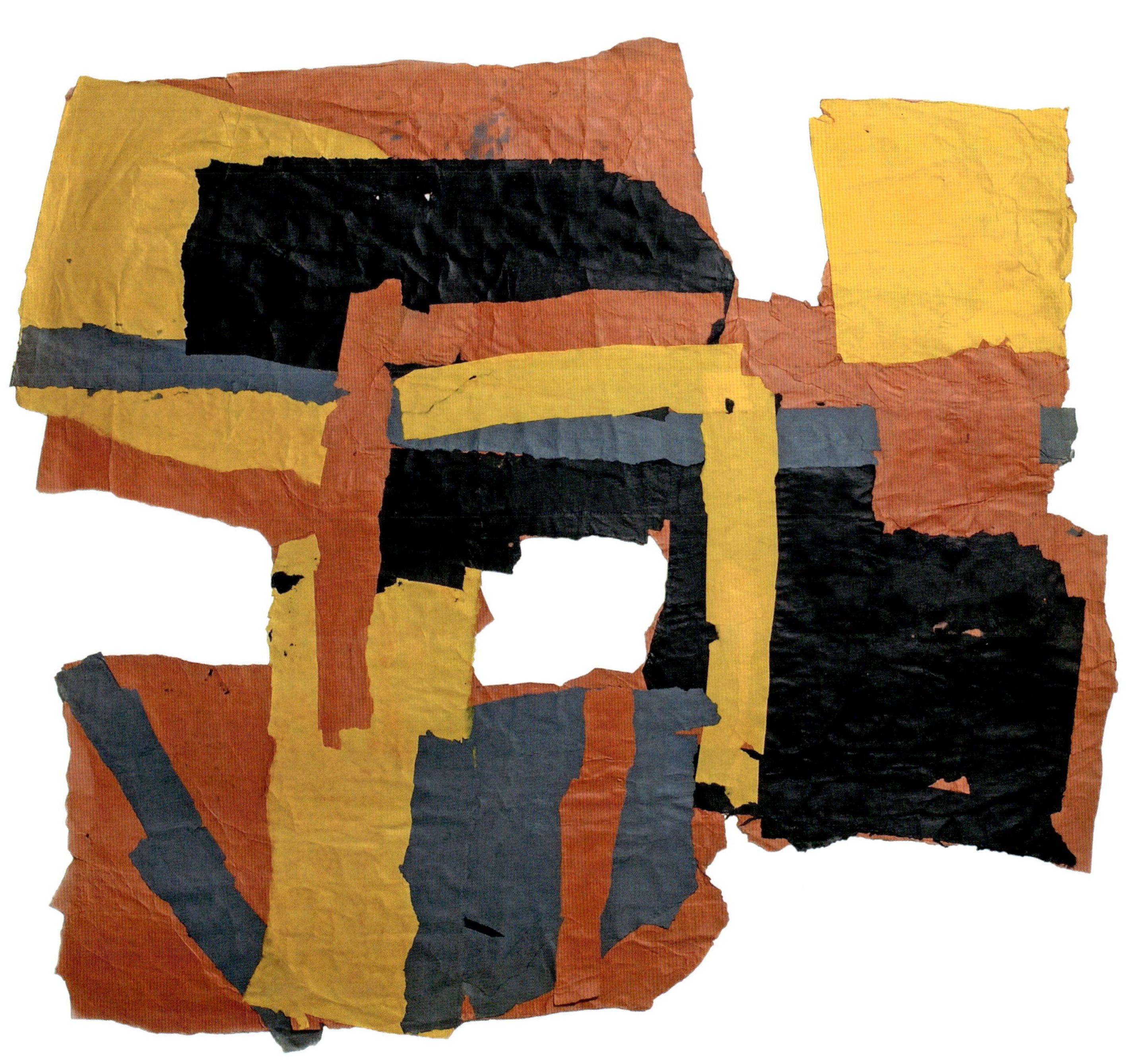

D-211　1972　Collage　106.7 × 124.5 cm (42 × 49")

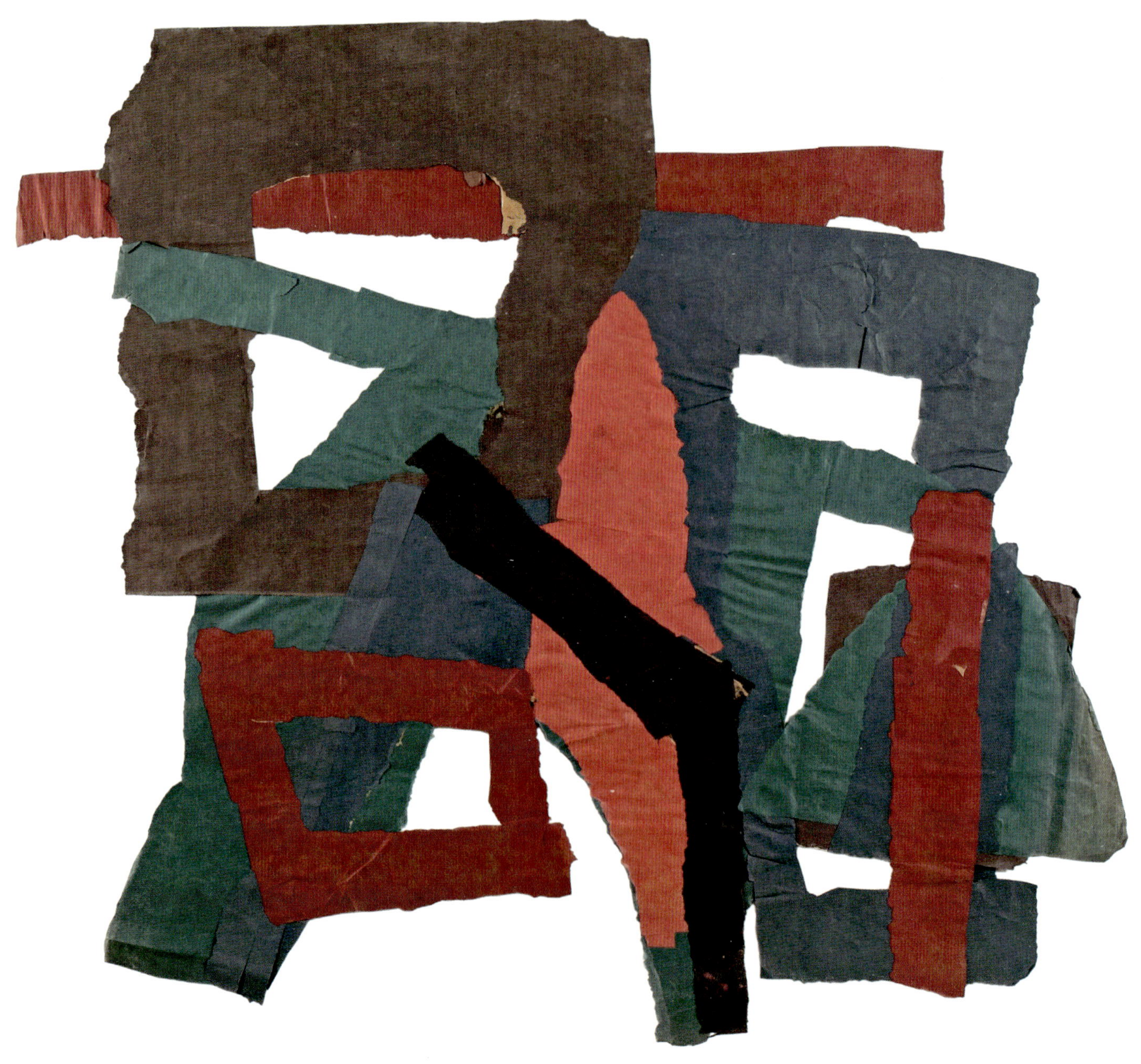

D-214   1972   Collage   114.3 × 124.5 cm (45 × 49")

to be framed straightforwardly, and floated in a kind of box frame. But what colour to mount them on or against? The act of framing these open-work collages would thus incorporate the owner's contribution to the work, and puts a new spin on audience participation.

The abstract imagery of torn paper in these works suggests a superimposed series of arches or entrances – perhaps architectural or organic (cave mouth?) – an emphasis on the notion of threshold which has an autobiographical element to it as well as a metaphysical one. Davison was entering into his kingdom, a kingdom of crumpled but reclaimed paper, of found colour and intimate shape. He was now using his very simple materials in increasingly innovative and radical ways, opening up new territory for art, and successfully transgressing the boundaries between painting and relief sculpture. A lot of the early 1970s collages have what might be called a rural palette, with browns and blues and greens predominating, though pink and red are beginning to assume a more important role. The imagery was growing more mazily convoluted, as the collage no. E-263 (see page 124) demonstrates, and begins to resemble some sort of industrial complex (as seen from the air) rather than the cell communication systems of the brain or the windings of the gut. The human reference was broadening out, owing no doubt to a major change of circumstance.

At the end of 1975, the Davisons moved from Syleham and took up residence in Southwold, painting their new house white from top to bottom – even the wooden floors. Although Margaret had been sad to leave her beloved Church Farm Cottage, she was recompensed by the presence of the sea on the doorstep of their new home, and in fact it was Francis who missed Syleham the most, dreaming vividly and

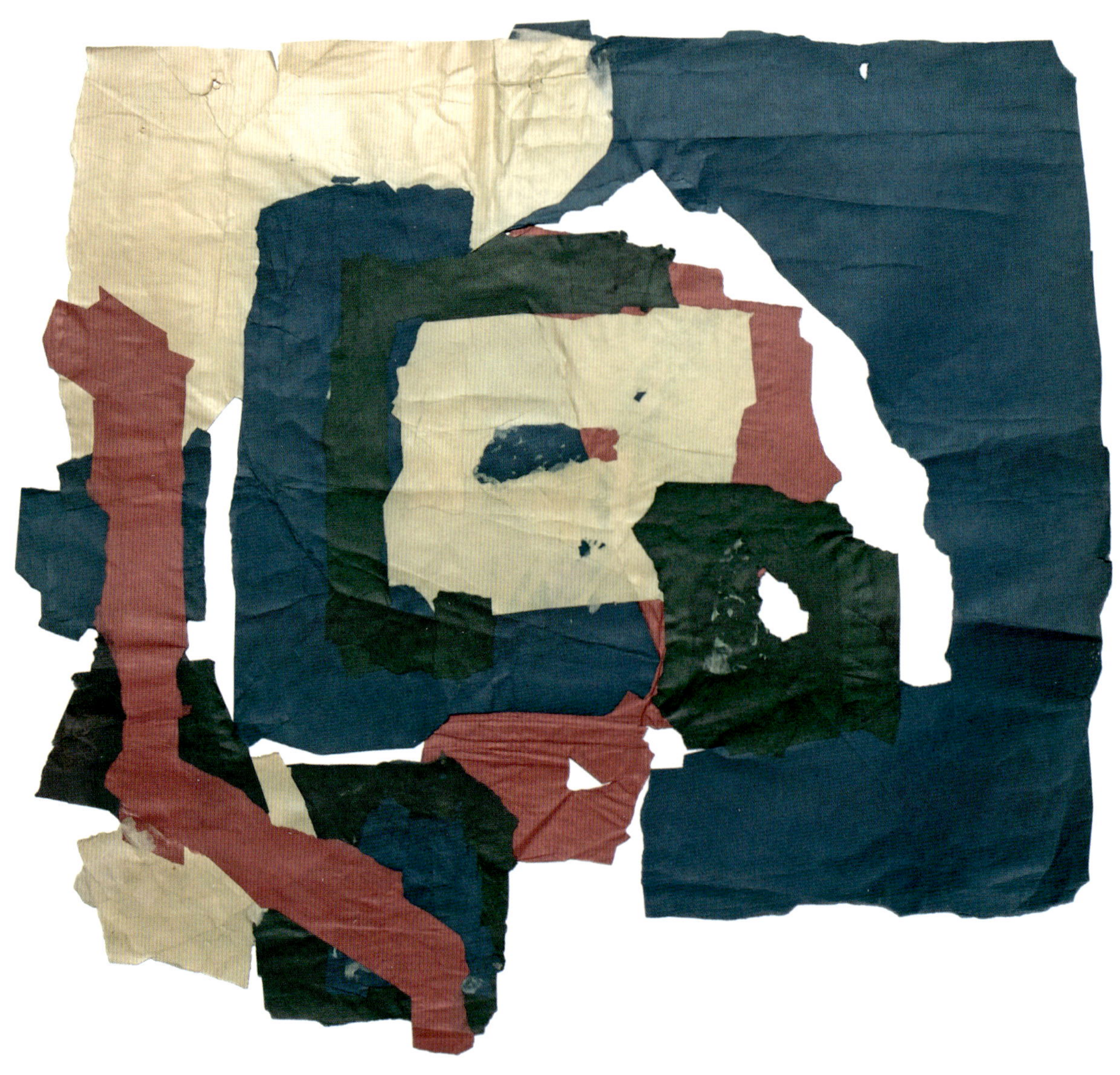

D-216   1971–3   Collage   100.3 × 109.2 cm (39.5 × 43")

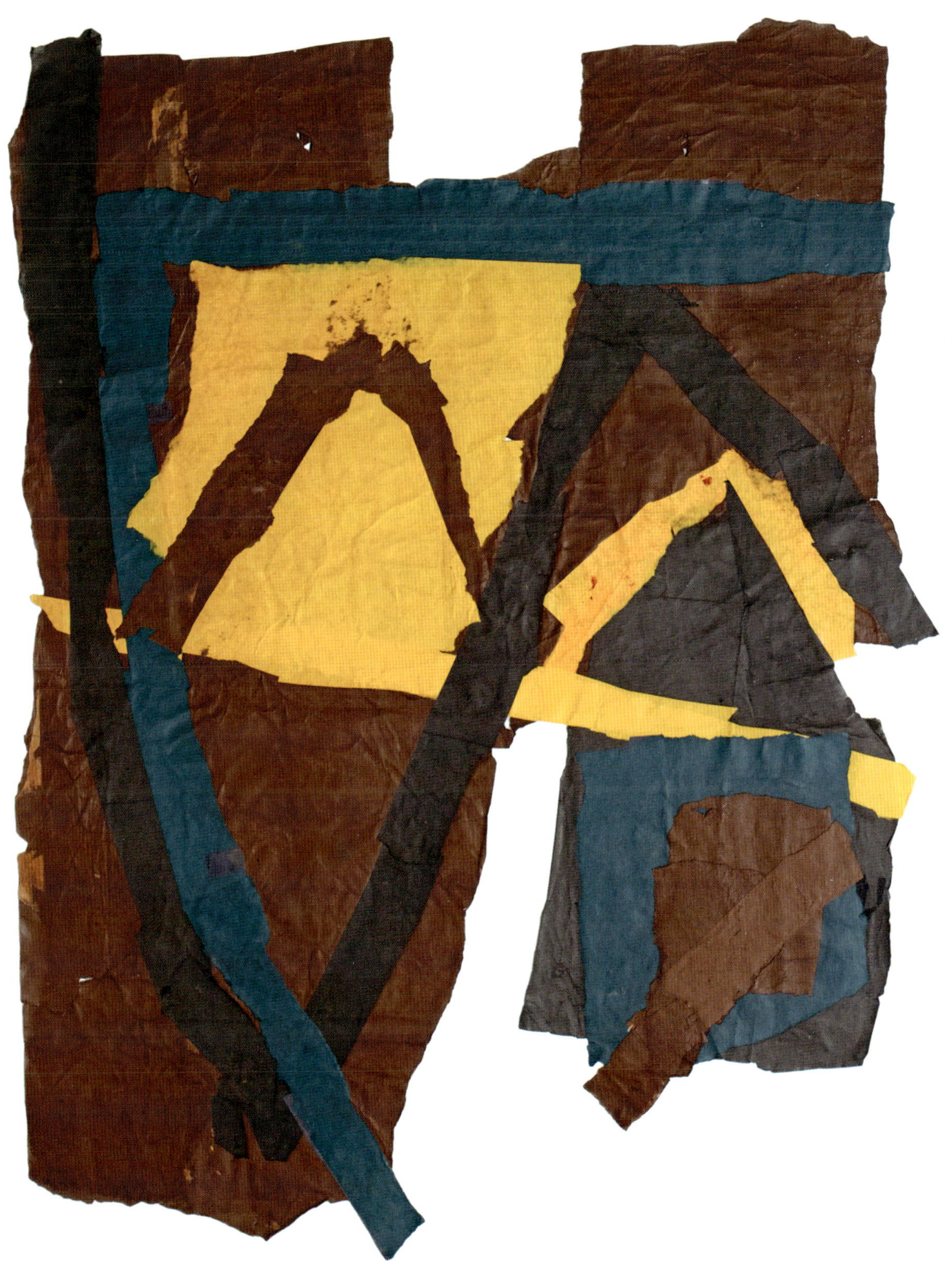

D-350   1972   Collage   139.7 × 104.1 cm (55 × 41")

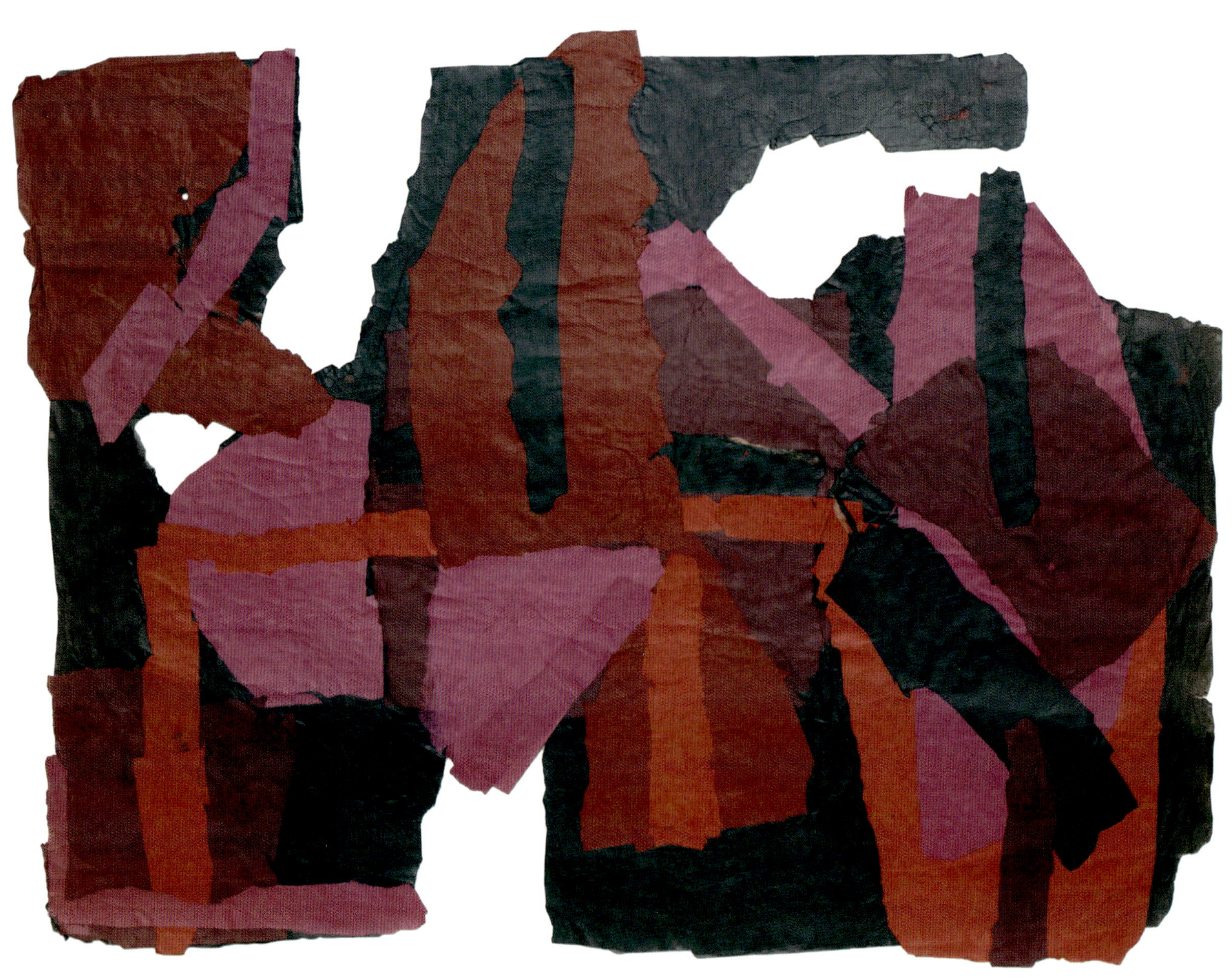

D-292   1971   Collage   114.3 × 142.2 cm (45 × 56")

unhappily about it. But at last he was able to concentrate entirely on his work – even if he had less space in which to carry it out. The garden studios that both he and Mellis occupied at Syleham had to be emptied, and large amounts of paintings and collages were thrown out and burnt. At Southwold there was no garden to divert them, and Francis now took no part in church life so he could concentrate on his collages.

At Southwold, Francis, naturally neat and tidy, did all the housework. Mellis was seriously incapacitated by arthritis, and though she did eventually cure herself, it took a decade of strict diet and exercise, including a daily sea-bathe. He took over the cooking, at a time when he was making some of his best collages, and could not spare the time. He worked in a small front bedroom measuring 12 foot square. Many of the large works were 6 foot in extent, so he wasn't left with much room for manoeuvre. He tended to work with a lowered blind, as he wanted his works to be seen in subdued light so that the colours glowed. This implies that it was less important to emphasize the broken uneven texture of the collaged surface, which a raking side light would have done.

By 1978 the works had become less rural, less green and brown, and much more colourful: the colour is more insistent and often raw. To what extent this was due to the new milieu in which he lived and worked, and how much simply to the kinds and colours of paper now available to him, must remain a matter for conjecture. Certainly at this point he started to cannibalize earlier works, tearing them up and re-using them, which makes the issue of dating his collages even more problematic than it already was. One particularly fine work from the period 1976–8, known simply as F-29 (see page 140), is an extraordinarily open and minimal composition,

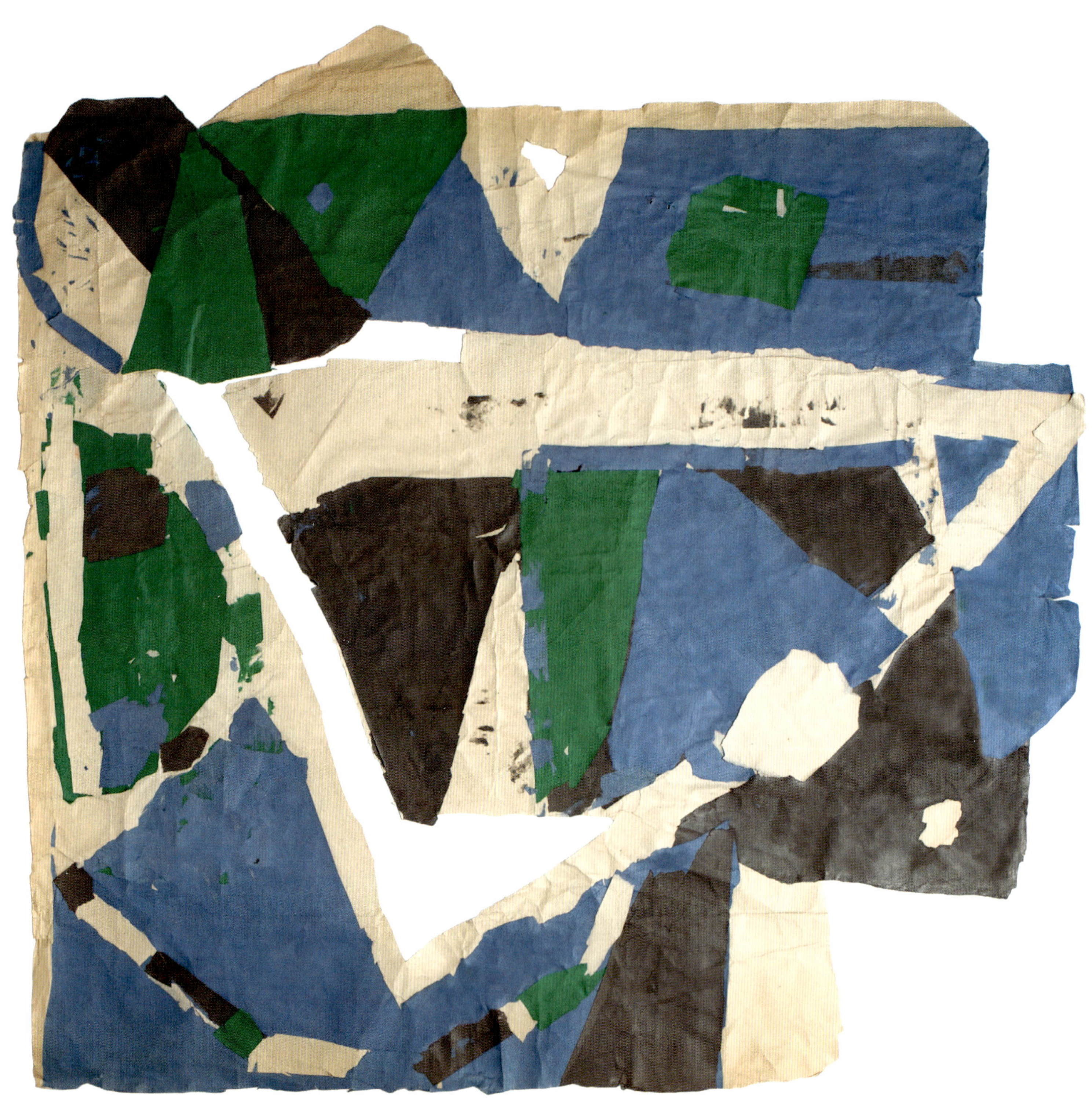

D-250   1972   Collage   144.8 × 144.8 cm (57 × 57")

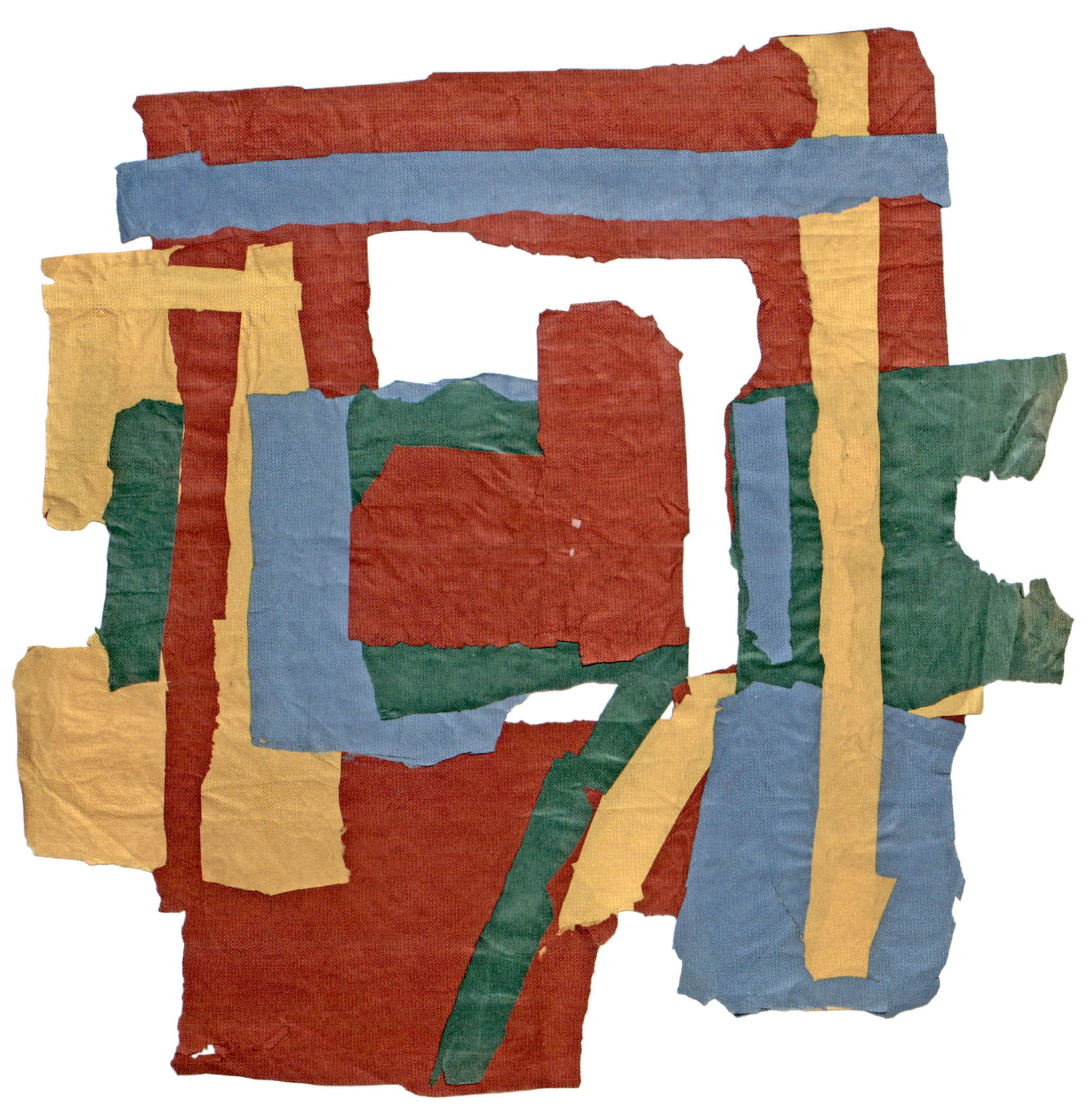

D-326   1972   Collage   119.4 × 118.1 cm (47 × 46.5")

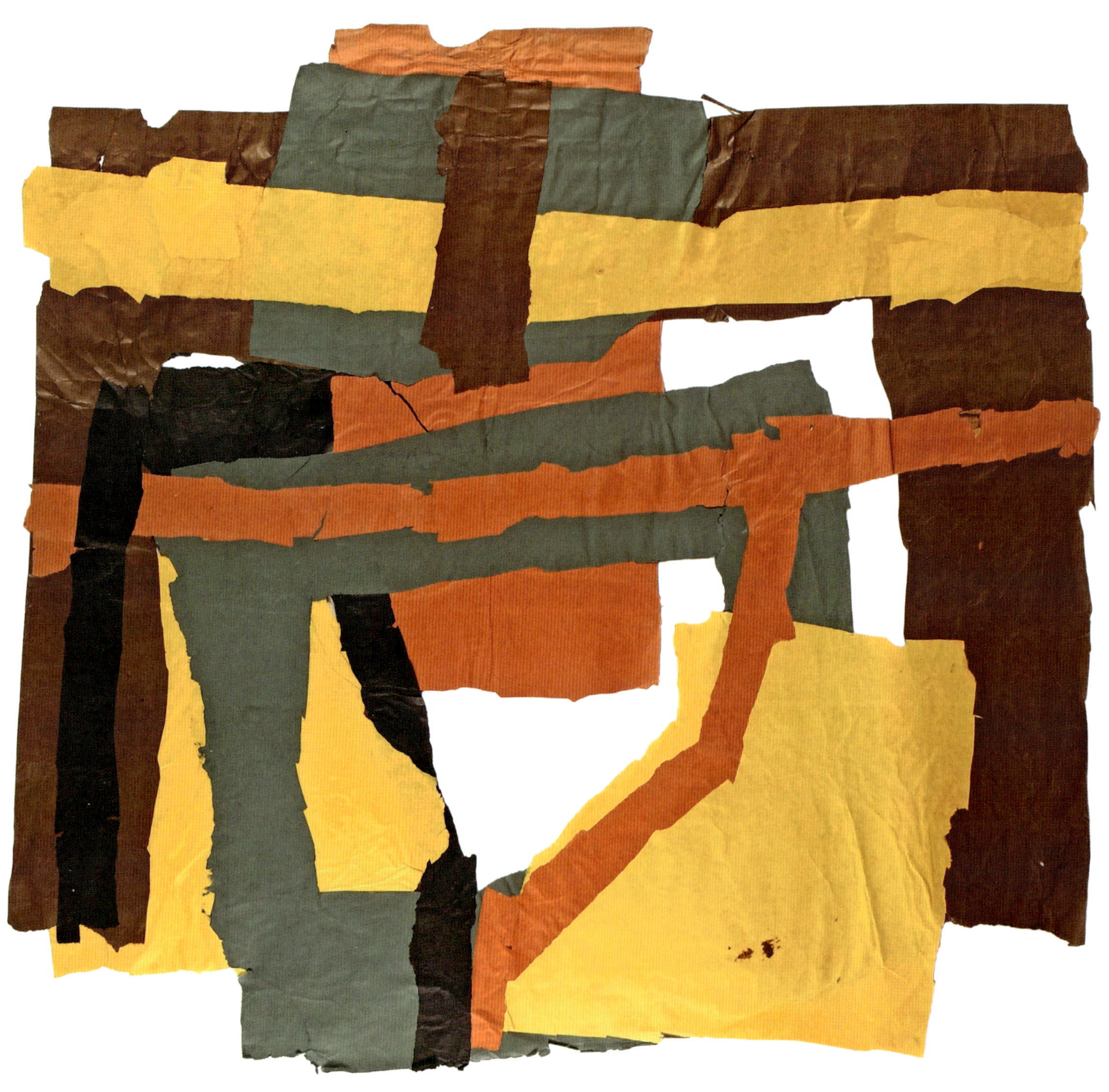

D-168   1972   Collage   127 × 146.1 cm (50 × 57.5")

loose and very painterly in handling, the line deliberately broken and intermittent – but no less powerful for that. It seems to signify two things: actual activity and traces of activity. To be more specific than that, one would have to invent a narrative (a notion entirely foreign to Davison's aims), or begin to speak in metaphors. Better simply to look at the work and ponder its various resonances.

By about 1978 Mellis was beginning to use collage again in her paintings, but Davison did not encourage this development and it was shelved for the time being. She had also begun to collect bits of driftwood that appealed to her, saved from the firewood she regularly gathered. In that year she made her first driftwood construction, but again this was a development in her work that Davison did not like, for he saw it as a direct challenge to his own supremacy. Undoubtedly in the pursuit of collage Davison had overtaken Mellis in originality and inventiveness, but it could be argued that in her late flowering of driftwood sculptures she equalled him again. Not surprisingly, Davison felt the challenge deeply, and Mellis had to be circumspect in exploring her new discovery. She was, after all, using irregular shapes of found colour and bringing them together in new configurations. Admittedly she was using wood and her work was altogether more three-dimensional than Davison's, but the parallel was too close for his comfort. In effect, it was only after Francis's death that she could really allow her work to take off; while he was alive she kept returning to painting in order not to compete too directly.

Latterly, Davison made working drawings for his collages, often on opened-out envelopes. Not only was this one of his wife's great strategies – her long series of envelope drawings of flowers was one of the most commercially successful

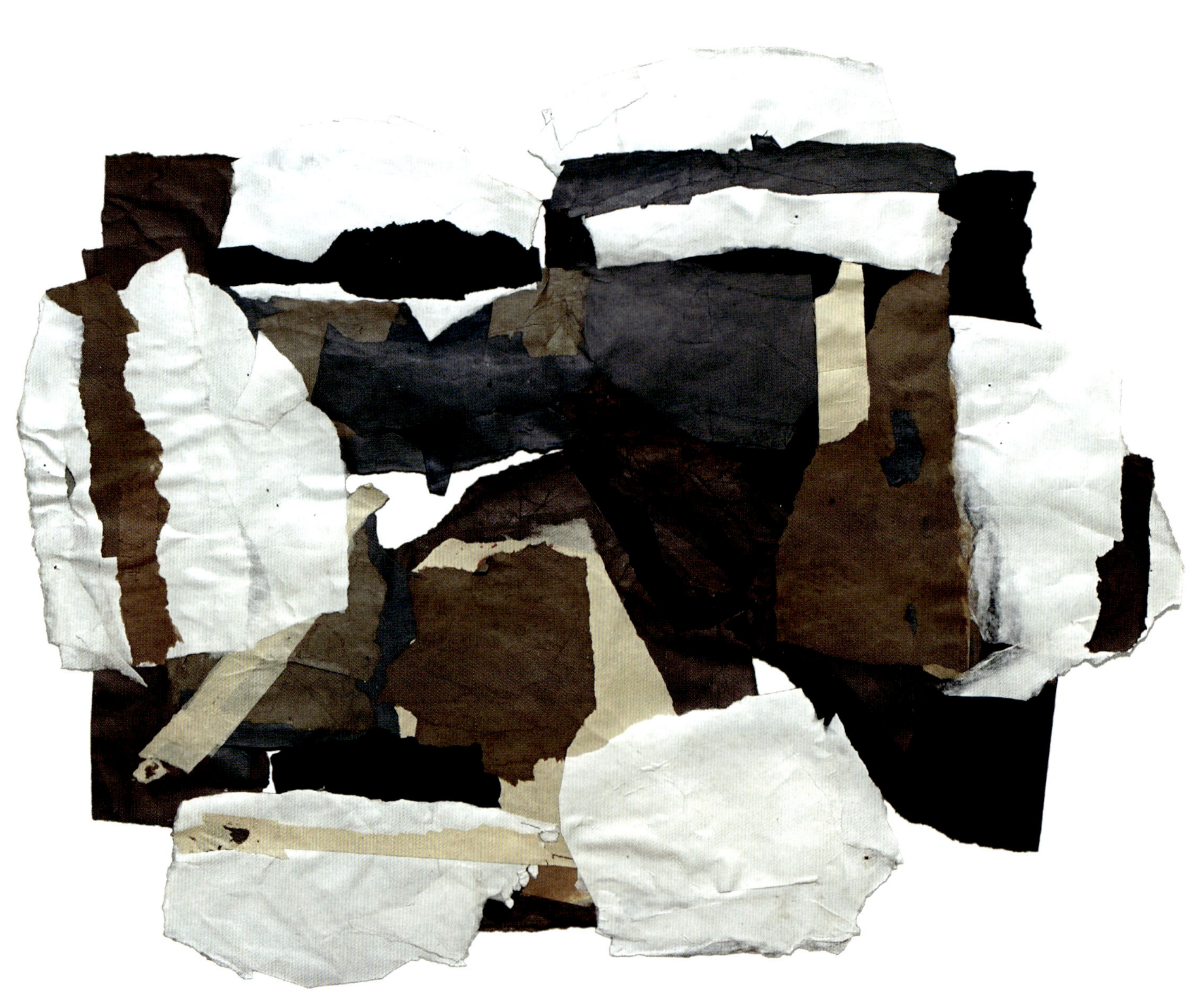

E-647   1976   Collage   58.4 × 72.4 cm (23 × 28.5")

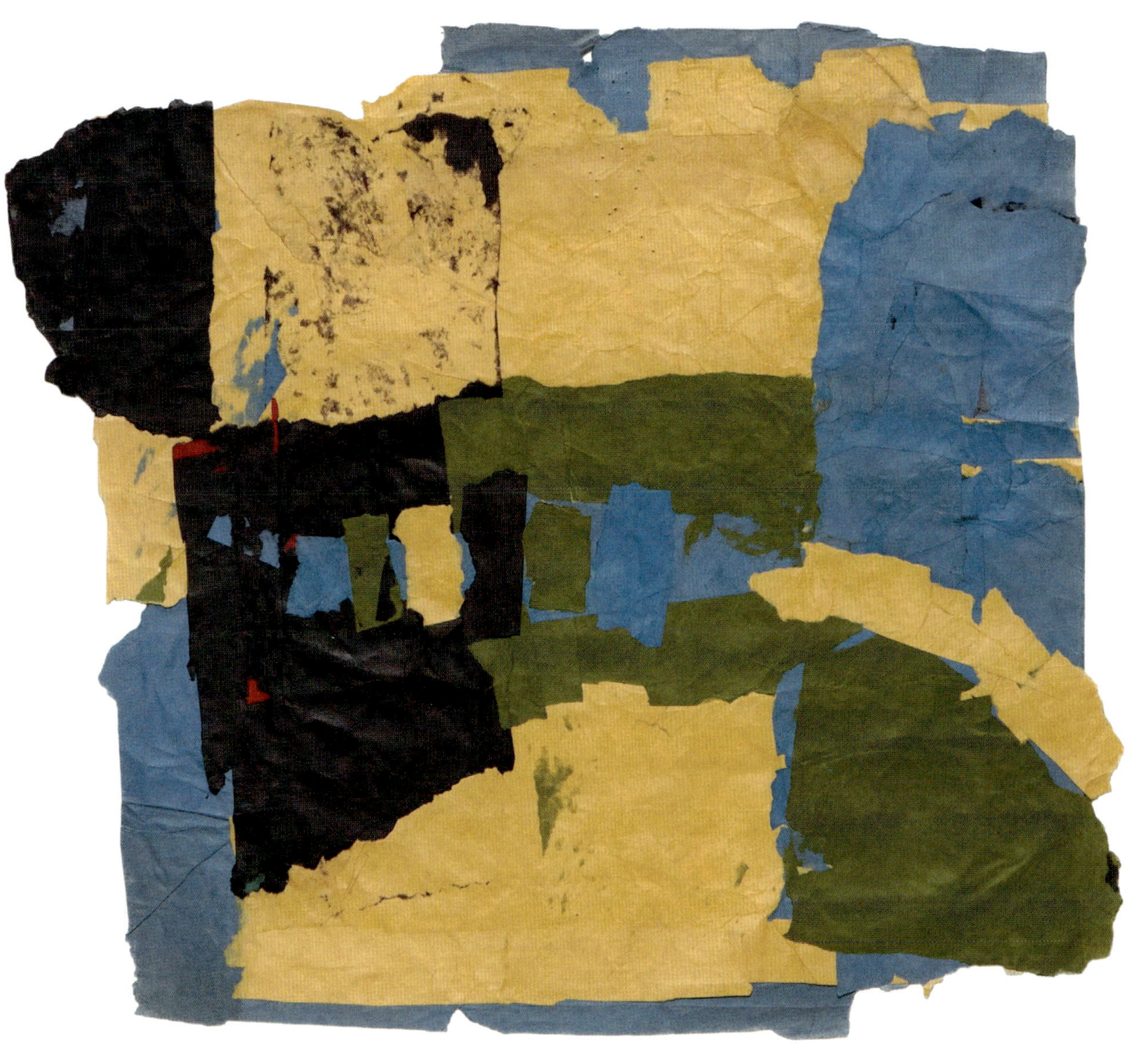

E-154   1974   Collage   57.2 × 69.9 cm (22.5 × 27.5")

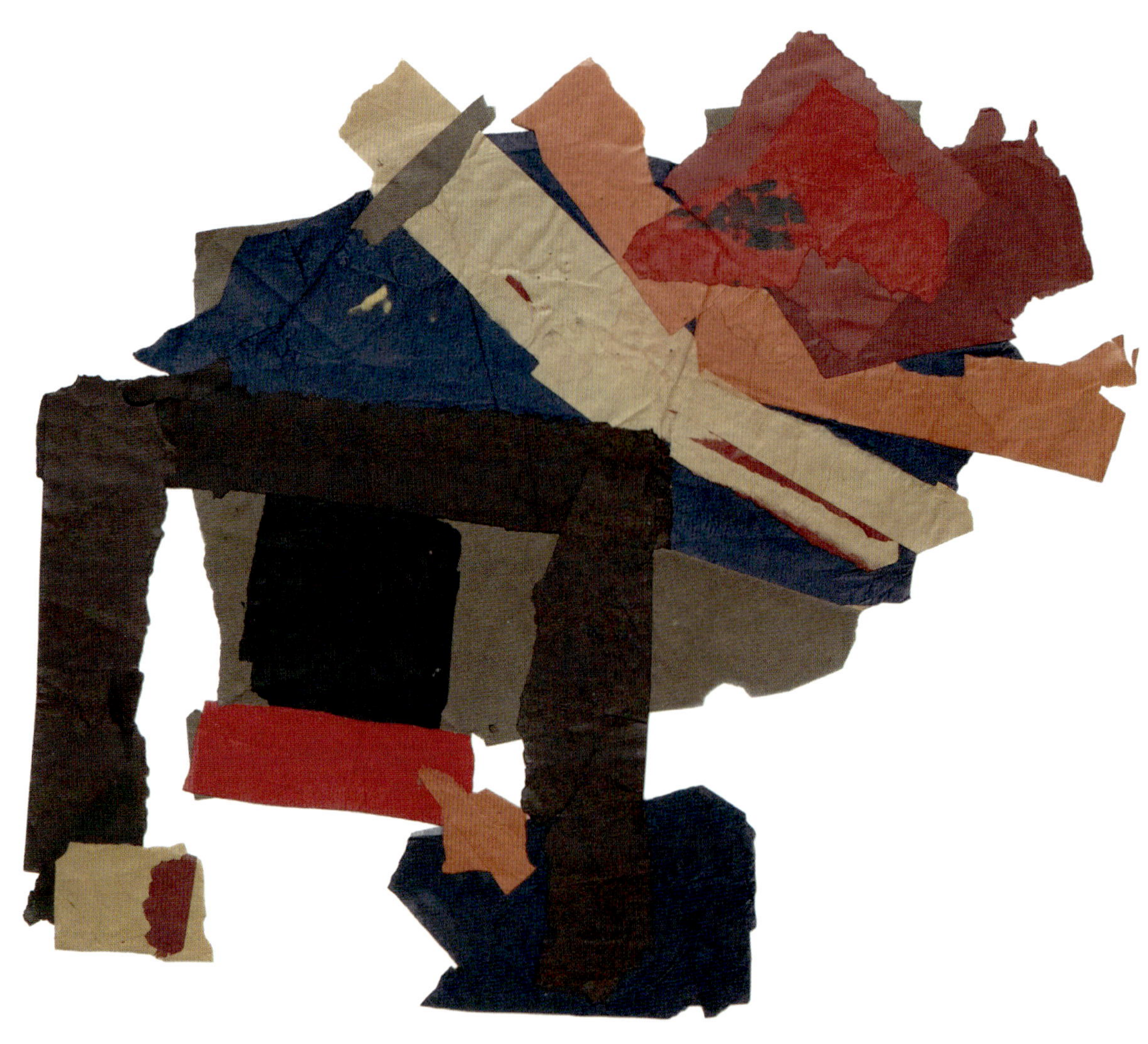

E-218   1975   Collage   53.3 × 61 cm (21 × 24")

of her enterprises – but Davison's drawings do resemble Mellis's late driftwood sculptures (precisely the ones he was not keen on her making), in that they look like bits of wood pegged together.

The atmosphere at home was not as strained as it might have been: Mellis made many concessions to her husband and was active in promoting his work at the expense of her own. When the art critic William Packer came to select some works for the first 'British Art Show' in 1979, of which he was curator, he was given the impression that she had been doing next to nothing recently in order to look after her husband. Packer, who was introduced to Davison by the regional officer of the Arts Council, recalls: 'He was a reclusive and rather tricky chap, and deeply suspicious of the whole enterprise, and I was told to be careful. In the event we got on very well. Everything was either on or under the bed in the spare bedroom, and dear Margaret Mellis was clucking over him like a protective hen all the time. It was altogether one of those special days that we have sometimes and, so far as the work was concerned, a revelation.' Packer included four Davison collages in his exhibition, which opened at the Mappin Art Gallery in Sheffield in December, and toured to Newcastle and Bristol the following year.

The later collages are multi-directional and luminous with colour. They look once again a little like aerial views (as some of Davison's earliest Suffolk paintings and drawings do), but this time the reference is to a much more abstract language than cartography. Perhaps the expressive abstraction of painters such as Peter Lanyon and Alan Davie is nearer the mark, both of whom spent much time gliding and observing the world from a very different perspective. Intriguingly, Davison did not work on his collages from

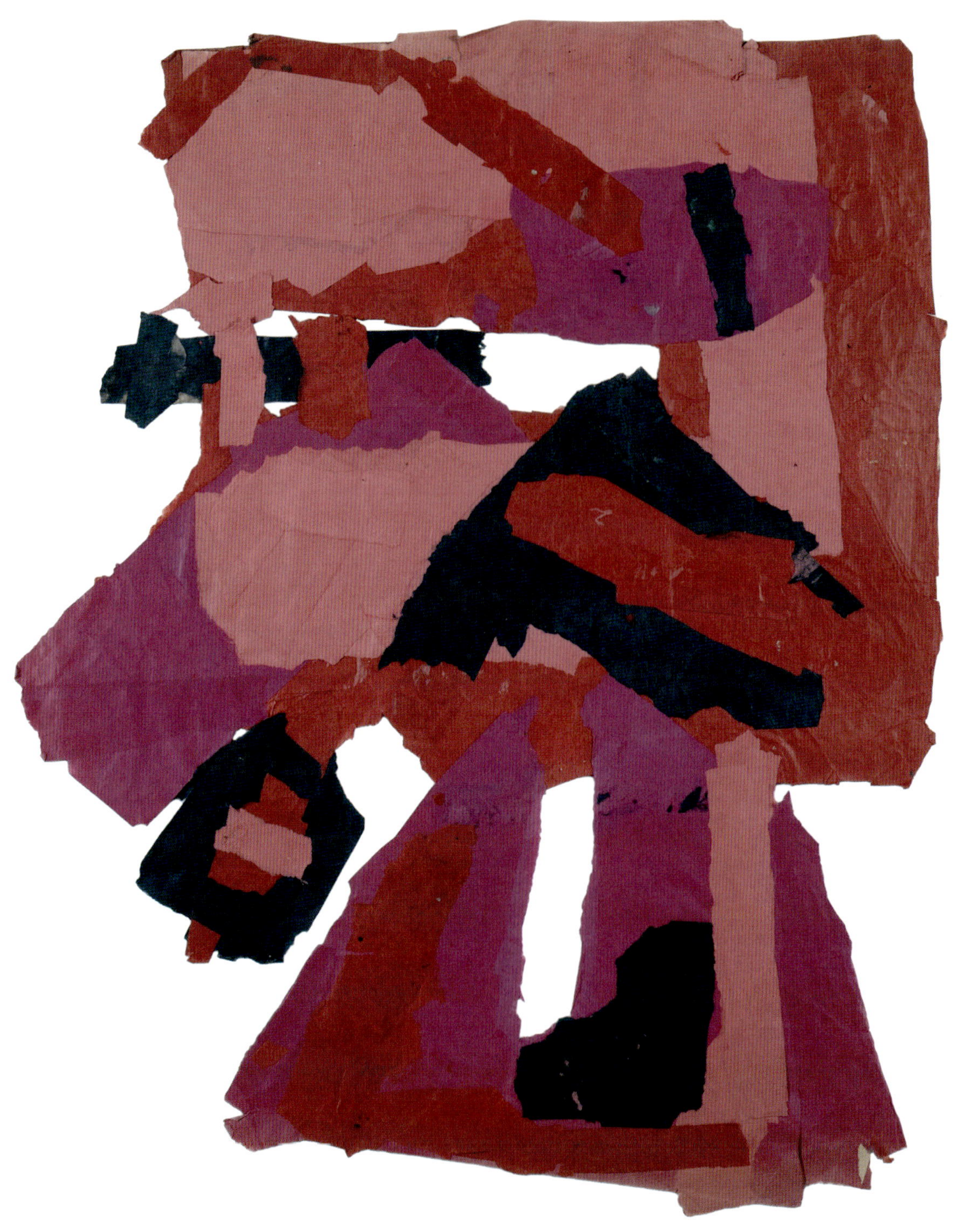

E-187   1974   Collage   104.1 × 81.3 cm (41 × 32")

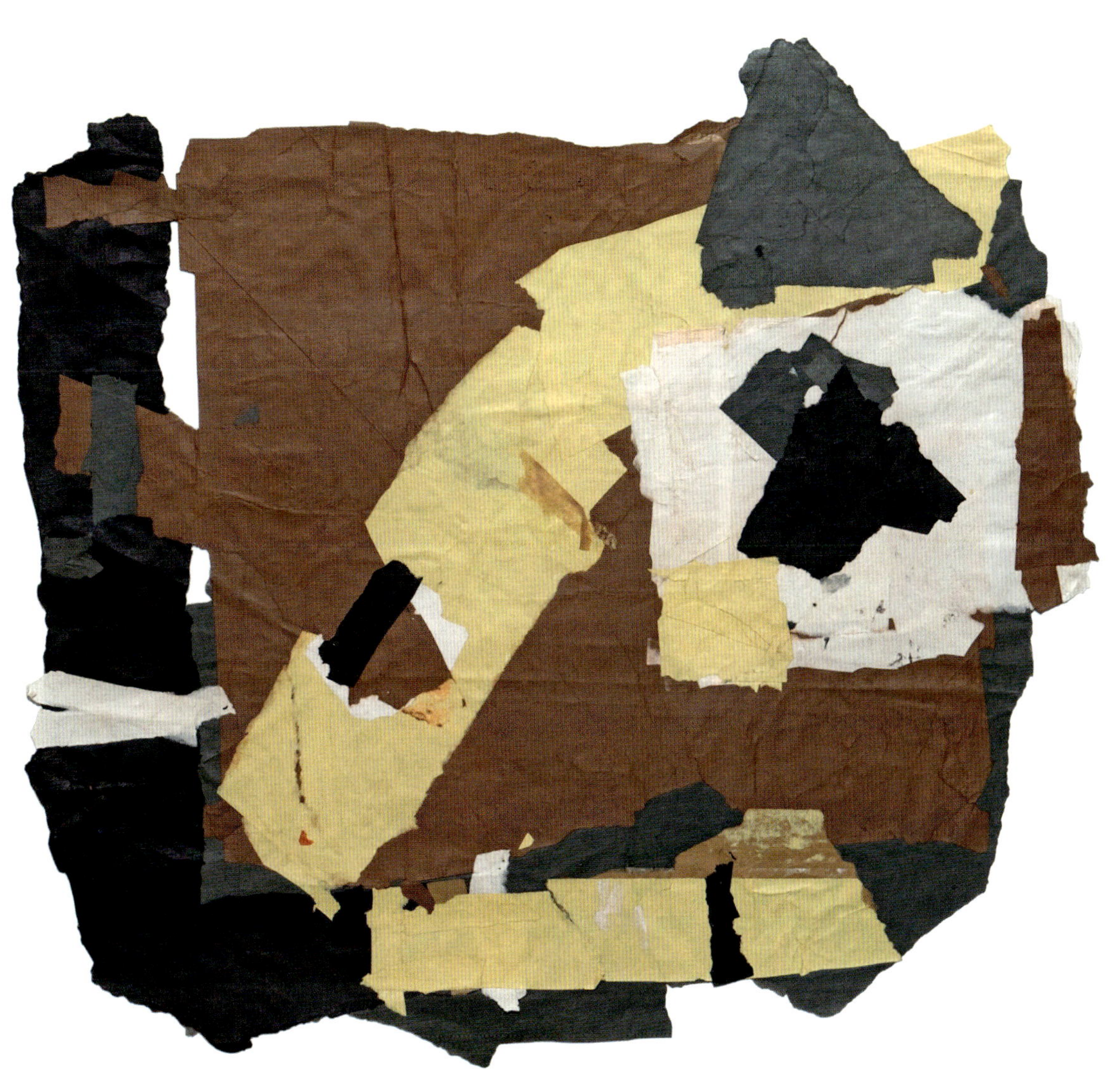

E-176 1974 Collage 69.9 × 66.7 cm (27.5 × 26.25")

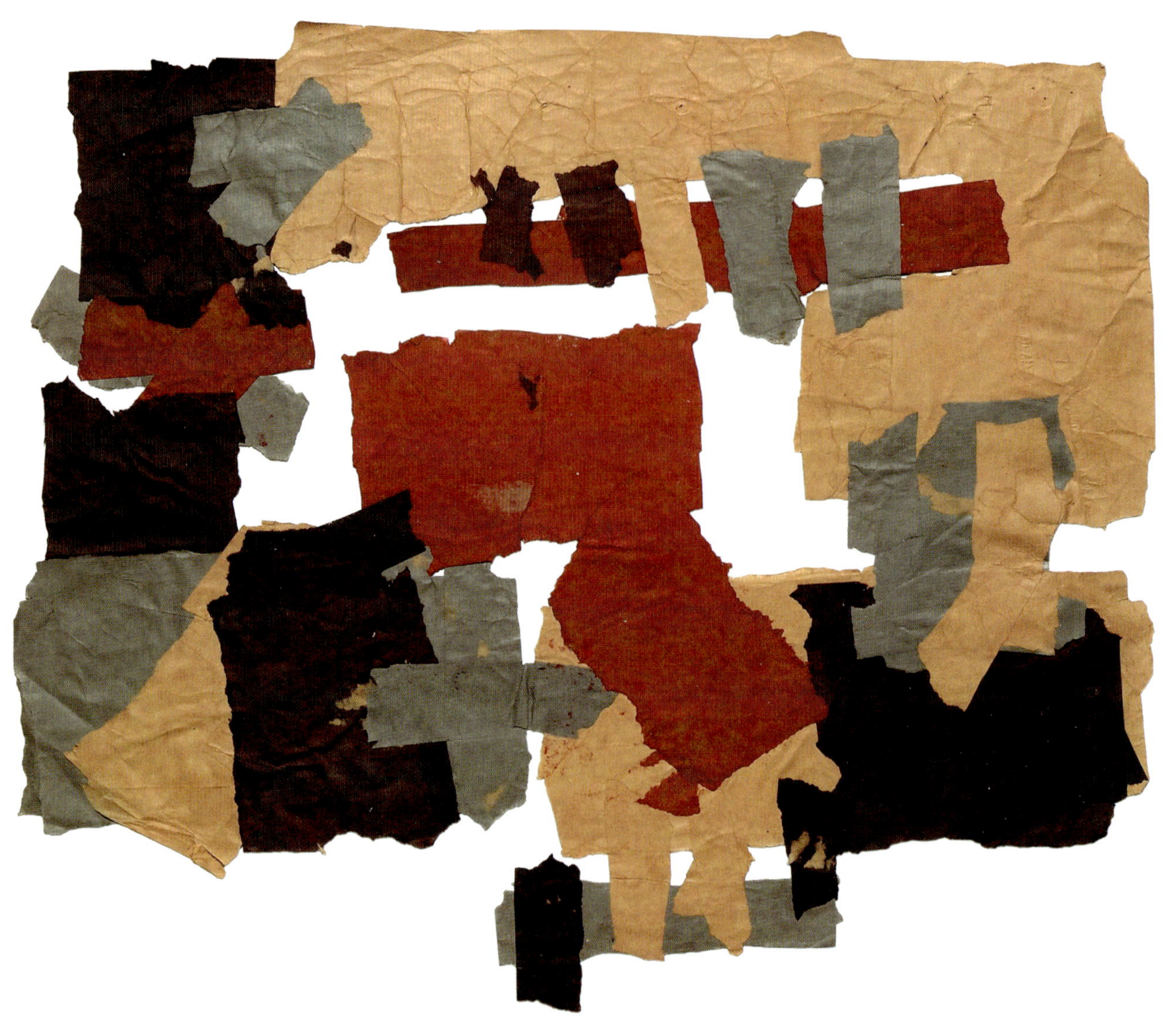

E-105 1973–6 Collage 73.7 × 85.1 cm (29 × 33.5")

above, on the floor, as this kind of viewpoint might lead one to expect, but rather on the wall. One method of determining which way up they might go as finished works (another perennial problem with Davison's work – he rarely left any stated preference) is to look for the holes in the corners left by the drawing pins.

As Alan Powers has noted, Davison seems to have known his own mind, and was astonishingly un-provincial in his work. He evidently had enormous reserves of confidence and self-belief, working as he did almost invisibly for most of his life. Inevitably this exacted a toll. 'There was much tension involved,' writes Powers, 'and a personal price to pay, although one would scarcely know it from the affirmative nature of the work. Had he not been living and working with another artist, perhaps he would have turned to something else, and even in these conditions, he worked privately and independently. His life is a model of selectivity, of knowing when to stay silent and unhearing.'

The collages do not allow of easy categorization or analysis because there is very little stylistic progression or development after the move to Southwold. (This is not helped by the artist's refusal to date his work, and by his habit of returning to work on earlier collages or incorporating bits of previous works in his current creations.) Davison evolved his visual ideas and they tended to go round in cycles, moving in and out of a pattern of response, investigating new areas but not actually straying very far from the model he had struck upon. This is not to say that he repeated himself: he was endlessly inventive with colour and form, and the effects he achieved are many and various. By employing shifts of tempo, scale and colour he ran the gamut of emotional and formal response in a body of work that is as

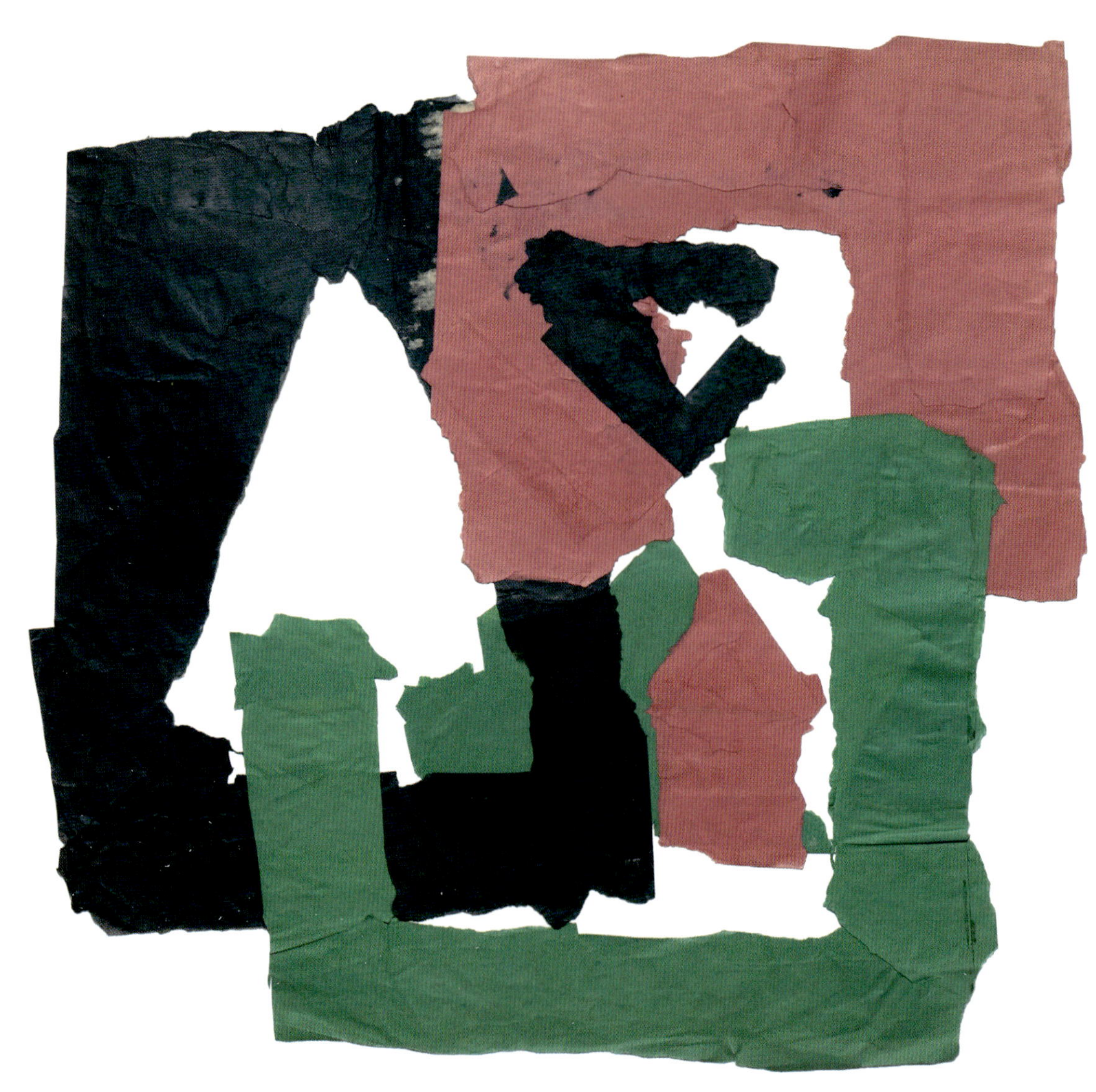

E-174   1974   Collage   73.7 × 76.2 cm (29 × 30")

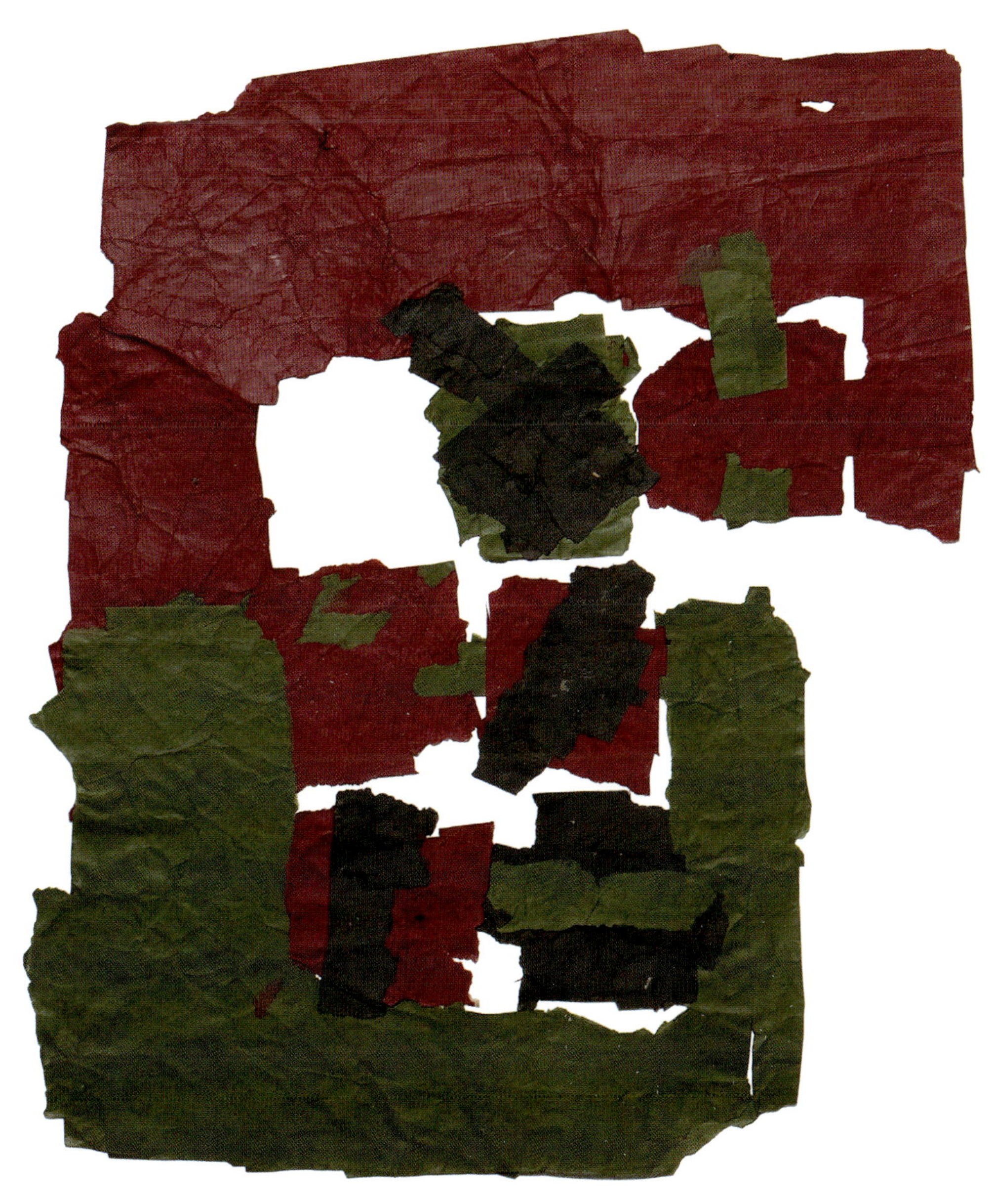

E-59   1973   Collage   78.7 × 66 cm (31 × 26")

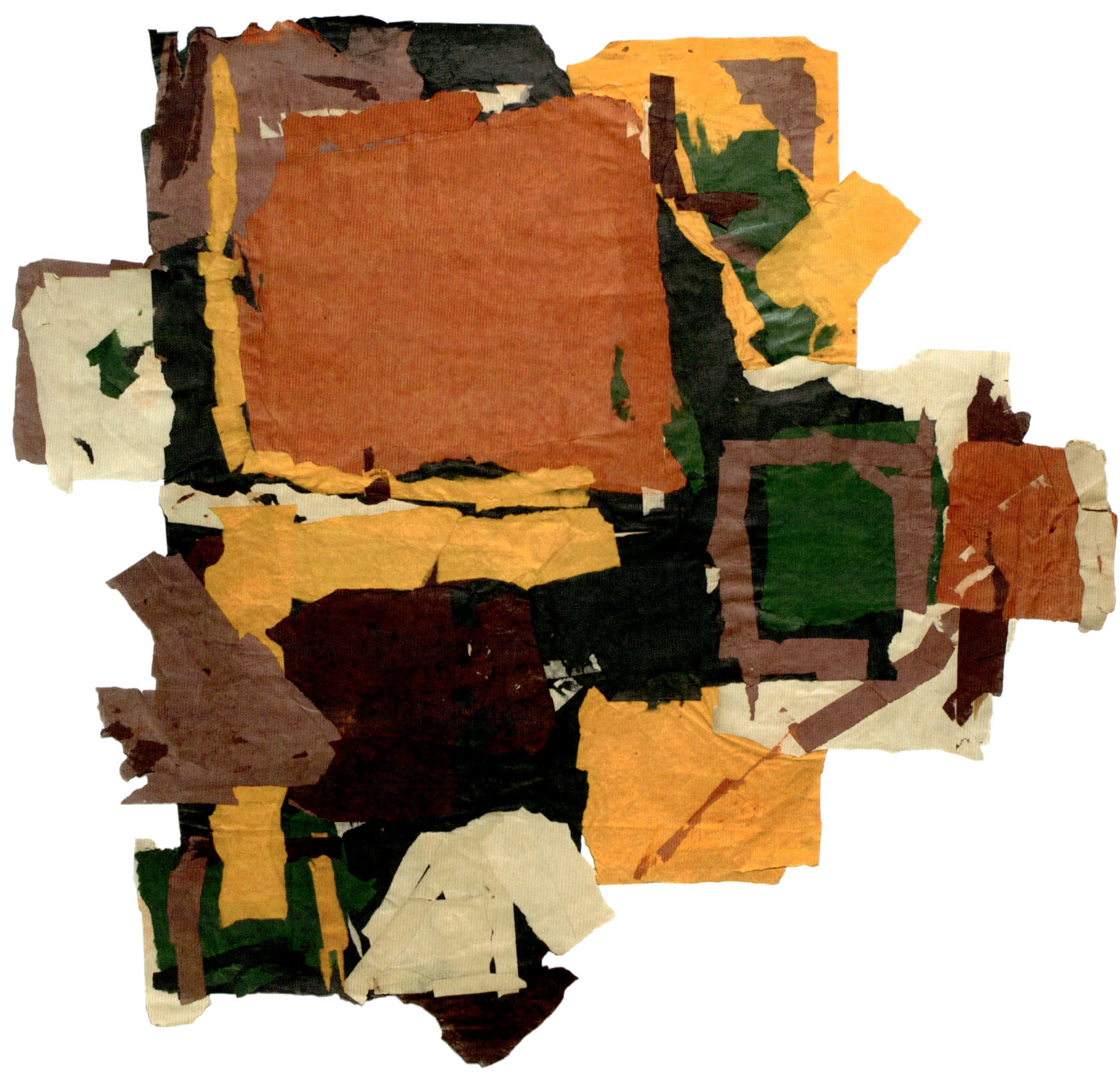

E-263   1975   Collage   115.6 × 121.9 cm (45.5 × 48")

rich and satisfying as it is exceptional. No one was working with paper in this way, and inevitably Davison's originality has (to some degree) gone against him.

A key strategy in the collages was breaking forms up with smaller forms – the roundish marks that look like paint dabs, the overlaid strips, the interrupted lines. In collage, you cannot simply paint over things to change them, and though you can layer over another piece of paper, the action is discernible. And if something is removed, that is also evident from the glue marks or skins of paper or colour that remain behind. In this sense, collage is a very *concrete* art form: the elements are physically real and present, and the process evident. There is, however, a self-contained group of final collages that Davison made while recovering from a prostate operation. He began to make tiny collages from envelopes which have a delicacy – one might say a frailty – that is genuinely moving. But these have a separate presence and identity to the bulk of the late collage work, which is vivacious in the extreme, however subtle its unfolding may be.

Packer's 'British Art Show' led directly to Julian Spalding organizing a Davison solo show in 1981 at the Graves Art Gallery, Sheffield, which in turn led to a further show in 1982 at MOMA Oxford, and finally to the major Arts Council exhibition at the Hayward Gallery in 1983. This was a great and serious accolade. Mellis recalled that Davison himself had to frame all his work on the kitchen floor as the exhibition's budget only ran as far as supplying the wood for the job. Afterwards he thought the show was a complete failure, as so few people seemed to be interested, but in fact it established his reputation and endowed him with a presence in the London art world he had previously lacked. It

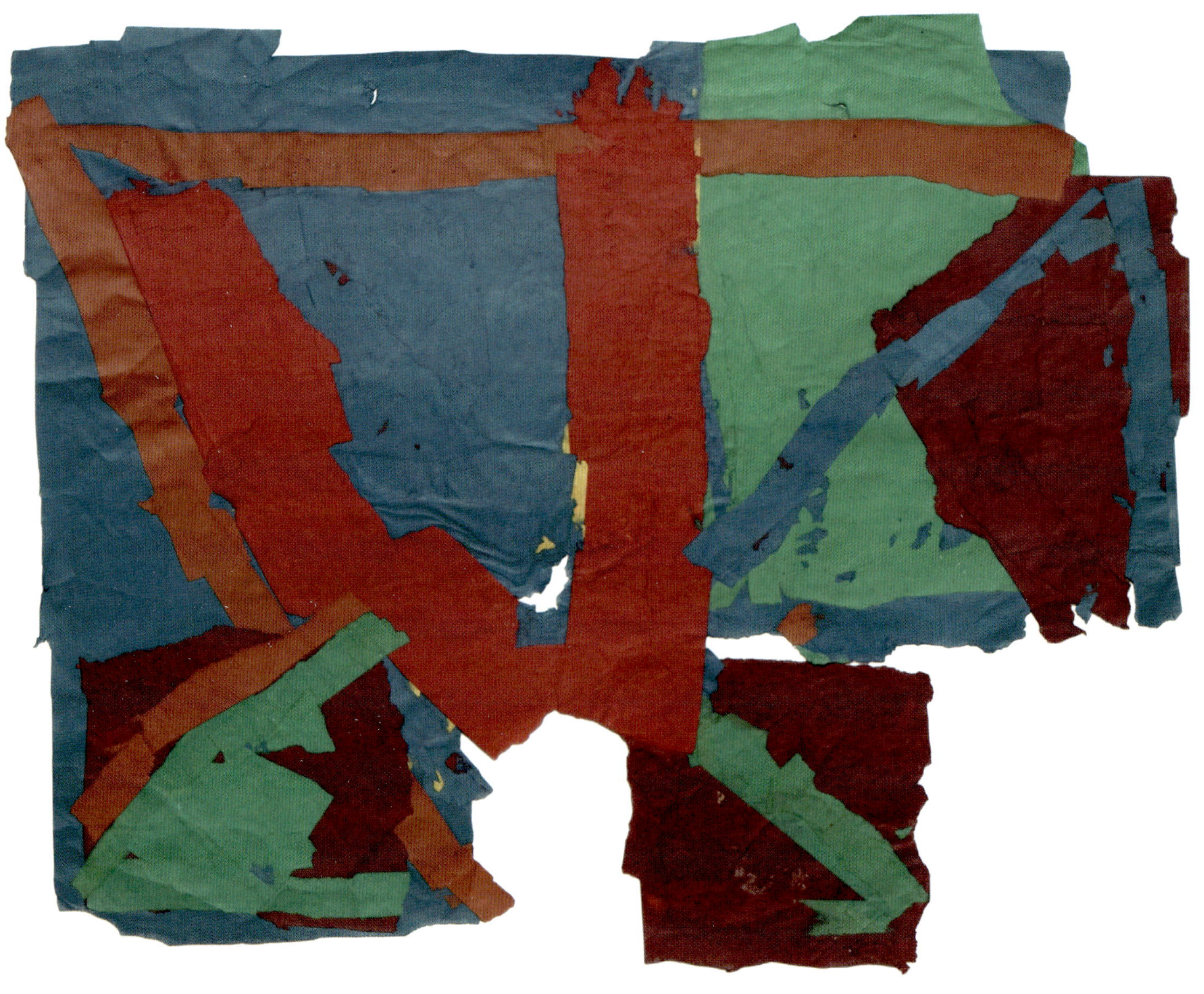

E-173   1974   Collage   66 × 81.3 cm (26 × 32")

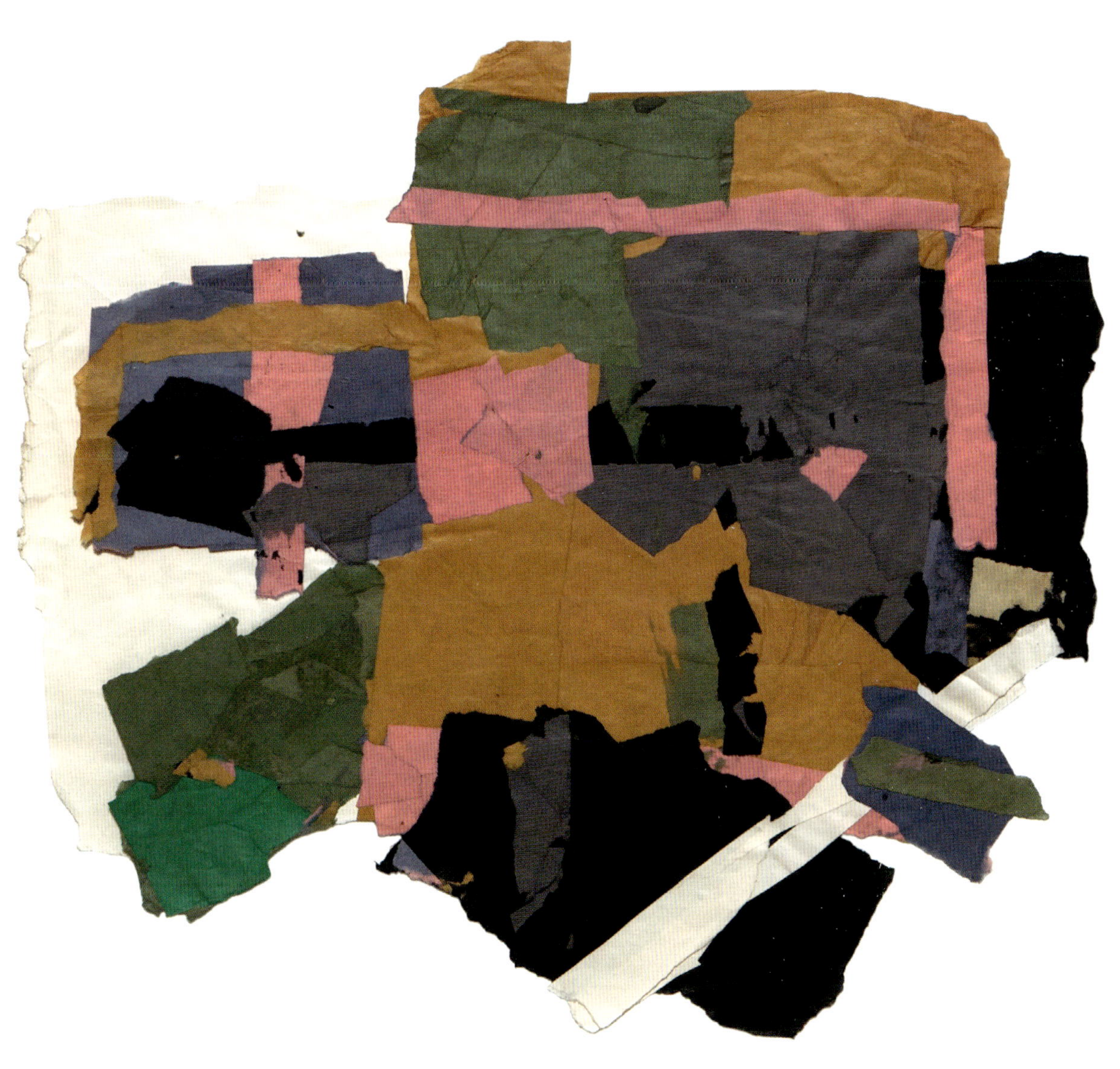

E-290 1975 Collage 57.2 × 61 cm (22.5 × 24")

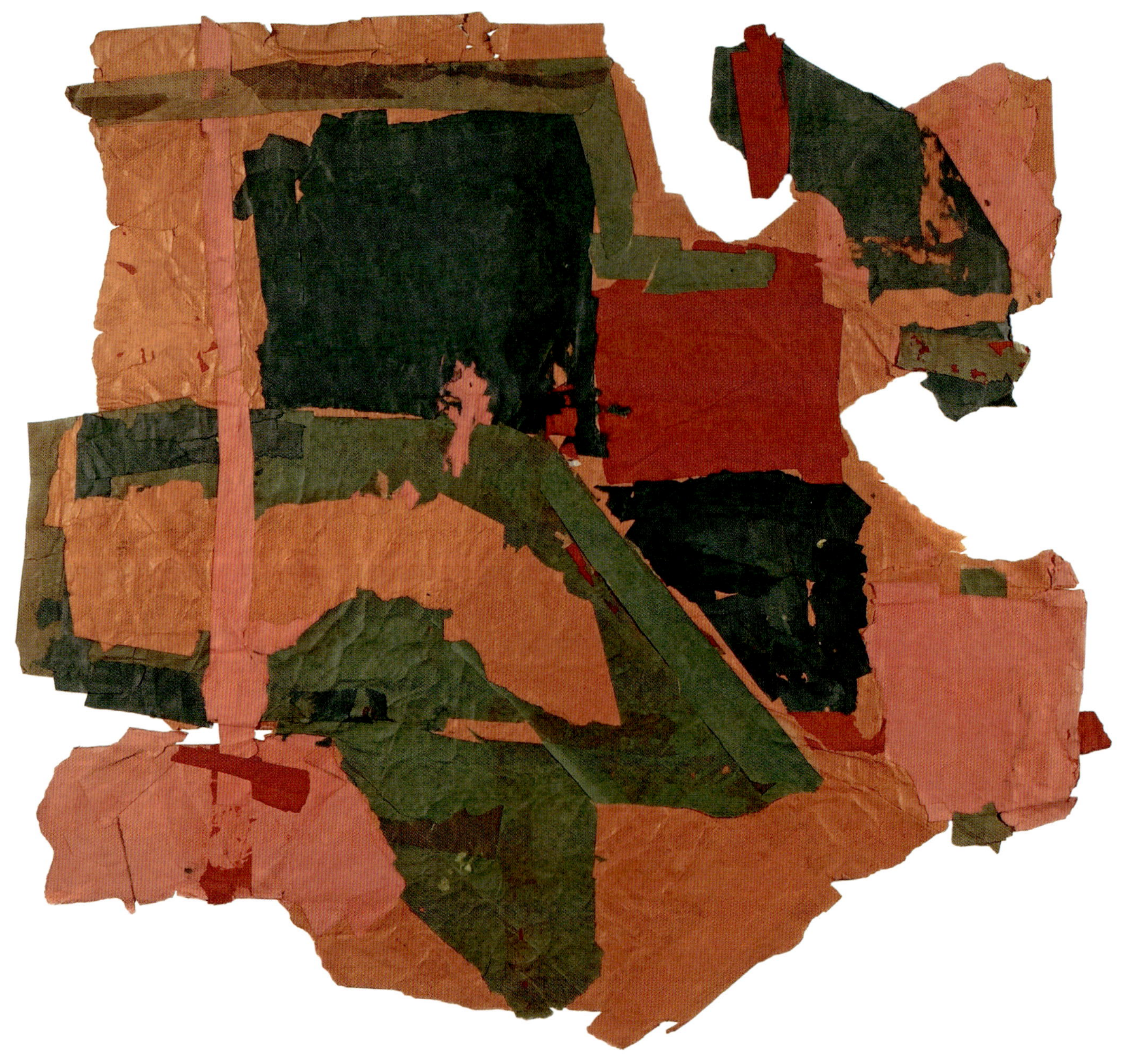

E-508   1974   Collage   100.3 × 107.3 cm (39.5 × 42.25")

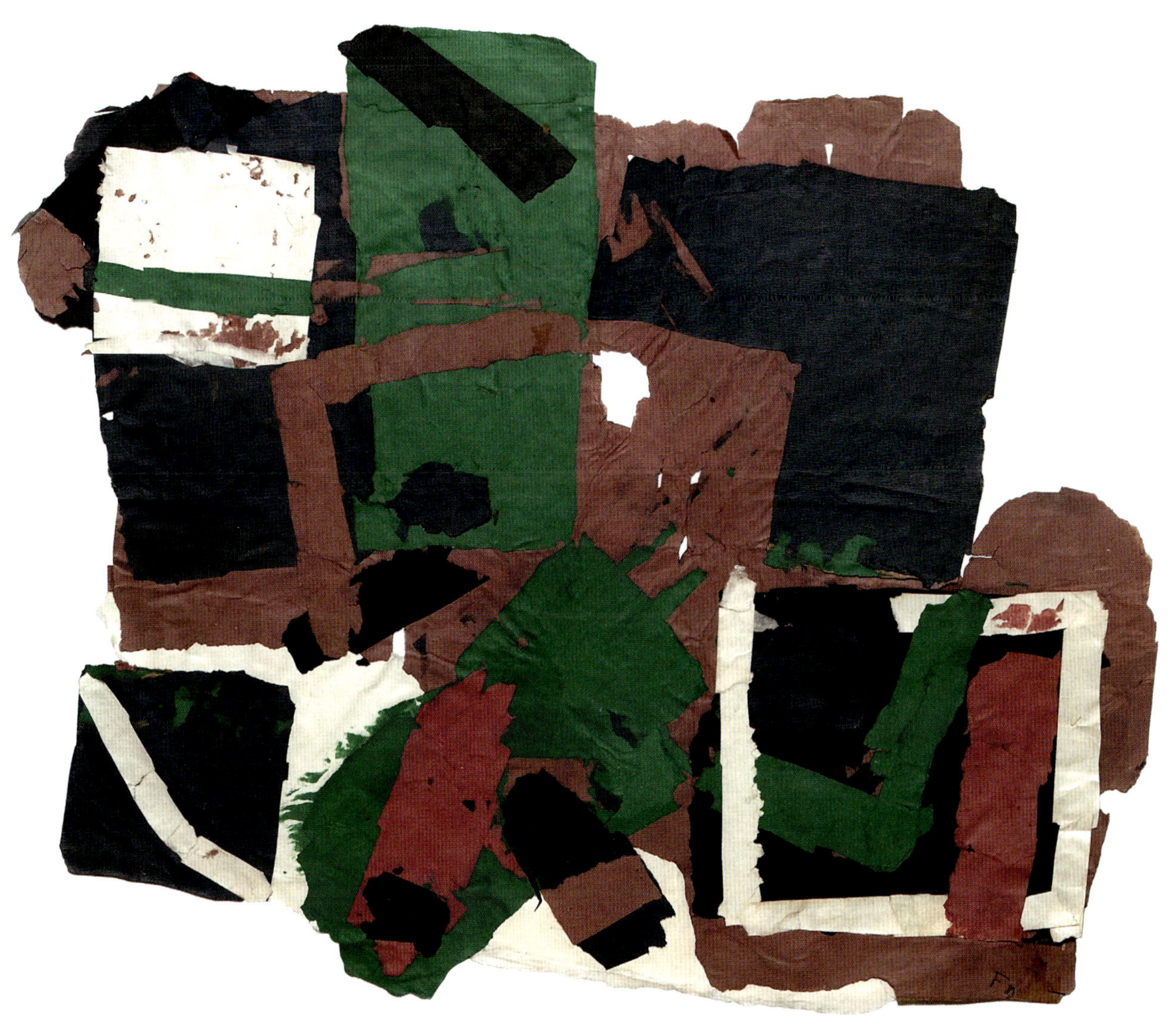

E-543   1973–6   Collage   78.7 × 93.3 cm (31 × 36.75")

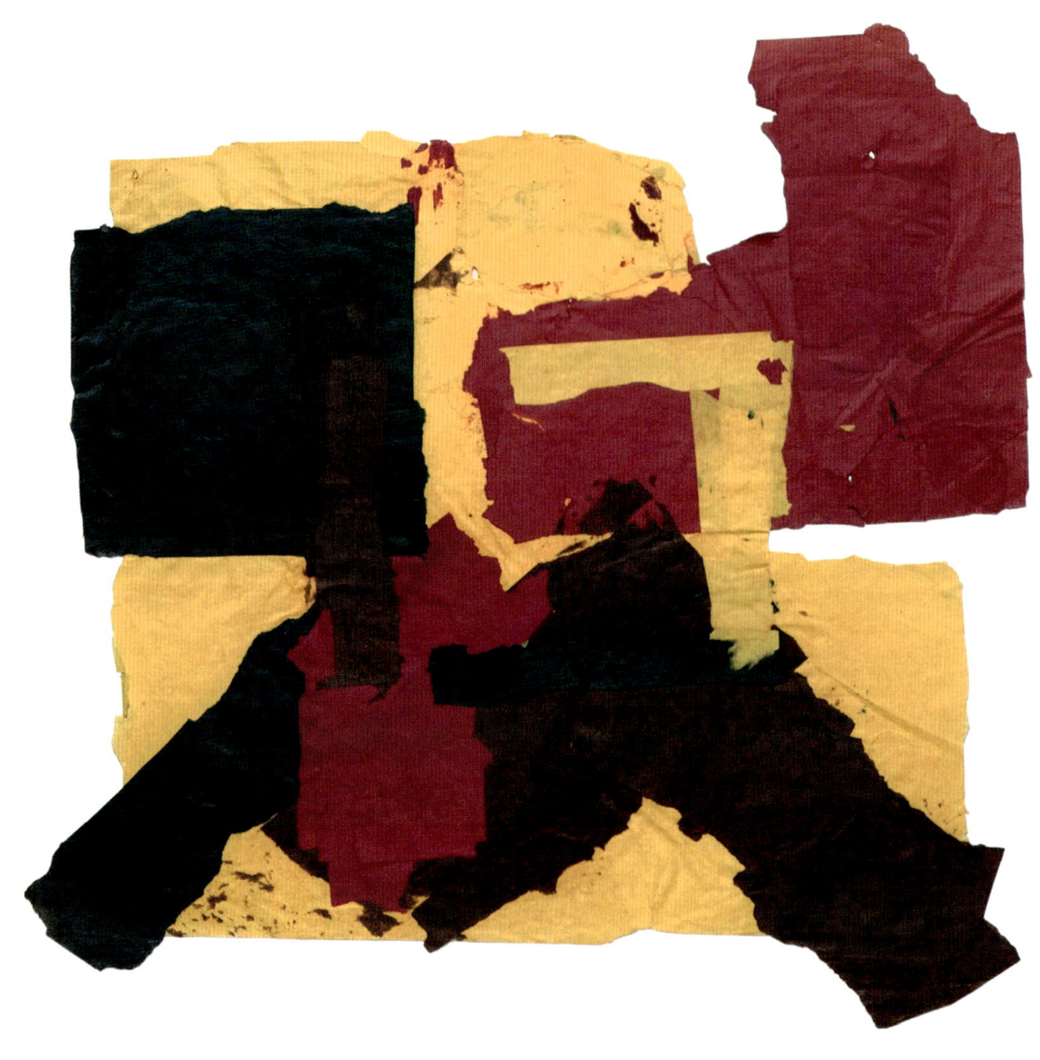

E-162   1974   Collage   77.5 × 78.7 cm (30.5 × 31")

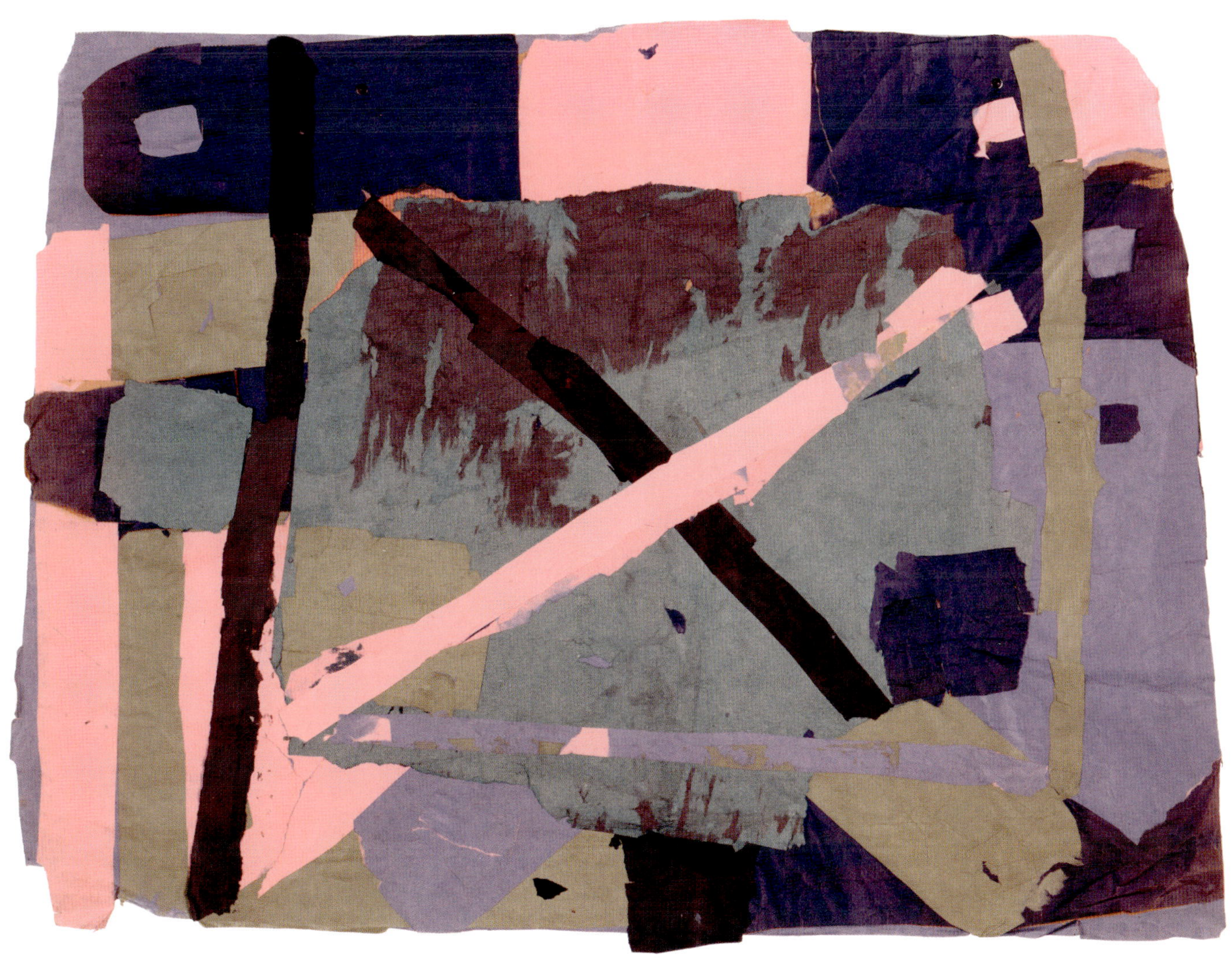

G-55   1978–84   Collage   80 × 101.6 cm (31.5 × 40")   Private collection

was both tragic and ironic that just at this juncture Davison began to grow seriously ill with a brain tumour, and although Margaret nursed him devotedly, he died on 6th August 1984.

During his last illness, Patrick Heron made a final visit to his old friend and Francis was not too ill for them to enjoy good talk. But he was too weak to tear the paper for his collages, and although Margaret tried to be his hands, this was a fruitless exercise. As Telfer observed: 'Who could replace his hands? He'd developed a whole history of tearing paper and working it. It was a very private activity.'

Installation photograph, Hayward Gallery, 1983.

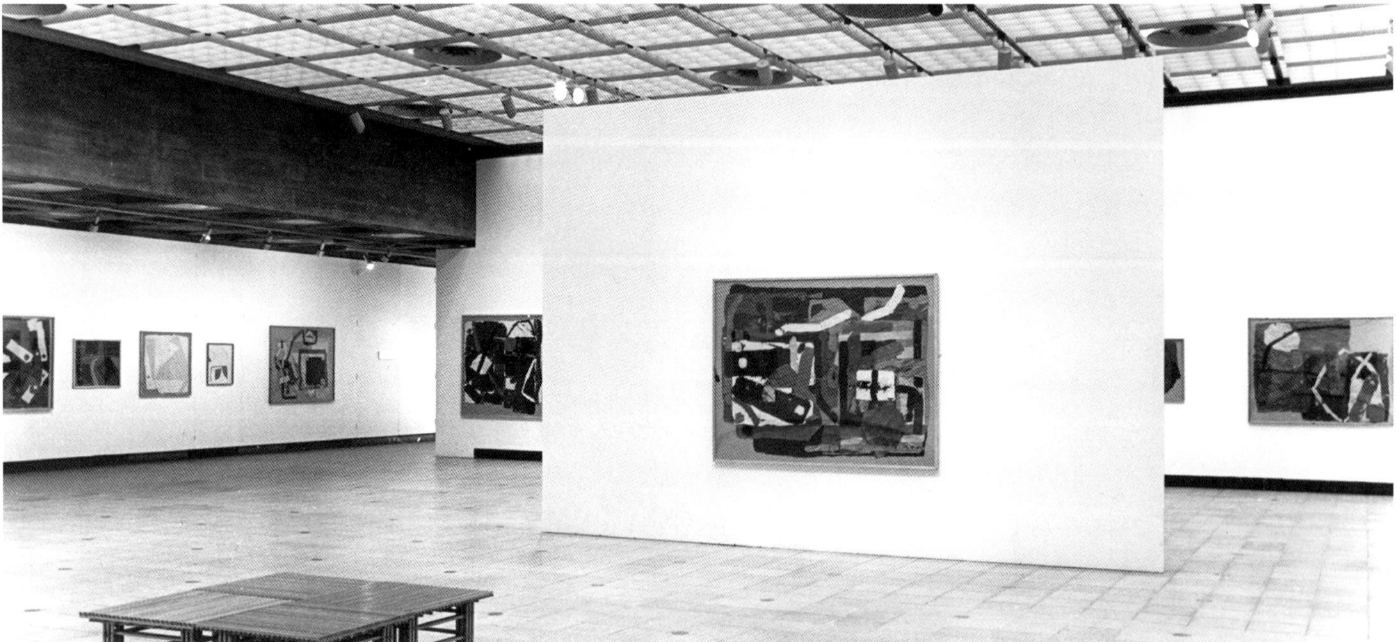

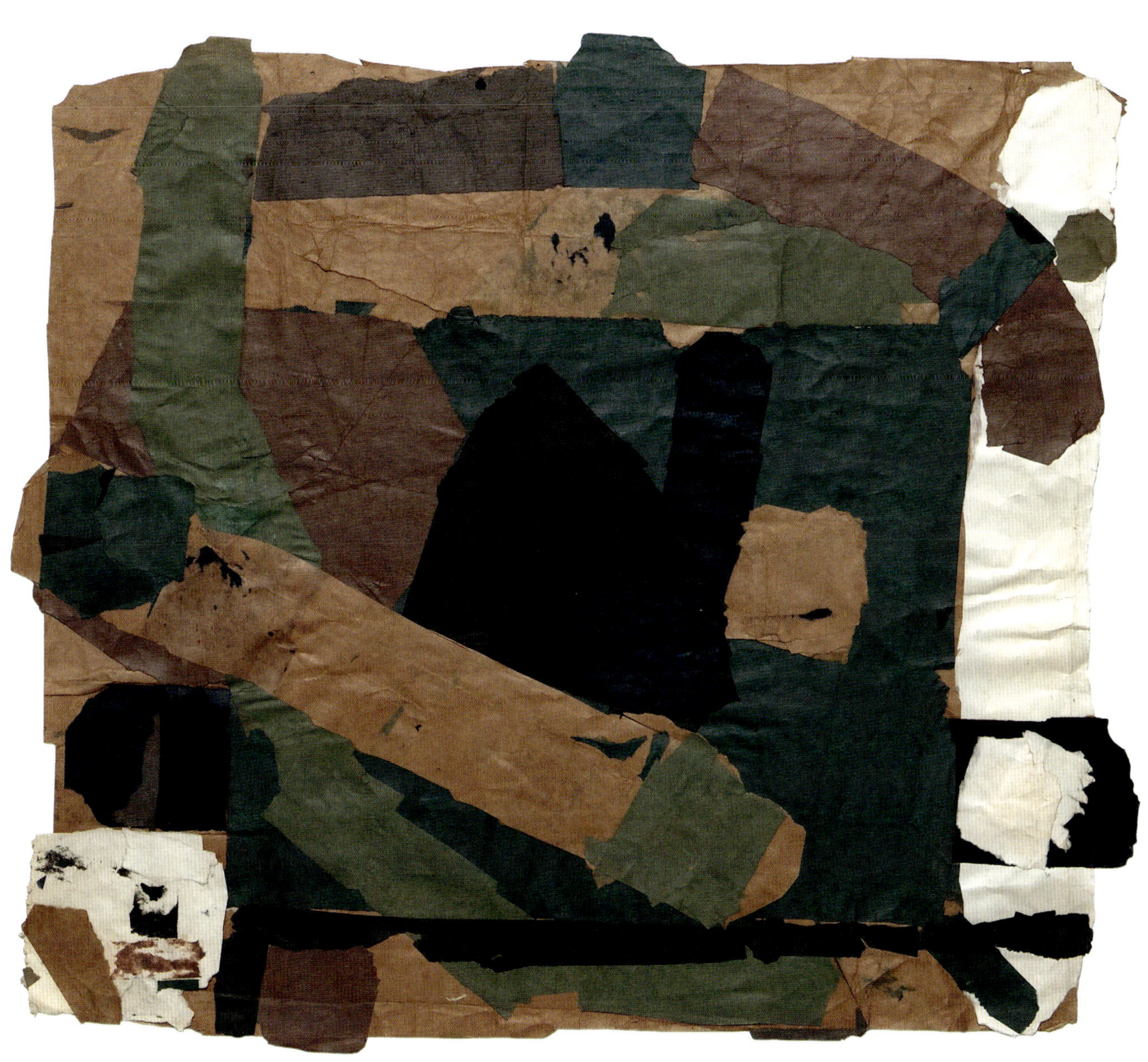

F-128 1976–8 Collage 70.4 × 77.5 cm (27.7 × 30.5")

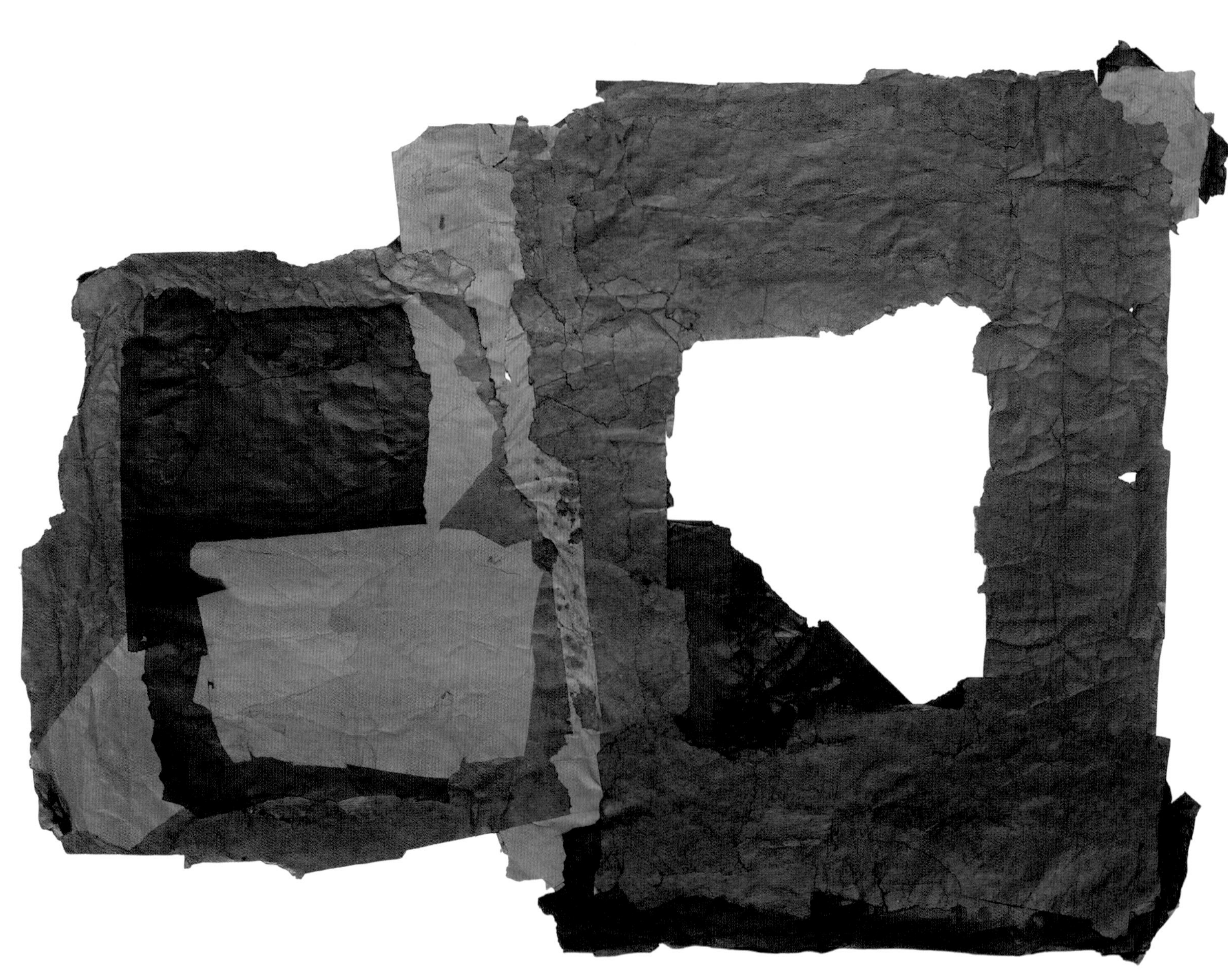

E/F-534   1973–6   Collage   87.6 × 118.1 cm (34.5 × 46.5")

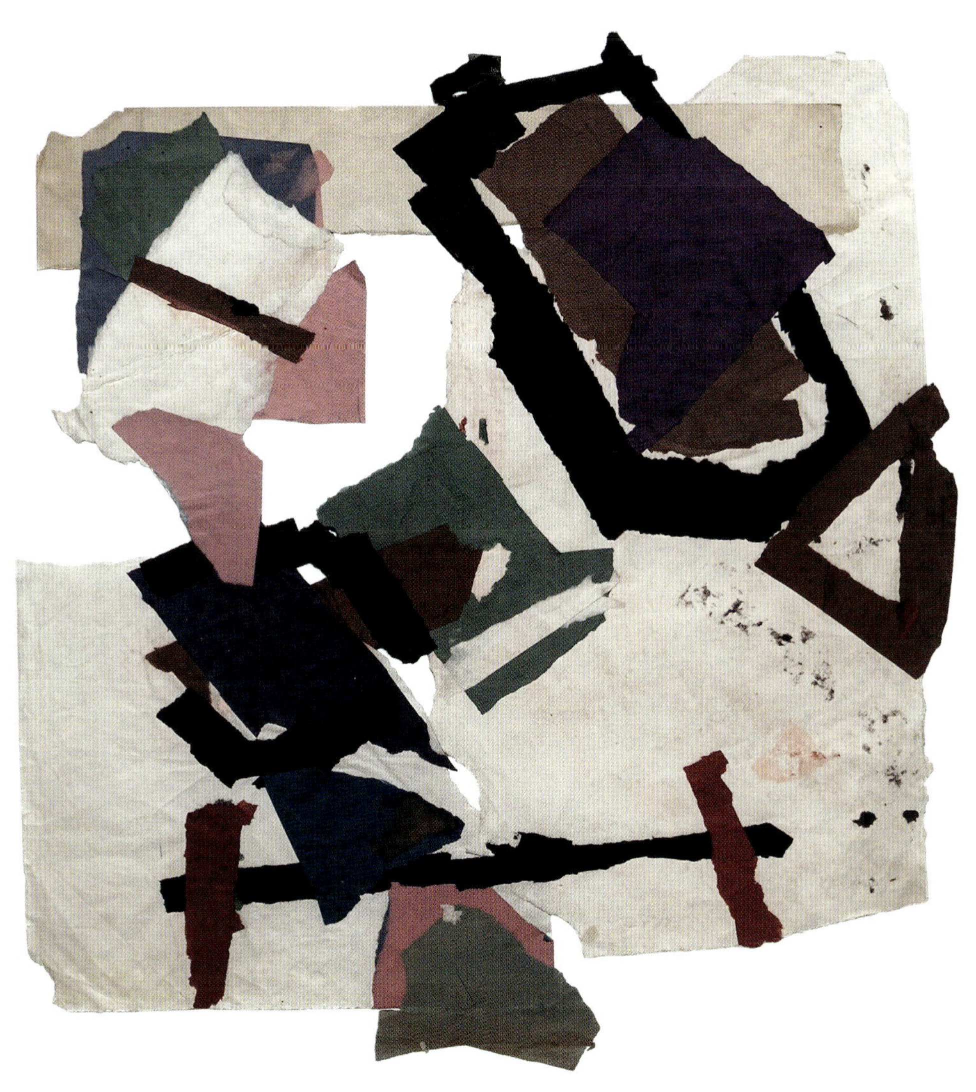

E/G-238 1975 Collage 71.1 × 65.3 cm (28 × 25.7")

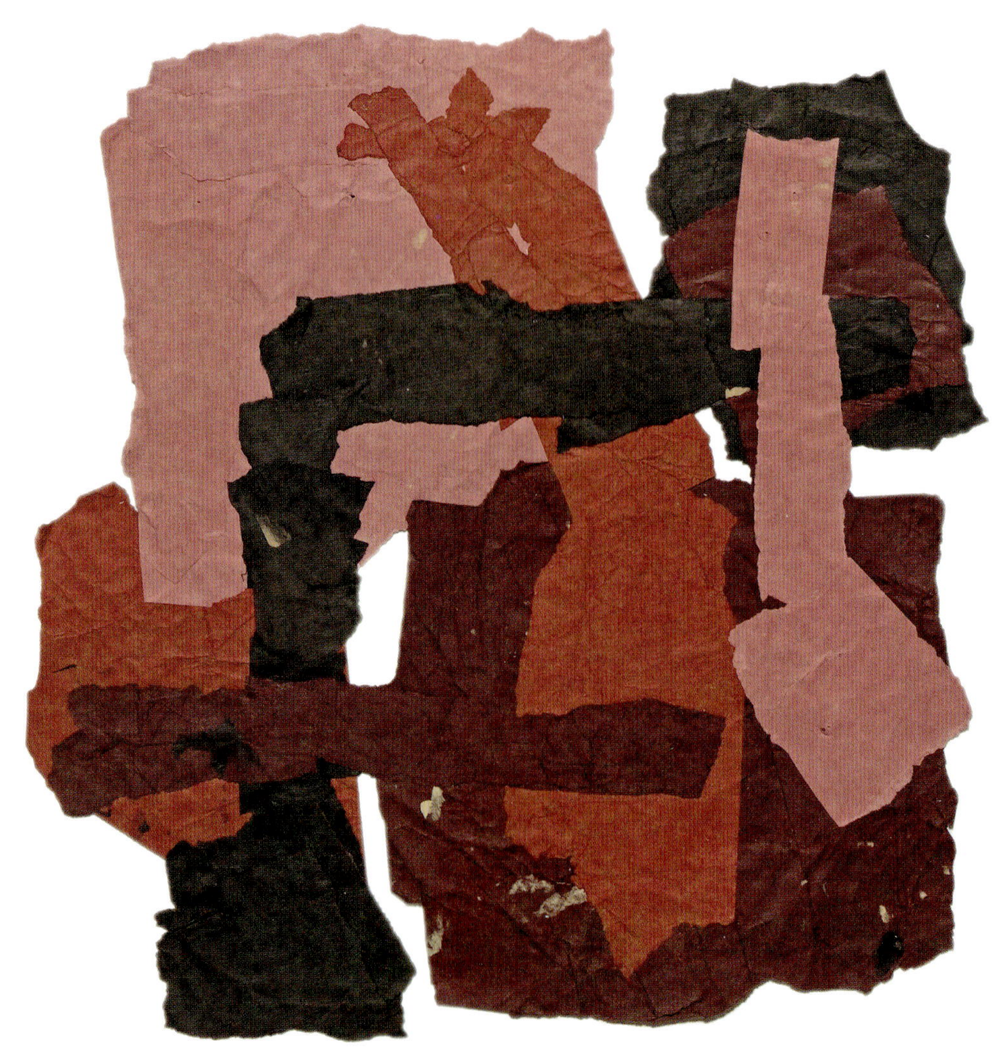

E-81   1973   Collage   63.5 × 63.5 cm (25 × 25")

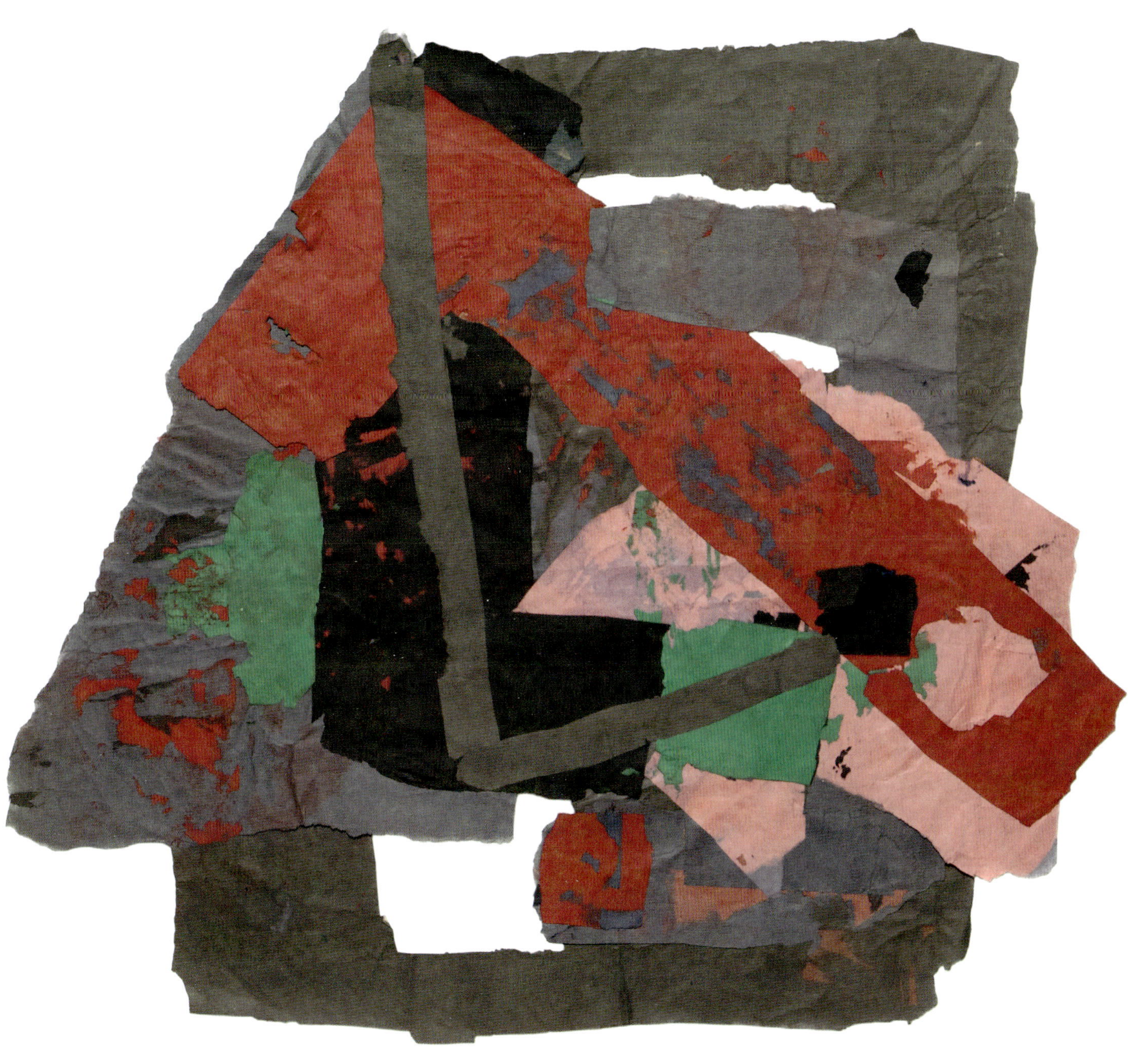

E/G-546   1972   Collage   94 × 100.3 cm (37 × 39.5")

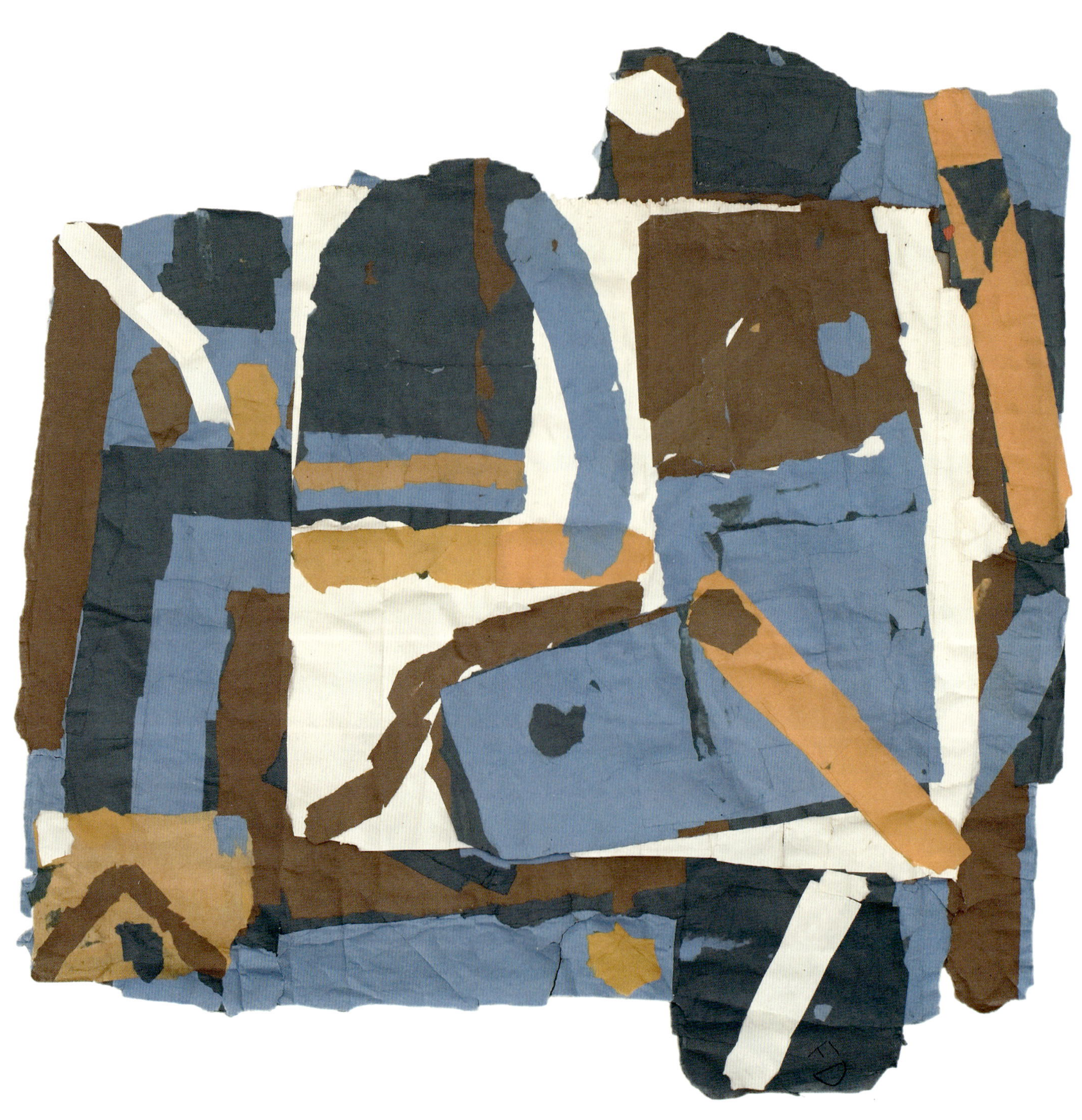

F-3 1976–7 Collage 114.3 × 124.5 cm (45 × 49")

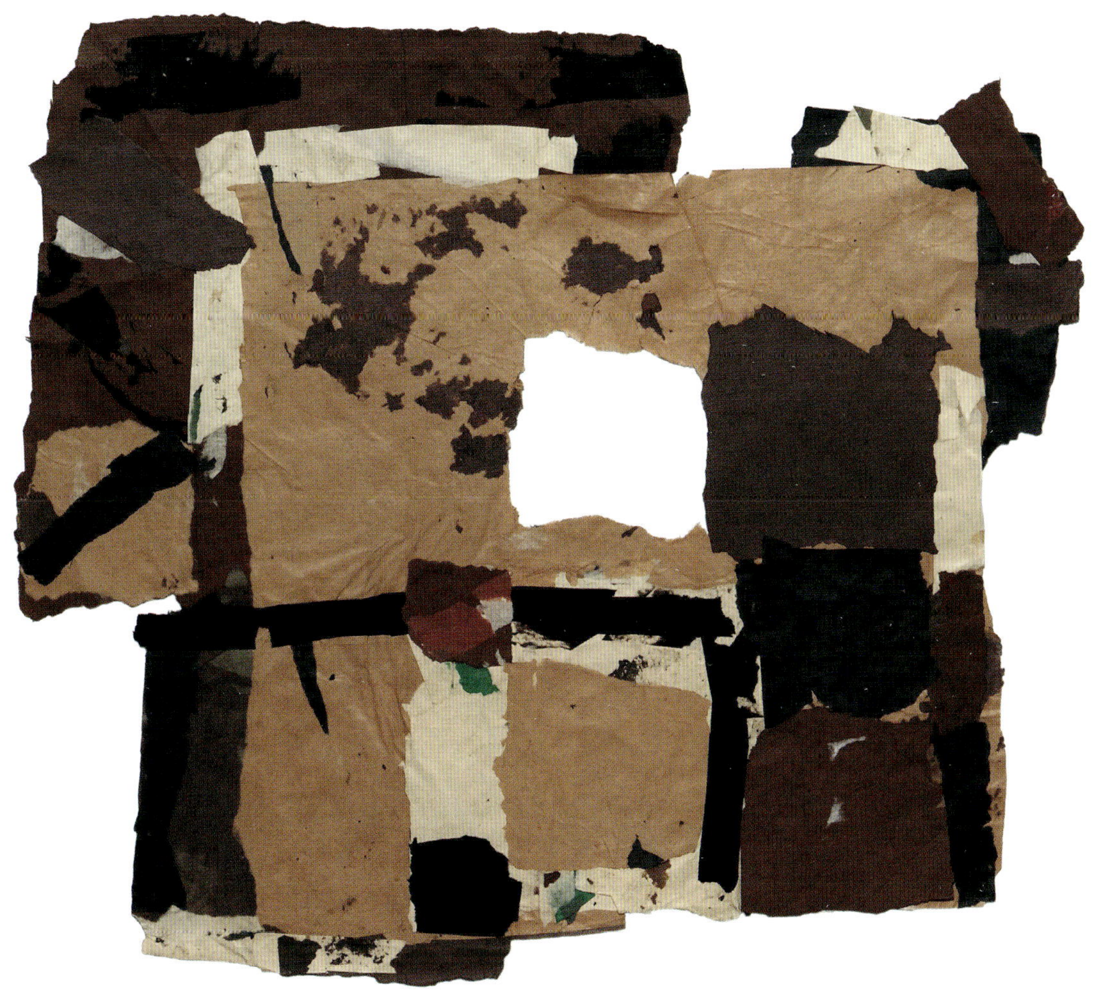

F/G-48   1976–80   Collage   62.2 × 69.1 cm (24.5 × 27.2")

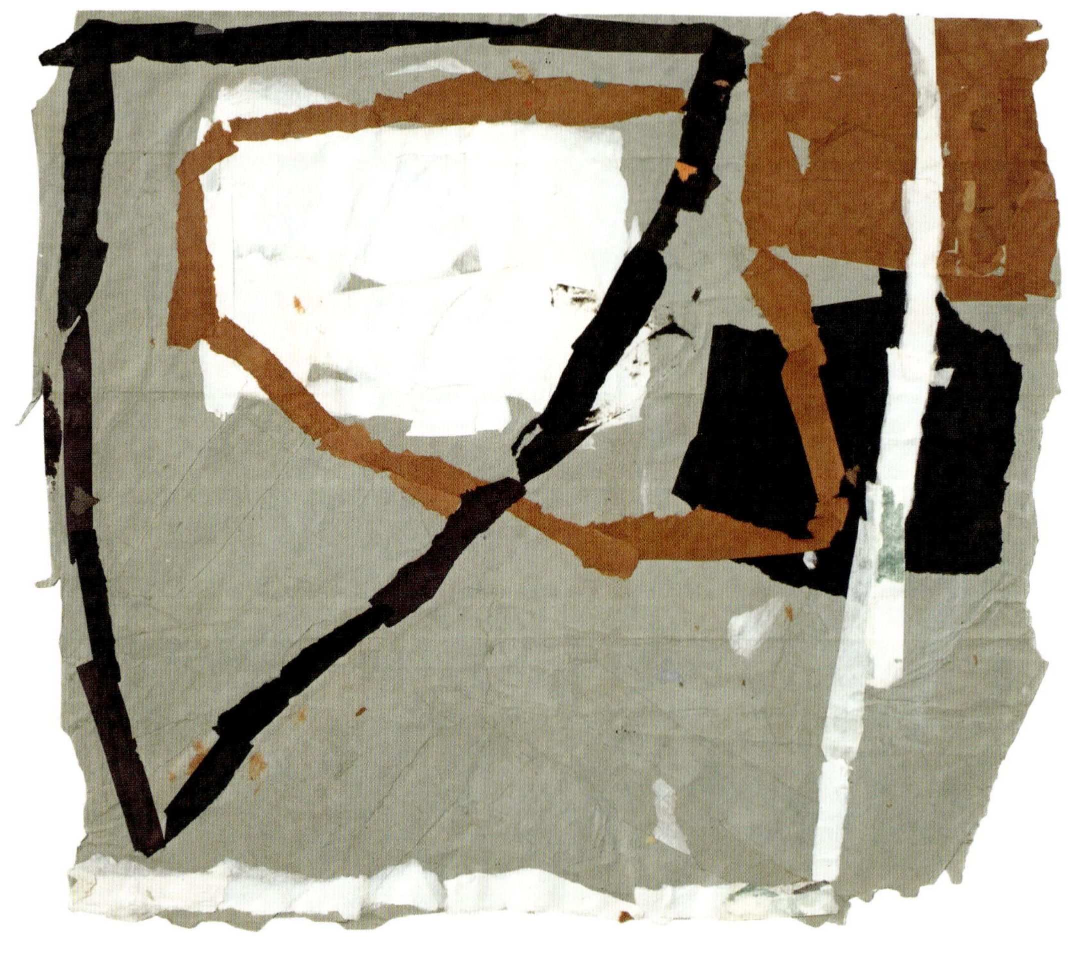

F-29   1976–8   Collage   58.9 × 66 cm (23.2 × 26")   Private collection

5
Posthumous Career

Francis Davison died with his life's work virtually intact, like some unknown amateur, or an Outsider artist who had sequestered himself from the world owing to mental instability. Some thought that his rightful home was St Ives among the pioneers of Modern British abstraction, but perhaps he needed the solitude of East Anglia for his work to germinate and mature.

After his death, there were three shows at the Redfern Gallery in London's Cork Street in the later 1980s and early 90s: a retrospective in May/June 1986, followed by 'Francis Davison: Works with Green' in the summer of 1988, and then 'Late Works' in August/September 1991. Interest was growing steadily, but there was no sudden conversion to the Davison gospel. In his catalogue introduction to the Redfern's retrospective, Julian Spalding noted that Davison's desire for anonymity at the Hayward had not been well-received: 'some reviewers found the lack of personal details and historical background offensive. One interpreted the artist's self-effacement as a publicity stunt in reverse. Another assumed that Francis Davison was a pseudonym.'

But there were serious attempts also to put Davison in context and perspective. In 1989, 'The Experience of Painting', an Arts Council touring show selected by Michael Harrison, included Davison among a group of painters. Devoted to 'eight modern artists' – Gillian Ayres, Jennifer Durrant, James Hugonin, Albert Irvin, Edwina Leapman, Kenneth Martin, Bridget Riley and Davison – it is very revealing that Davison the collagist should be positioned in this way within a group of high-ranking painters.

Mel Gooding, another admirer of Davison's work, compiled the catalogue. The main Davison text was edited by Gooding from his conversations with Margaret Mellis (conducted at Southwold in September 1988) about Davison's methods of working. In it she described how she had to invent titles for the collages in order to distinguish them from one another. Her titles were essentially descriptive such as 'Flashing light and dark colours' or 'Crossed paths', and the dates she gave were only intended to be approximate, and might cover a span of several years.

Gooding divided the Mellis text into sections. I quote it here extensively because it is so revealing of the man and the art. The last three sections are reproduced in their entirety. Under the heading 'The Reality of Art' Mellis said:

> Francis was reluctant to title his works, or to date or classify them in any way, because he wanted you to look at the collage itself, without any preconceived ideas which might have been suggested by the title. In exactly the same way he felt that dates were irrelevant. People always look at those other things first, the things round the edge, title and date and so on; and that stops them seeing the work itself.
>
> In the earlier paintings and collages, there is sometimes a reference to things in the world, a house and a hill, or a road perhaps, but even then he turned those houses or hills into shapes that work together, they are not houses, they are shapes, *but we read them as houses*. So it is not much of a step from representation to non-representation …
>
> Francis wasn't trying to do anything for the viewer. He was dealing with his own experience. When his inner feelings have *become* the material, that is where the satisfaction lies. So these collages present us with something that is nearer to our true experience of the world than a picture of something which can

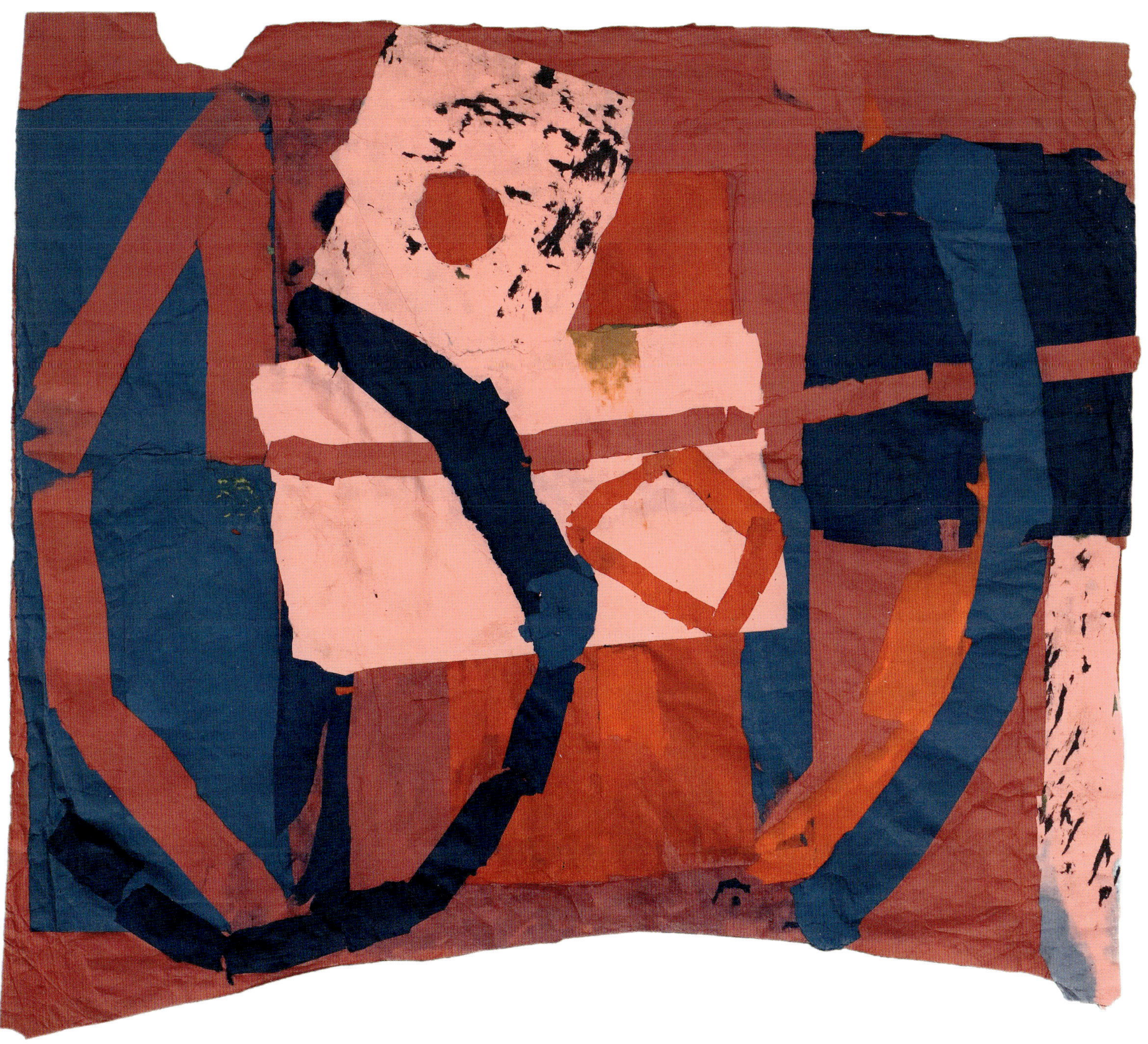

G-53   1978–84   Collage   83.8 × 94 cm (33 × 37")   Private collection

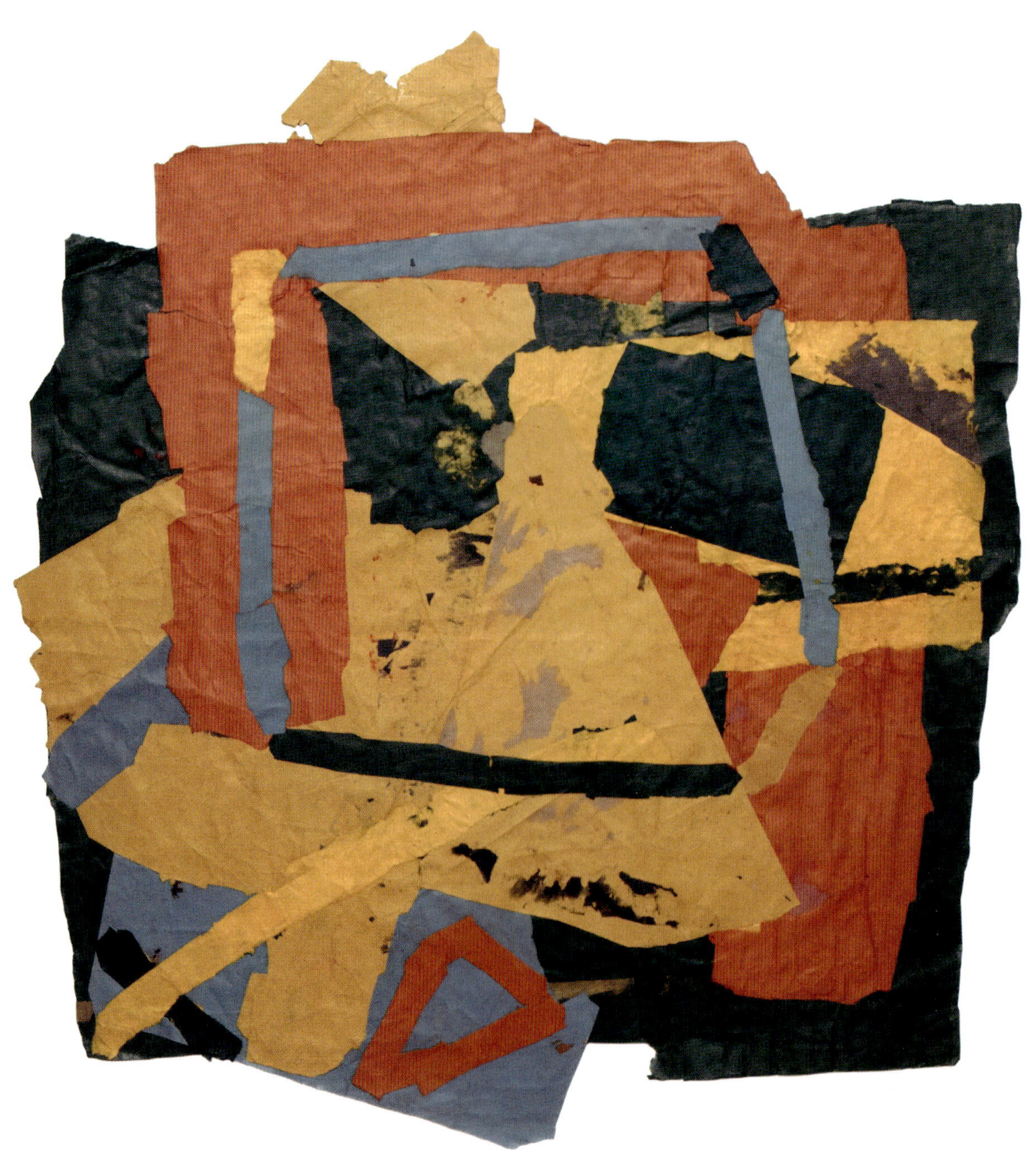

G-429   1978–83   Collage   104.1 × 92.7 cm (41 × 36.5")

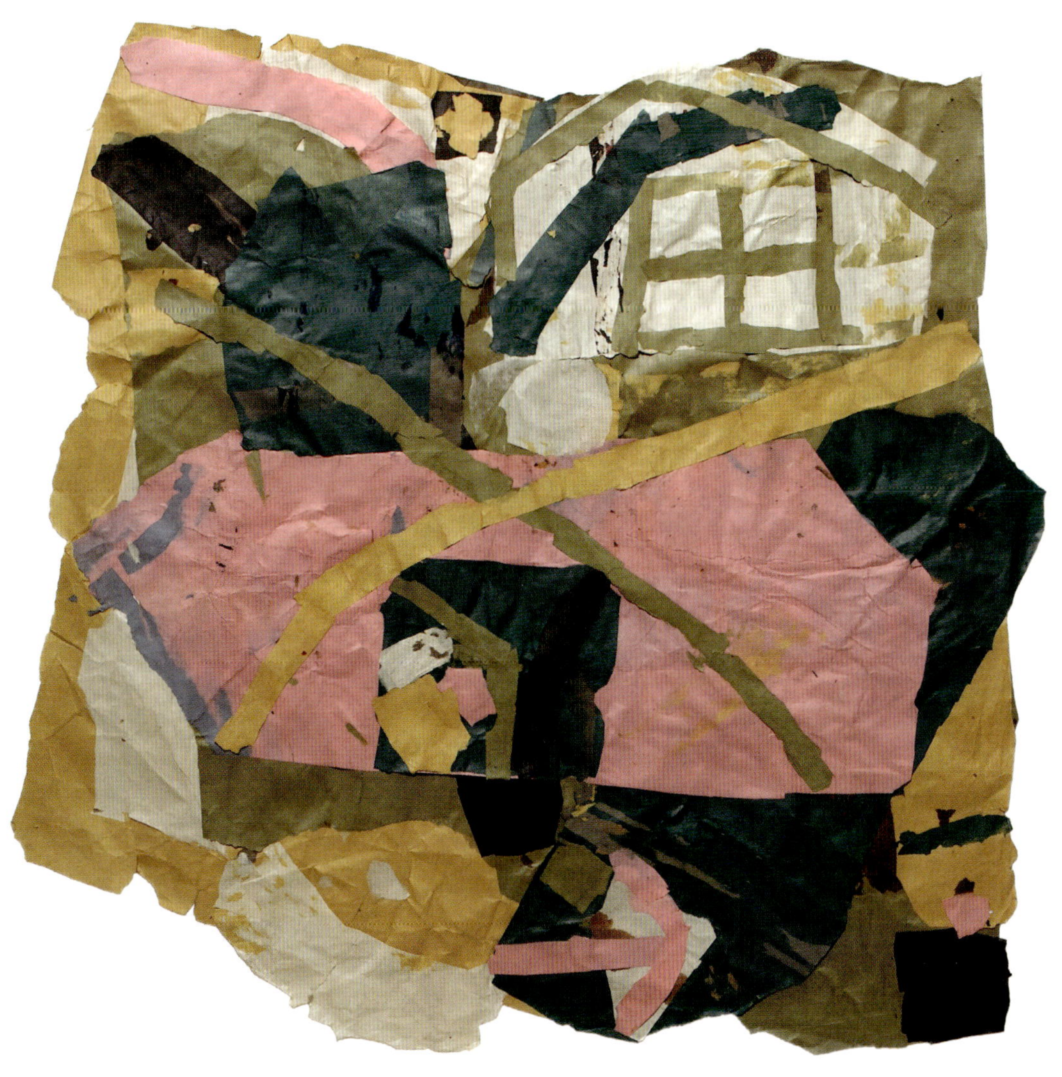

G-600   1981   Collage   88.9 × 88.9 cm (35 × 35")

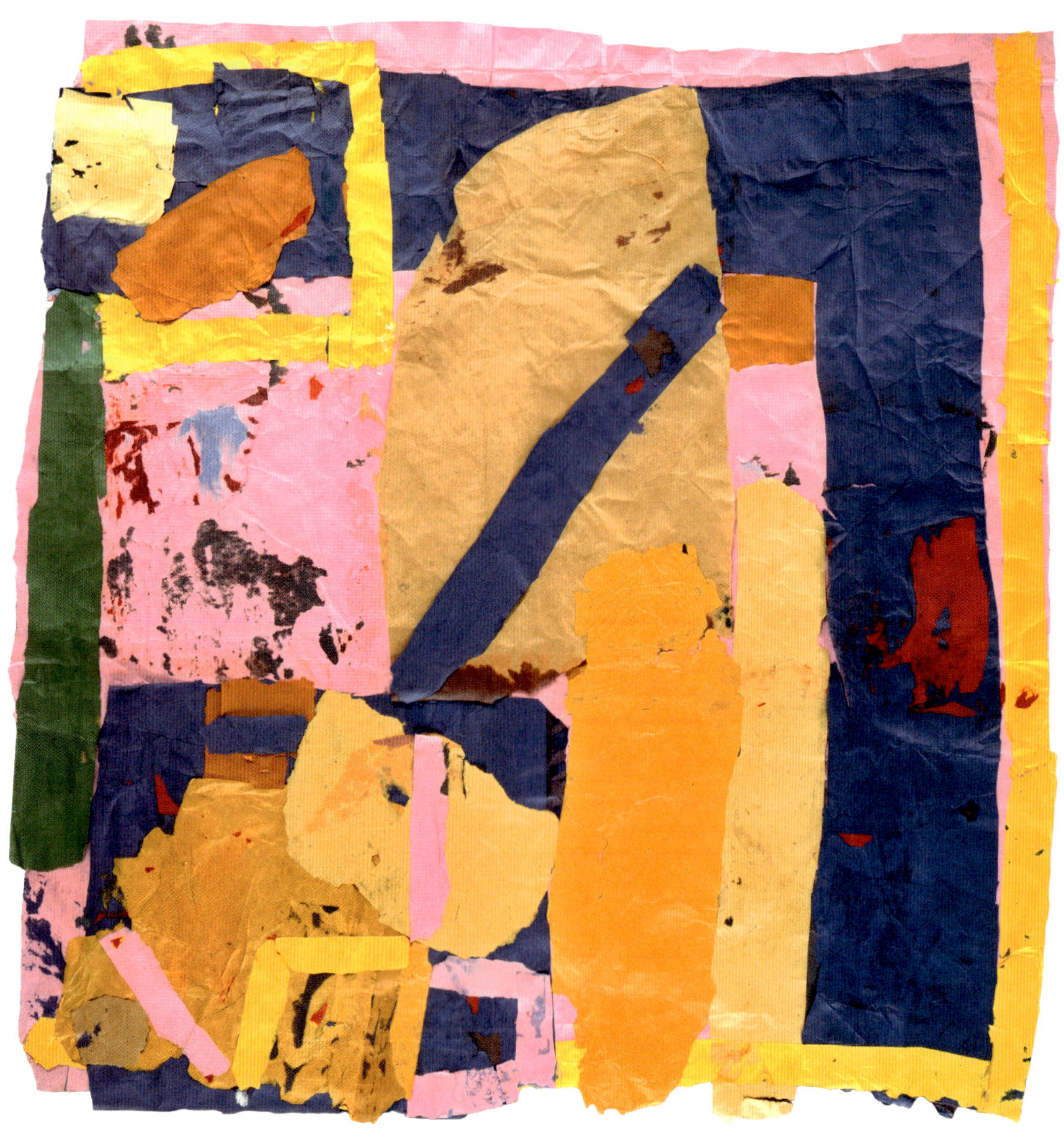

G-4   1978–82   Collage   124.5 × 116.8 cm (49 × 46")   Private collection

only present one aspect of it. I think that is why painters move from representation to abstraction, because it gives them greater scope and freedom, and helps them to avoid being cluttered up with pre-conceived ideas. Art is more than a matter of emotions, it is perceptual, and conceptual; it is many things simultaneously.

Making the work

The medium of collage gave Francis tremendous freedom, and it worked for him because of his very strong sense of structure and design. The way he approached it meant that he was able to work with the total surface the whole time. There was nothing precisely preconceived in this manner of working: it was a process of spontaneous discovery that would go on until the work was made. At the end, everything looked right, the right coloured shape in the right place.

Francis always said he was the only true collagist, because other people painted their paper, or put other things in, things that had other associations. He didn't put anything extra in. He just worked with these used papers. They had to be *used* papers, they couldn't be anything else.

Chance and intention

Francis's work was both completely spontaneous and controlled, two opposite things. There is always more than one thing happening at once; which is why they are interesting.

Some people might think that there was a great deal of chance and accident in the making of the work, but there aren't any accidents in it at all. *There is nothing there that is not intended.* Say you put a piece of blue on here, or green, and it isn't right, it doesn't work, you just take it off again, until you find the right shaped colour. And that is not chance. It is a matter of judgement and intention.

I used to think that there were a lot of chance things which happened to come right because of the rhythm of the working as it were. But when Francis was half-paralysed, and I had to hold his papers so that he could tear them, I found out how absolutely *precisely* he worked. There was enormous control, and

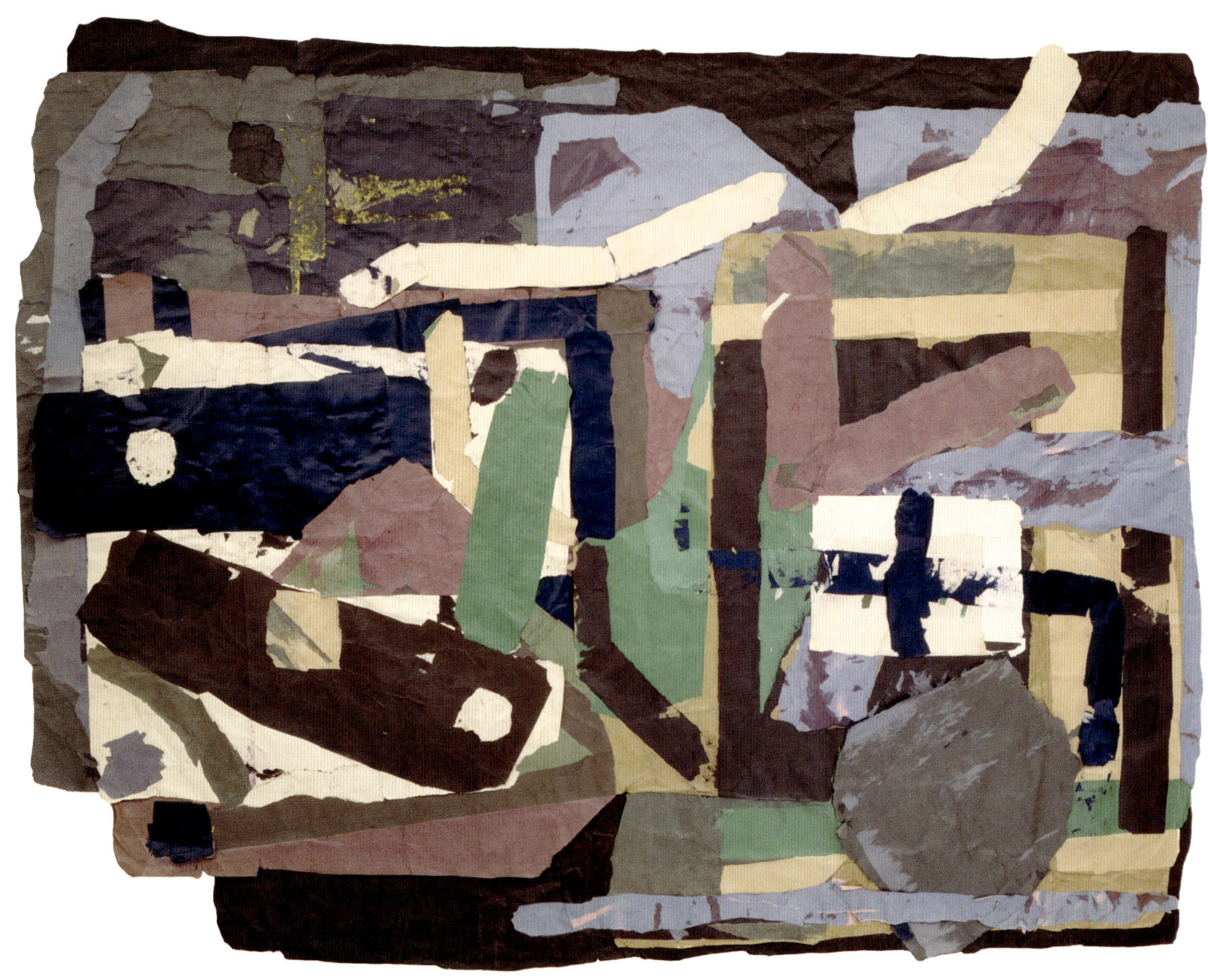

G-11   1982   Collage   147.3 × 185.4 cm (58 × 73")   Private collection

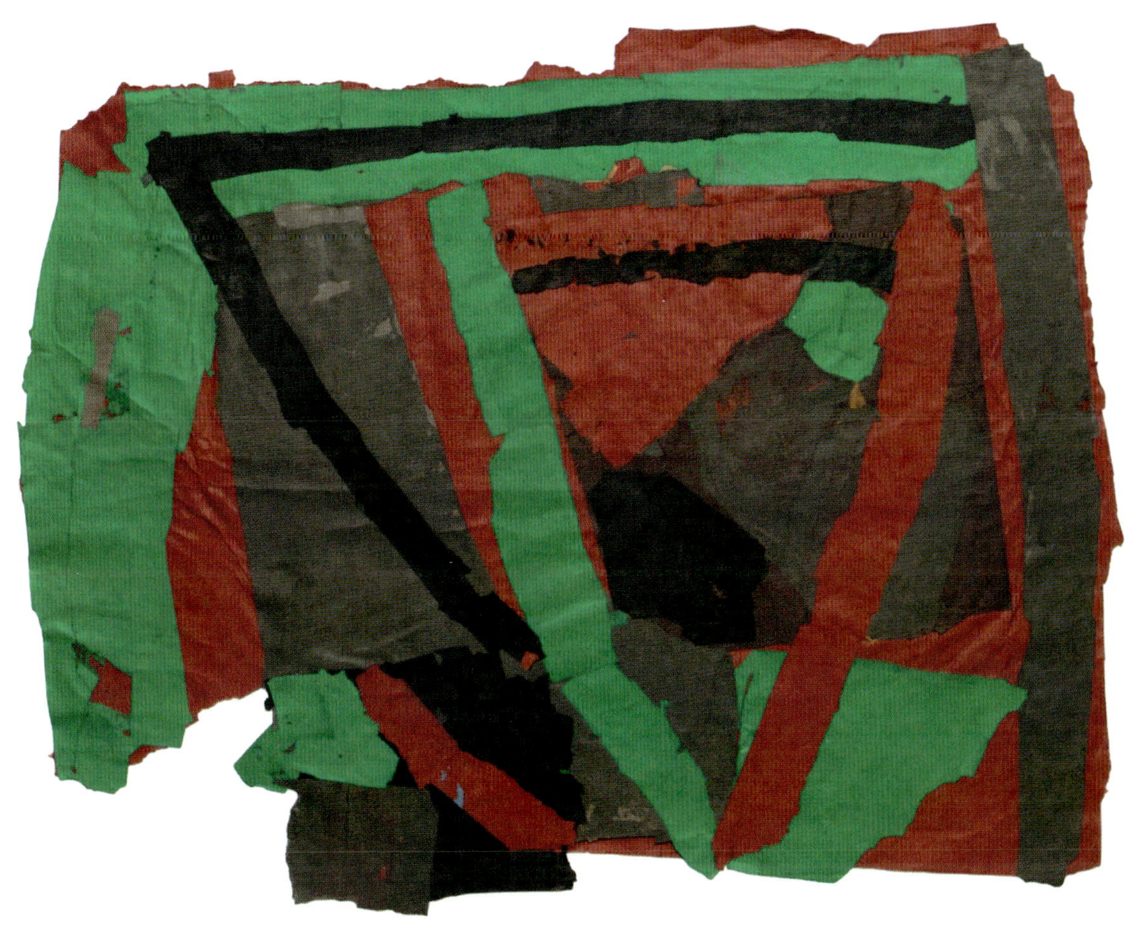

G-355 1978–83 Collage 88.9 × 108.5 cm (35 × 42.7")

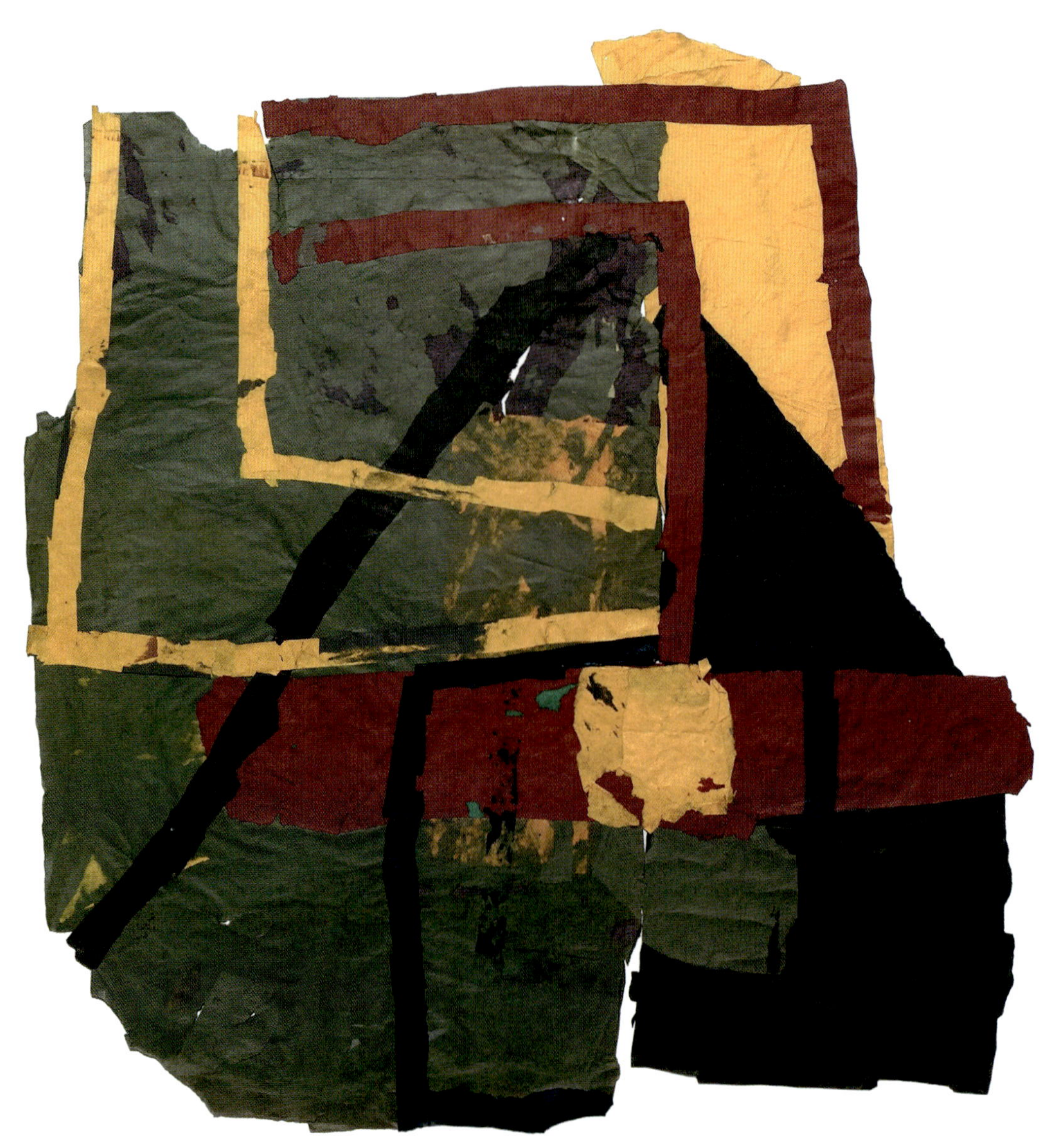

G-420   1978–83   Collage   99.6 × 90.2 cm (39.2 × 35.5")

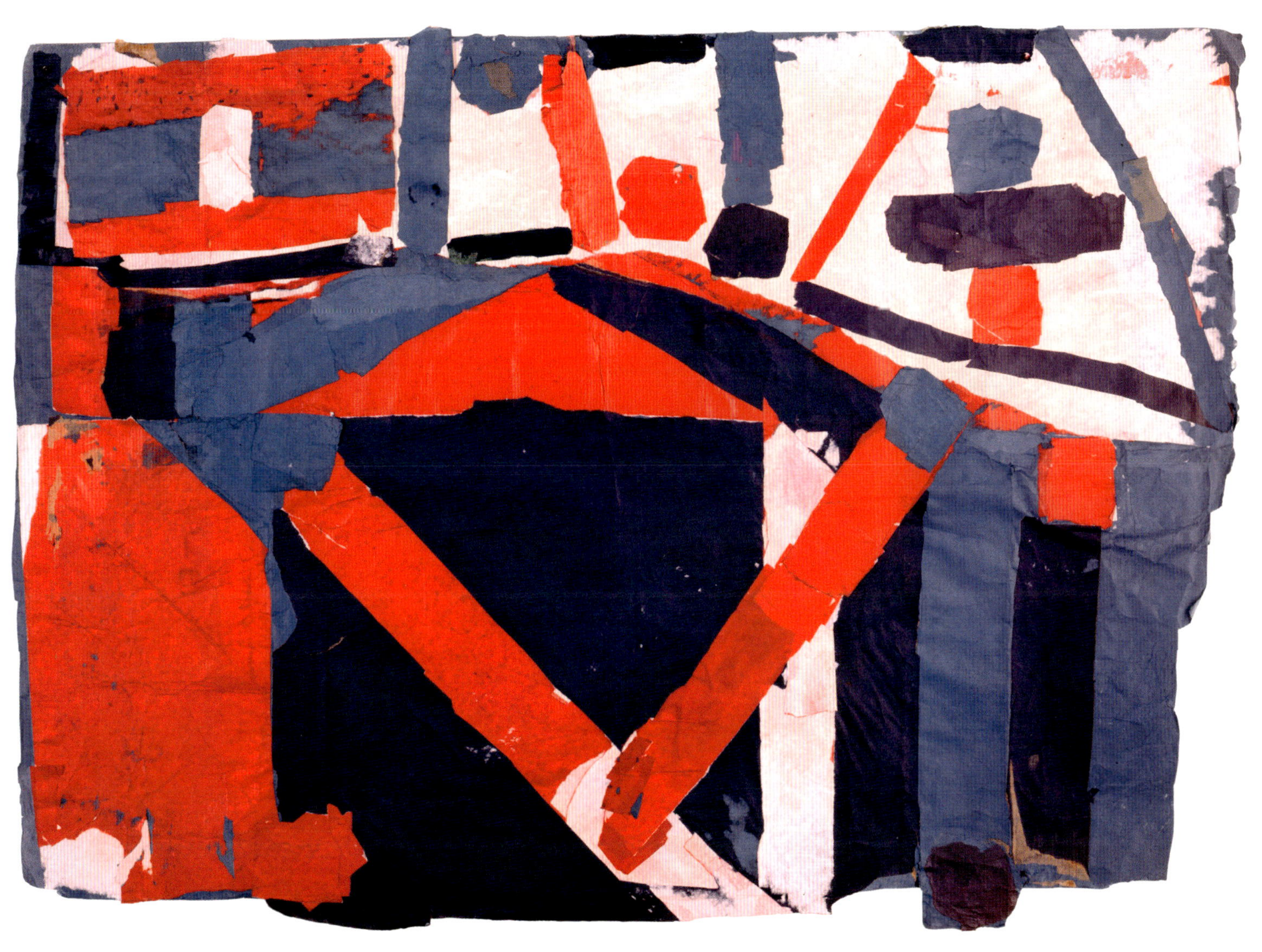

G-60 1978–84 Collage 101.6 × 137.2 cm (40 × 54") Private collection

every tiny little bit of paper was torn and nitched to *exactly* the shape he wanted. This spiky bit here at the top, that little bit down there which is not quite rounded, this piece of blue which shows underneath in a sort of circle, where he has torn a piece off; each of these things is meant to be like that. His control was much tighter than I could possibly have imagined.

Structure and colour

These pieces work in a total way, with shape and colour and depth all giving an experience that is simultaneous, because of the structure underneath. It is very tight, yet they look quite loose and free. Francis used only used papers, so his colours are entirely *found*. But they are all put together so that they have a tonal relation, and a spatial relation; and the colour relation comes right when you get the tone and the structure right. 'Right' means that every single bit of the picture works in about six different ways: you have all these things going on at once and they all relate to each other: backwards and forwards, flat surface against depth, colour through form.

When something has gone wrong with a painting or collage, you tend to think it is the colour that is wrong, but it almost always turns out to be the shape or structure. Colour only works in amounts; it depends on *how much* blue, *how much* red, and how it's touching the other colours. To get colour to work you have to concentrate on the forms and the structure.

It is like music. People don't expect music to be a copy of something, do they? They realise it's a relationship of sounds to each other. What makes the music is the structure of the sounds, and it is exactly the same with painting and collage. The difference is that music is one sound *after* the other, whereas with a picture you are getting it all at once, there isn't any sort of progression. Your eye may move from one thing to another, but you are aware of the total area, and you don't have to look in any particular direction, it's not structured in time. I don't know why people have to expect paintings to represent something; they don't expect music to, they listen to the whole thing. And you ought to look at a painting or a collage in the way that you listen to music.

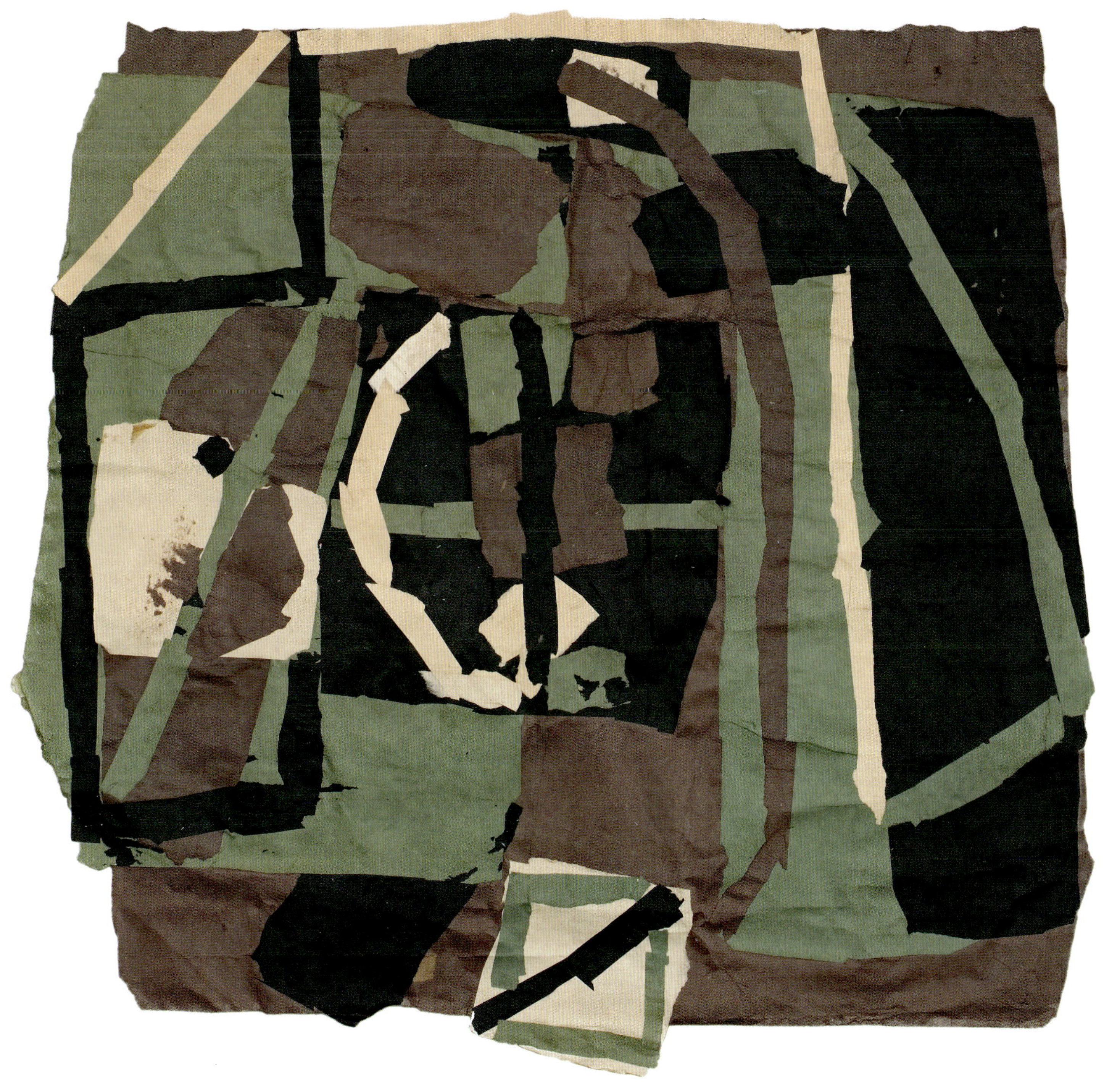

G-52a   1978–83   Collage   118.1 × 124.5 cm (46.5 × 49")   Private collection

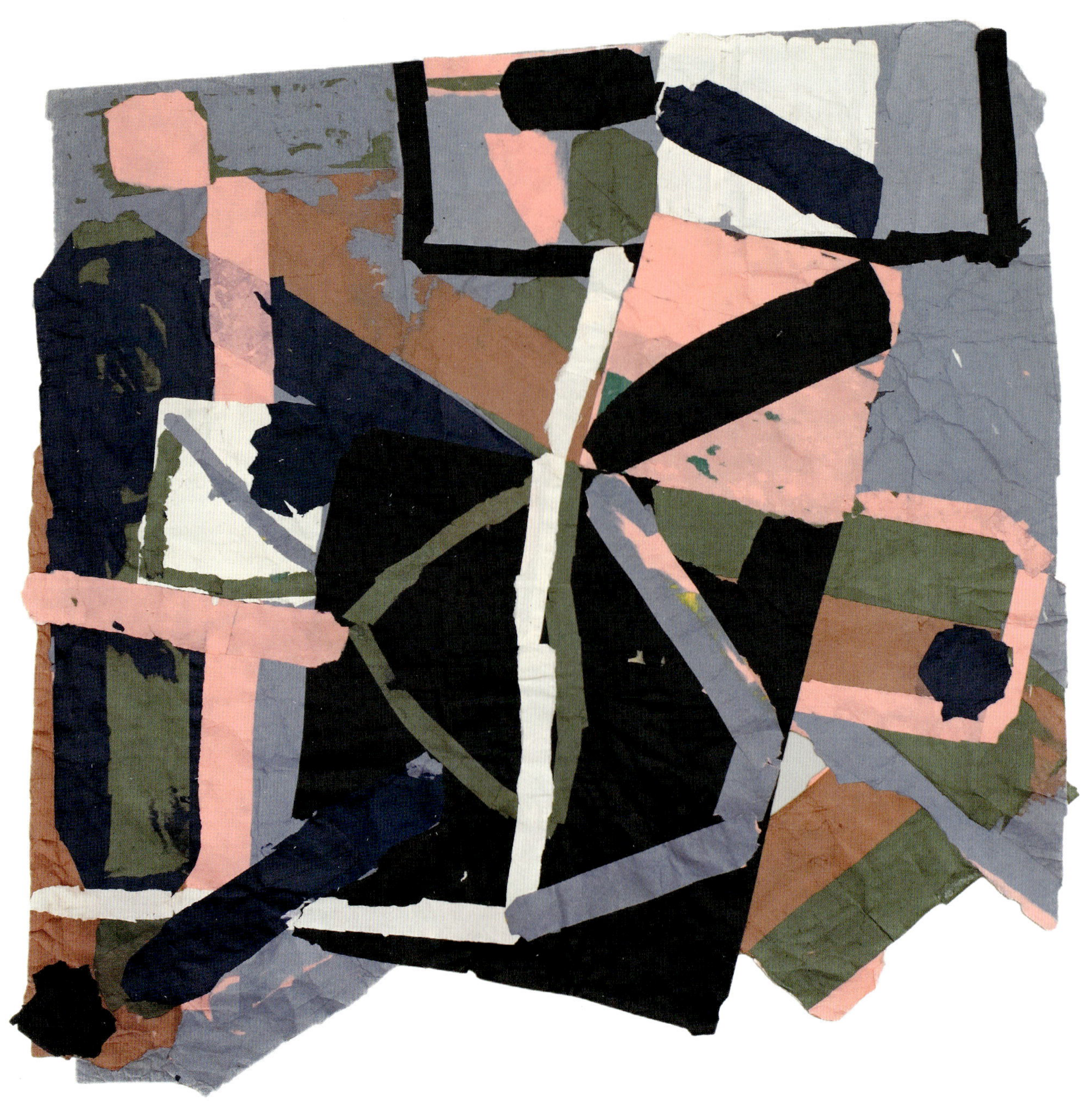

G-52   1978–83   Collage   118.1 × 124.5 cm (46.5 × 49")   Private collection

The photograph of Davison reproduced in 'The Experience
of Painting' catalogue (taken by Mellis) is dark and moody,
more like a painted portrait that a photographic record.
His eyes are shadowed and his thick dark hair is chopped
in a boyish pudding-bowl style. He is posed unknowably in
shadow against a dense backdrop of foliage. The photograph
gives very little away; in fact, it may be said deliberately to
withhold information. In other words, a very appropriate
image of a man obsessed with anonymity.

In 1996, Davison was given the Aldeburgh Festival
Exhibition, held at the Peter Pears Gallery in June. In the
brochure note, Julian Spalding predicted that Davison would
come to be seen as the John Sell Cotman of his generation.
In the new century, there have been various commercial
shows of Davison's paintings and collages, principally
at Austin/Desmond in London (2003, 2006, 2012) and
at Goldmark Gallery in Rutland (2010). There was also a
superb museum exhibition of his collages at Kettle's Yard in
Cambridge in 2007–8, organized by long-standing Davison
supporter Michael Harrison. But there is still much to be
done in terms of showing the range of this little-known and
seriously underrated artist.

For example, the very late small collages, fragile as confetti,
were in a rather lamentable and uncared-for state, all stuck
together in a corner of the studio store. David Archer from
Austin/Desmond noticed that they had all been individually
numbered and he took the time to separate them out and
restore them to their former glory (see pages 168–71). In
fact, they became the subject of an exhibition at Austin/
Desmond in 2012, and for Archer they represent a distillation
of everything Davison was trying to do. For him, Davison's
larger works reflect the somewhat aggressive physical

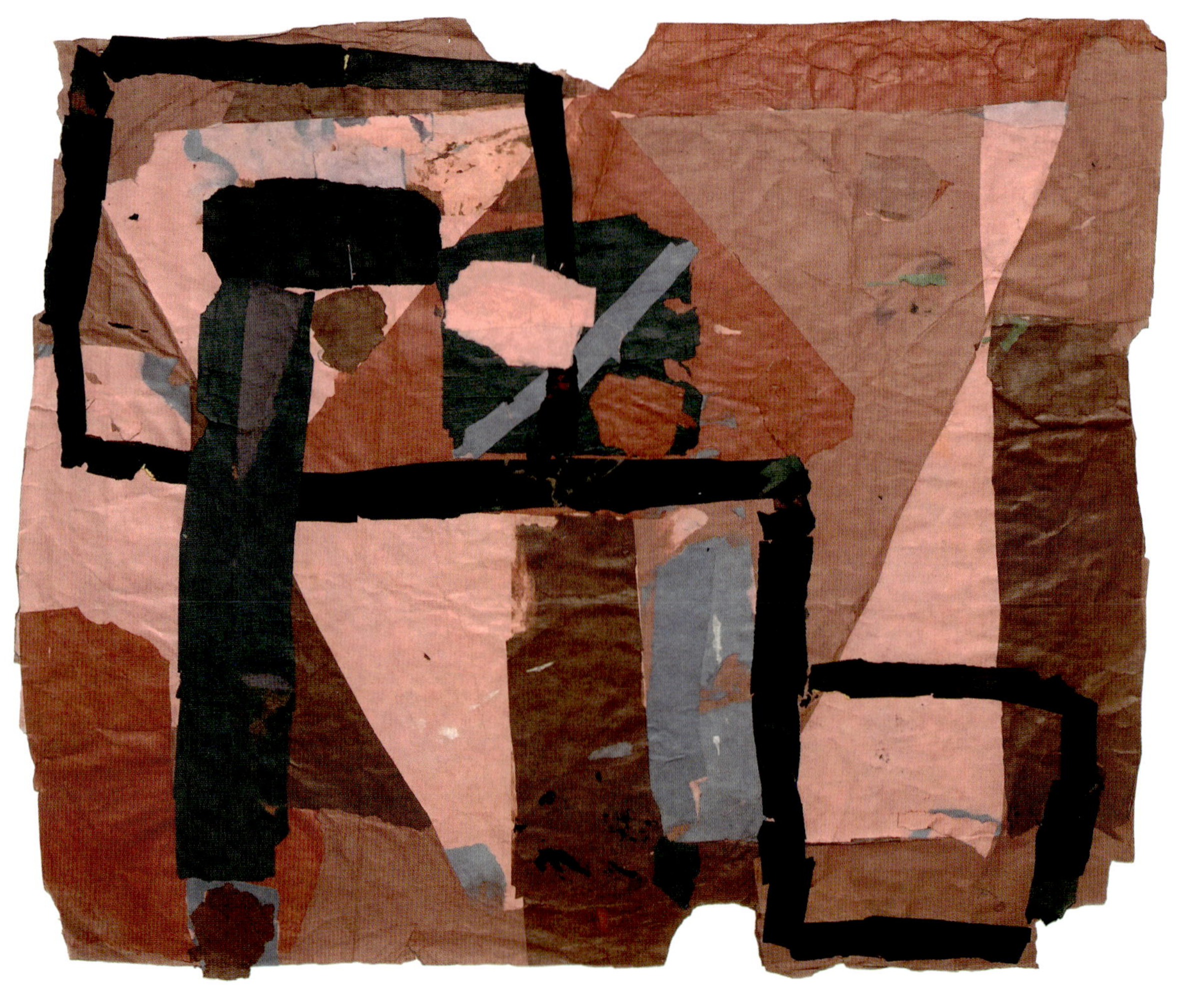

G-476   1978–83   Collage   91.9 × 108.5 cm (36.2 × 42.7")

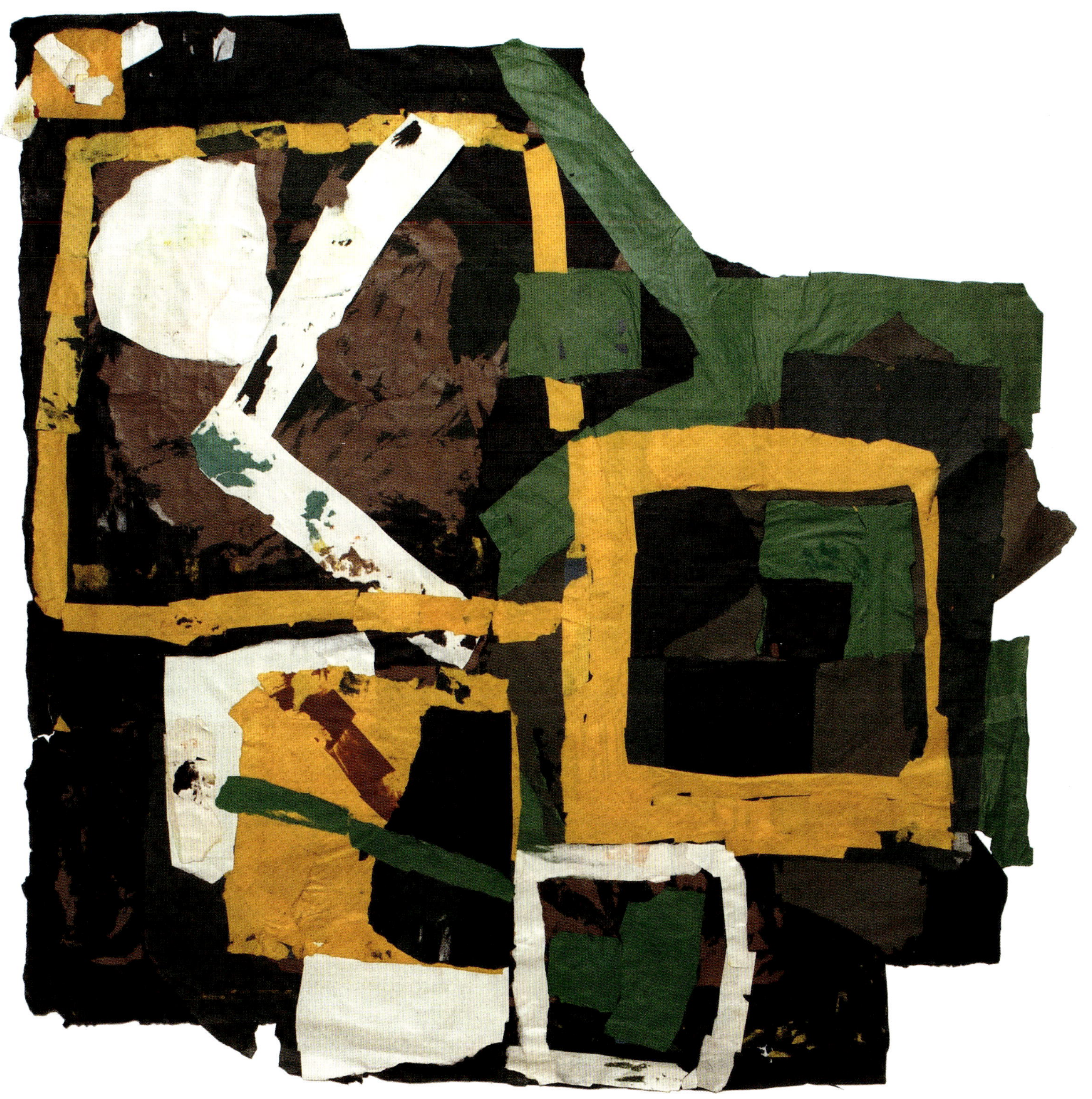

G-340 1978–83 Collage 144 × 144 cm (56.7 × 56.7")

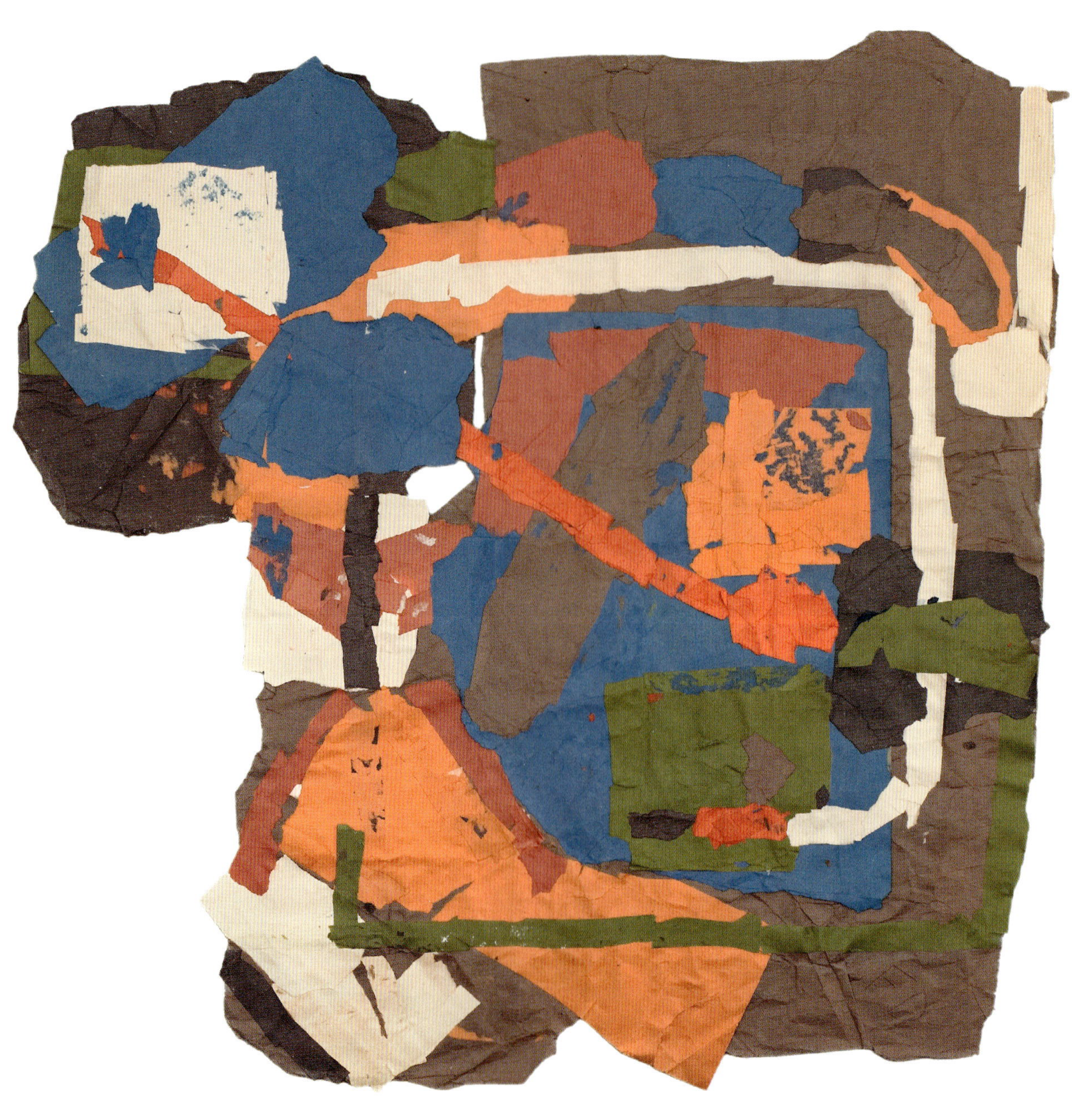

H-22   1982–4   Collage   142.2 × 132.1 cm (56 × 52")   Private collection

personality of the artist, whereas these late collages, made after an illness, suggest his vulnerability. This, in Archer's opinion, offers increased access to the work for the general public. He sees a new humanity to Davison's art as his physical abilities declined, and he compares this late period to the similarly late flowering of both Victor Pasmore and Ben Nicholson. (Examined in a 2008 Austin/Desmond exhibition of their later work entitled 'The Thing Observed'.)

These final collages by Davison are little more than A5 in size and are composed entirely out of envelopes. Given Mellis's interest in using envelopes for her work, it's not difficult to imagine the two artists fighting over the morning mail; except that Davison was now so physically reduced that Mellis, in her typically supportive way, would have happily allowed him all the raw material he wanted even if it meant depriving herself. Looking at these delicate and lovely works it is not always possible to tell which way up (or round) they go, for Davison was always elusive about specifying the orientation of his collages. This was part of his urge to anonymity, and suggests a desire for spectator involvement: the viewer decides (if the work is unframed – or even if it isn't) which way to look at the work. Archer concludes that Davison was less concerned to make a statement with his envelope collages. The large earlier works had been declarative and emphatic: the small late ones were insinuating and allusive. They have what Davison himself in an early published poem referred to as 'gracewillow ease'.

Was part of Davison's self-imposed remit to make paper sculptural? Not really. Obviously he wanted the torn edges to be part of the image, and occasionally passages curl up or stand proud because they have not been glued absolutely flat. This was no doubt allowed if not actively encouraged

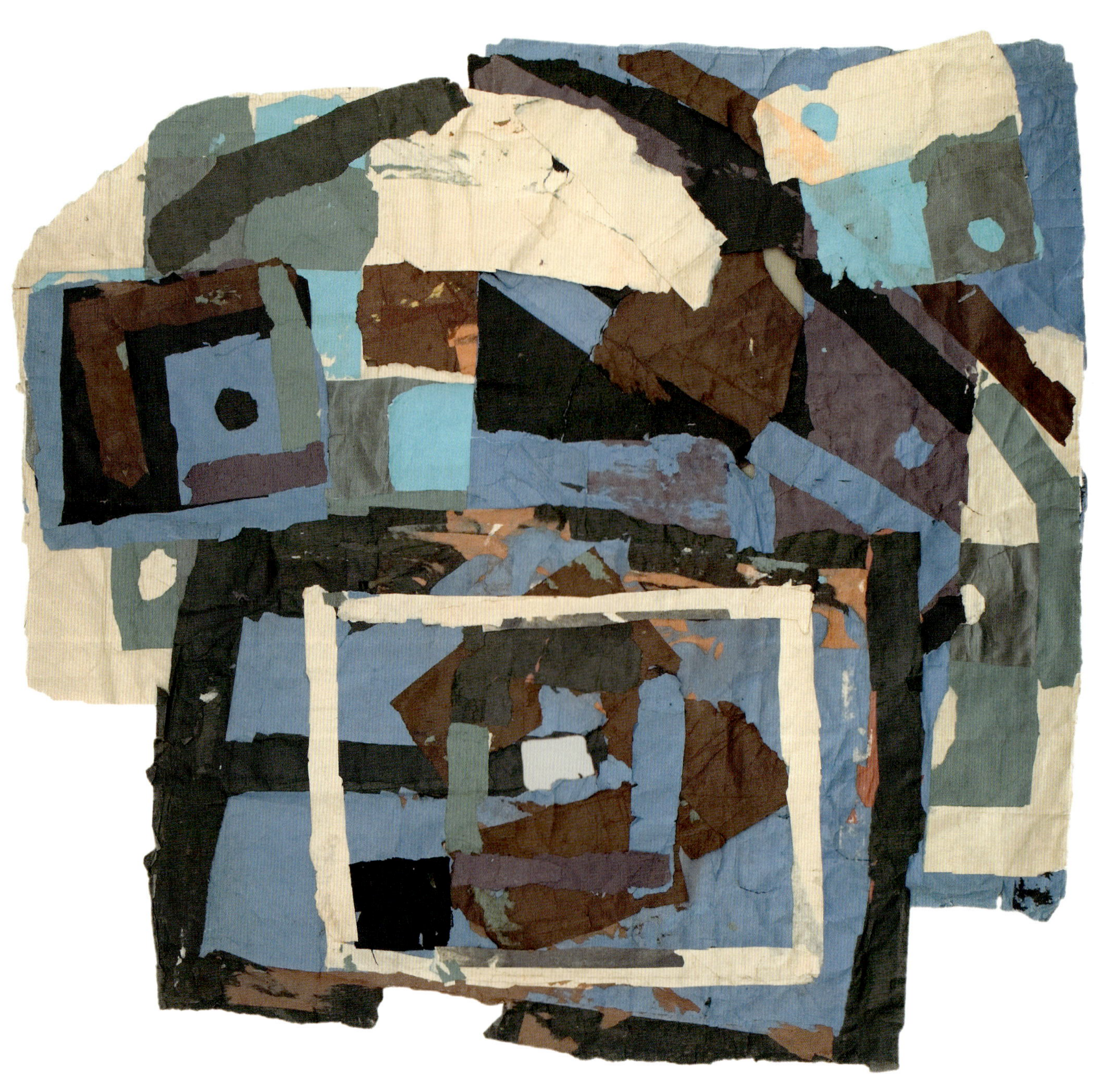

H-23   1982–4   Collage   144.8 × 147.3 cm (57 × 58")   Private collection

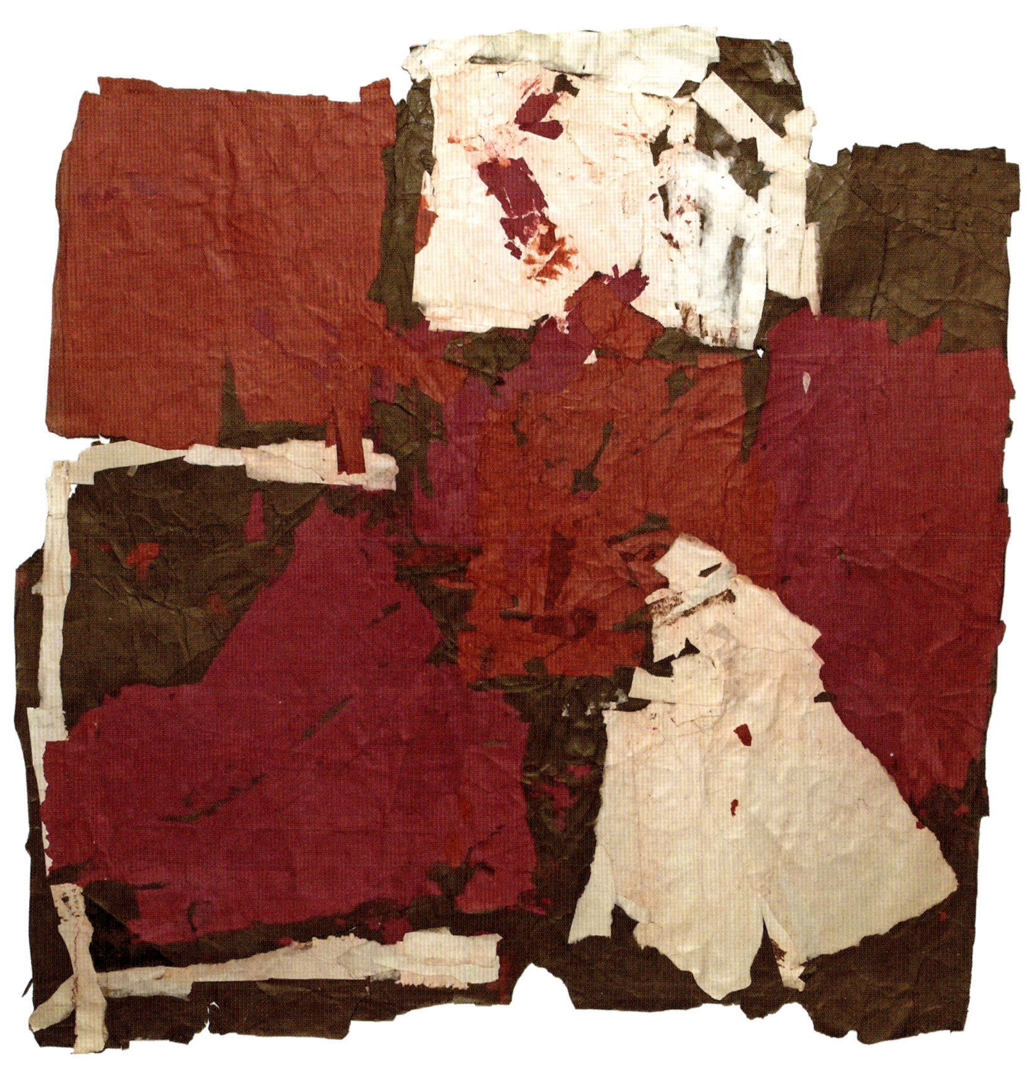

G-314   1978–83   Collage   110.5 × 109.2 cm (43.5 × 43")

in order to provide variation in texture and make the work more three-dimensional. However, the materials did not generally dictate the forms of the collage because Davison was concerned to modify his raw material by tearing and juxtaposition, changes in emphasis, rhythm and direction within the composition. Obviously choice guided the selection of one paper over another: as Mellis pointed out, in a Davison collage everything was intentional.

Telfer recounts that Francis once said: 'It isn't so much that you're looking at the collage as that it's looking at you.' This is less about being paranoid, and much more about the autonomy of the art object, endowing it with a life of its own – or releasing the life already there. There is an ancient Welsh myth recorded in *The Mabinogion* about a woman made from flowers, Blodeuedd, who falls in love with someone other than her husband and is punished by being turned into an owl. The story is brilliantly re-told in Alan Garner's novel *The Owl Service* (1967), in which some children find a dinner service with owl decorations on it. They feel compelled to trace the owls onto paper and liberate them from the plates, but by doing so they re-awaken the legend, with the inevitable consequences. This kind of release is what Davison evidently found in his art – a version of the idea of the artist acting as a conduit for some power outside himself.

For Davison, collage making was an art of intuitively judged decisions, of relationships and revisions. He told Telfer of a dream he had about being attacked by his collages (he called them his 'collies', perhaps symbolically). He was cornered by them at the back of a room and they were snapping at him. Telfer interprets the dream as: 'an indication of how he was more or less directed by another part of himself when he was making the collages, which he didn't want to or need to control.' This supplements Mellis's interpretation of Davison's absolute and conscious decision-making. Taken together, these two explanations may begin to account for the complex reality of Davison's remarkable collages.

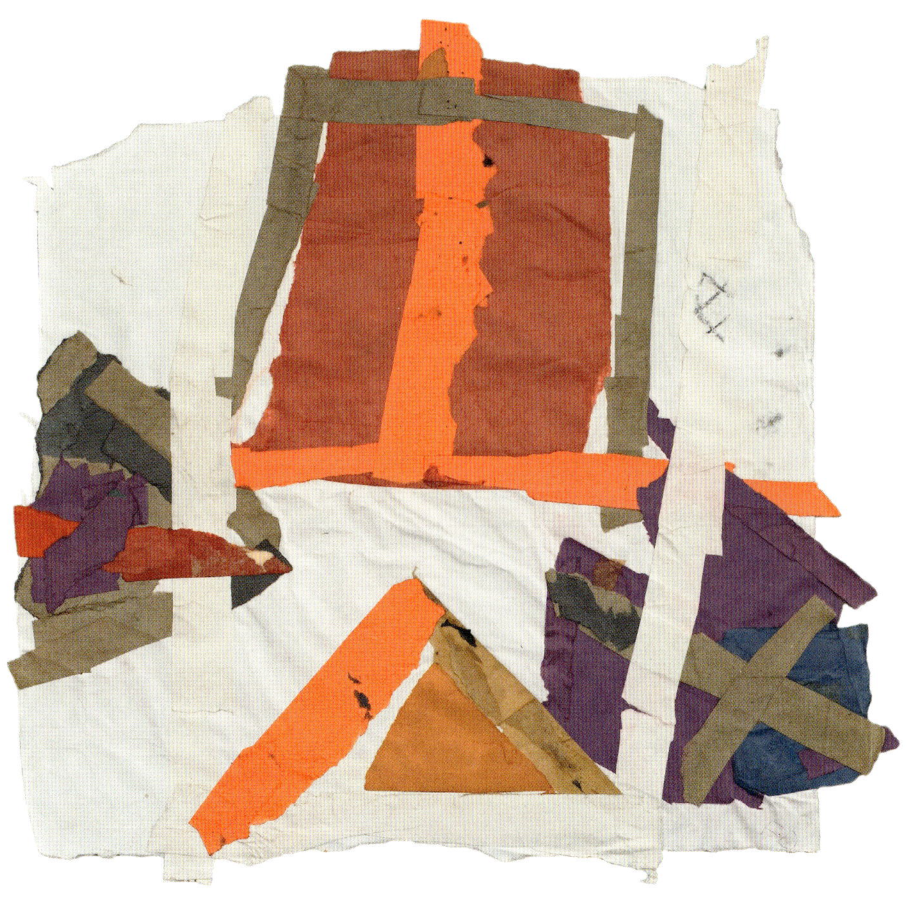

H-21   1980–2   Collage   45.7 × 47 cm (18 × 18.5")   Private collection

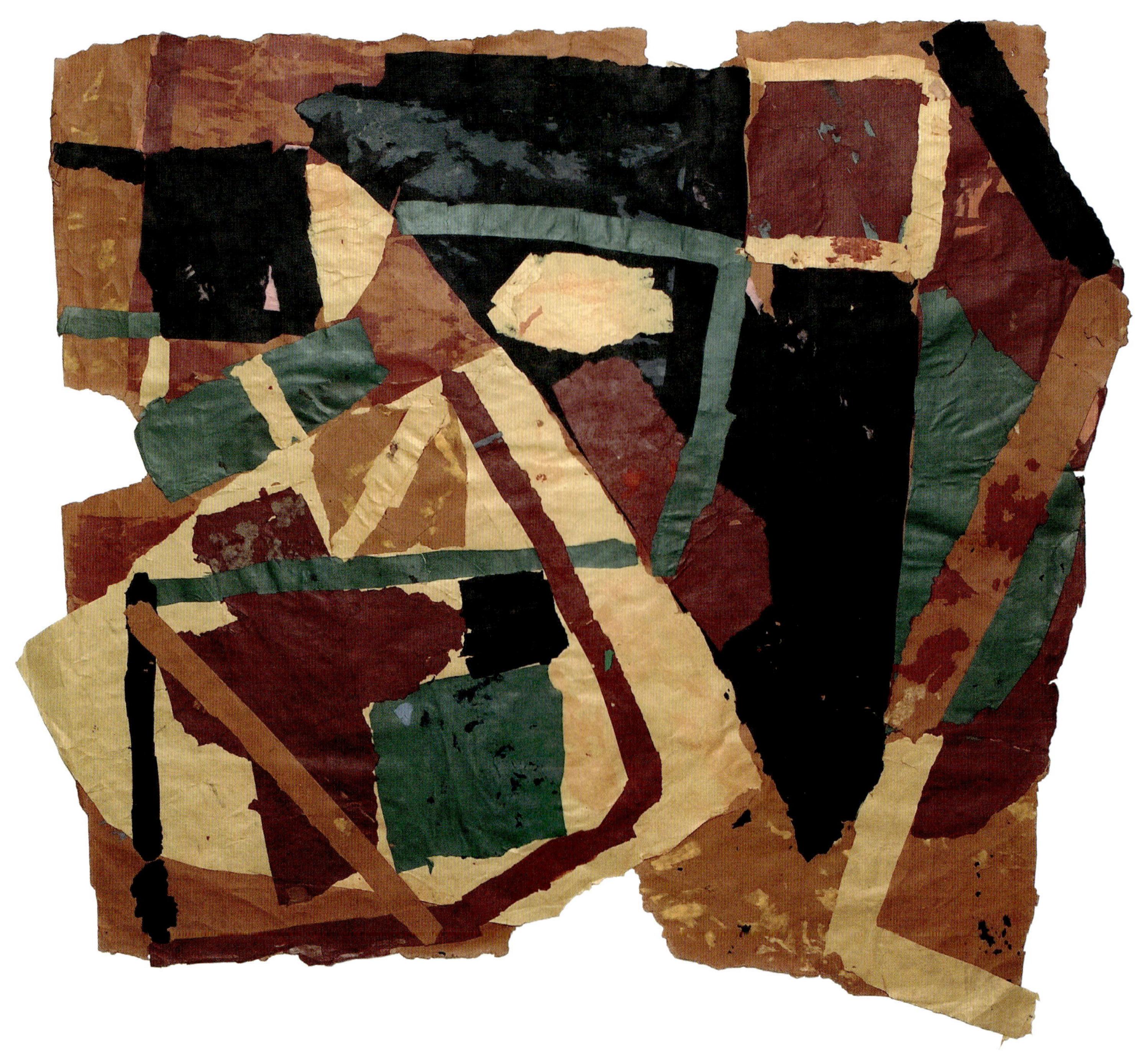

G-500   1978–83   Collage   132.1 × 144.8 cm (52 × 57")

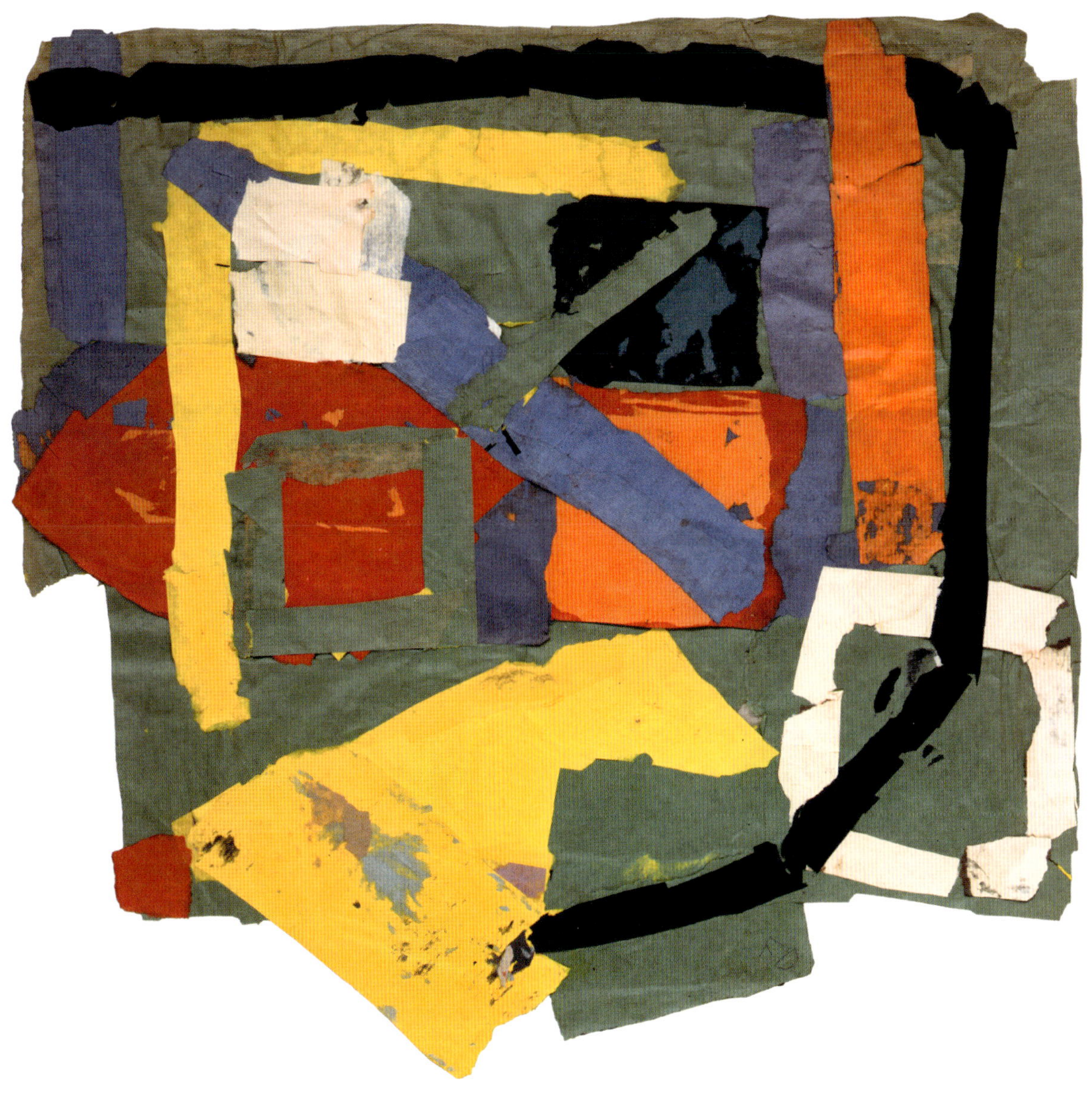

G-2   1978–82   Collage   94 × 94 cm (37 × 37")   Private collection

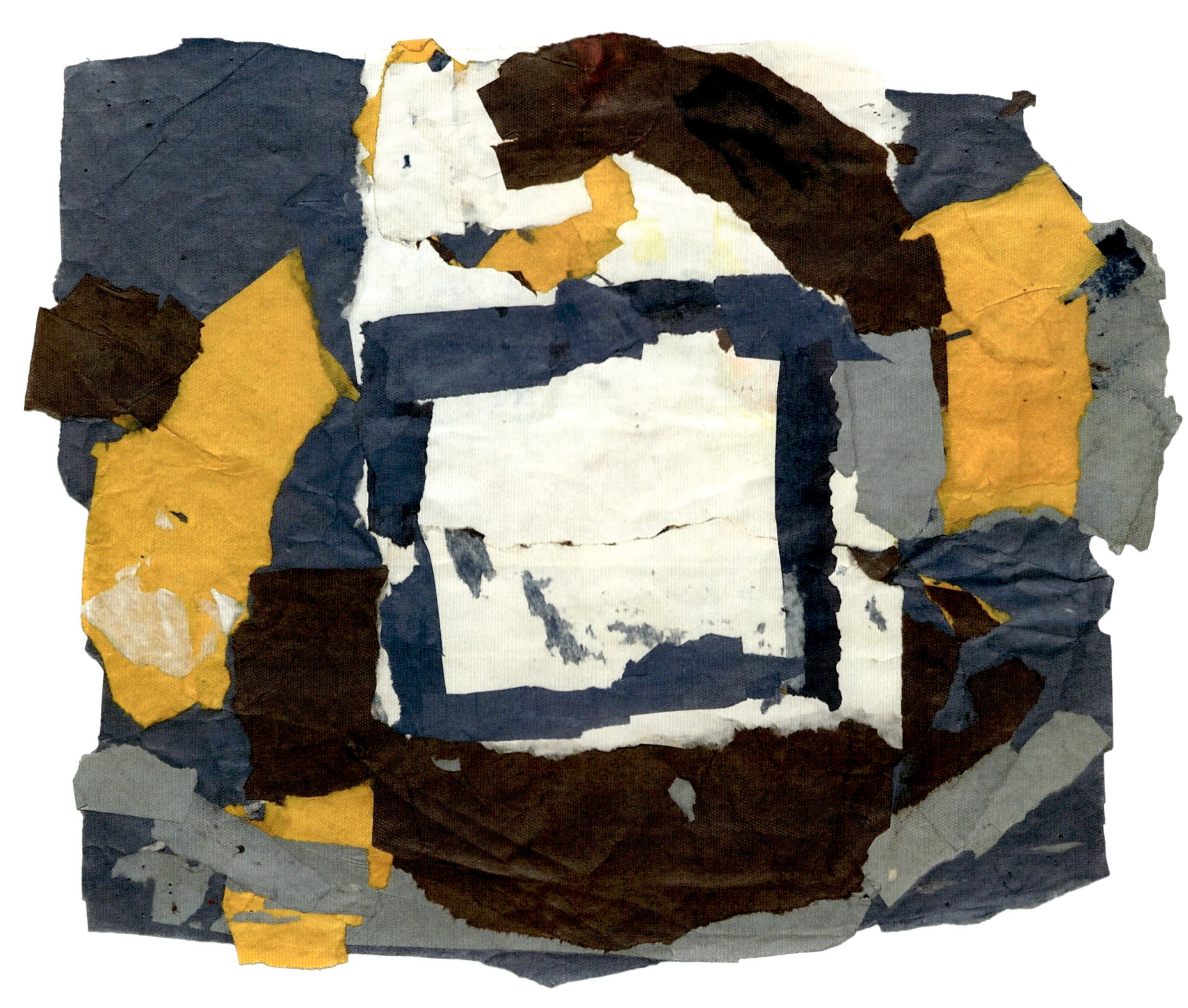

G-318   1978–83   Collage   c.76 × 84 cm (c.30 × 33")

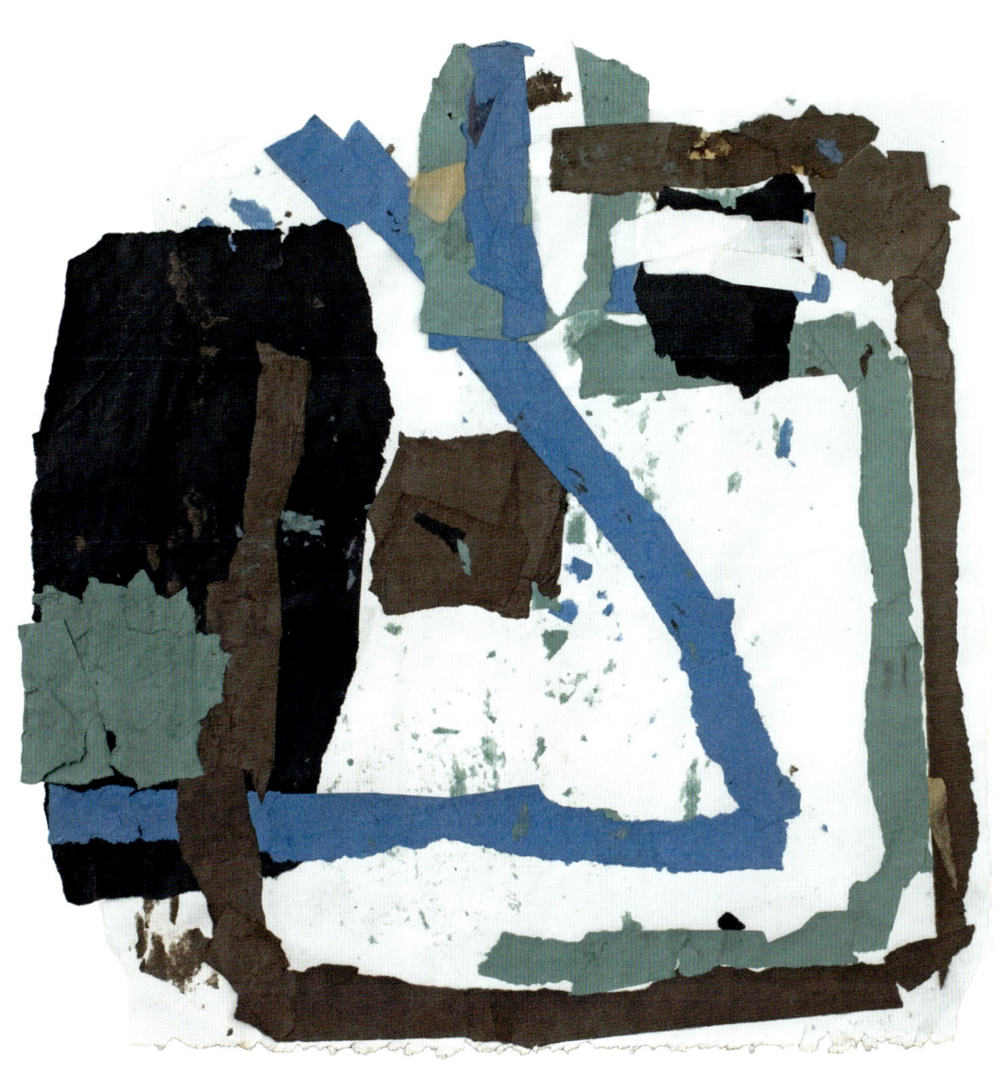

H-9   1983–4   Collage   59.7 × 55.9 cm (23.5 × 22")   Private collection

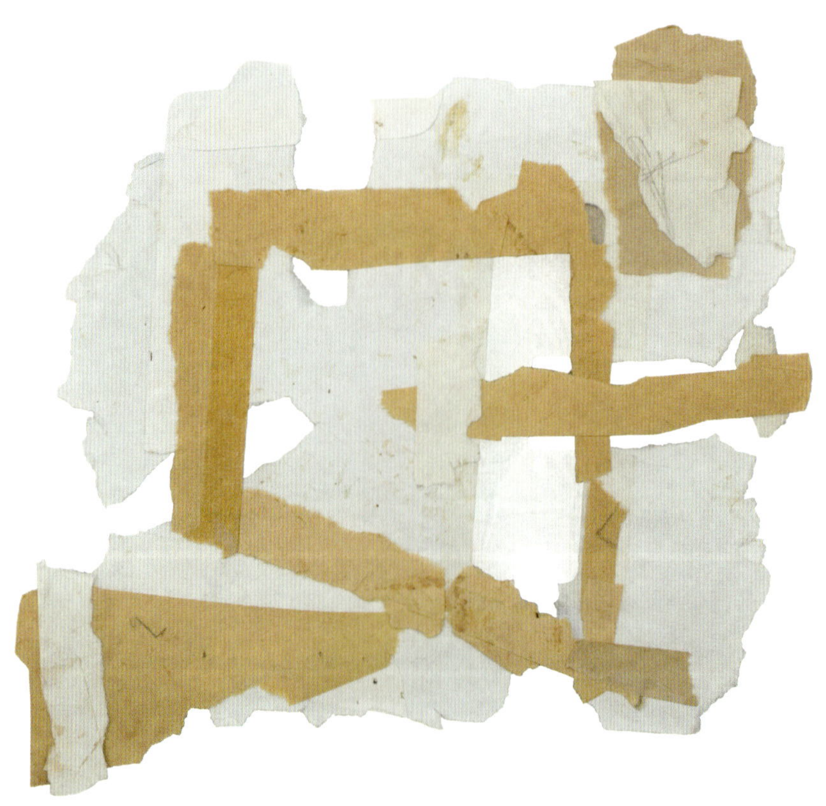

HL-59   1983–4   Collage with envelopes   21.3 × 21.3 cm (8.4 × 8.4")

HL-24 1983 Collage with envelopes 20.3 × 23.4 cm (7.9 × 9.2")

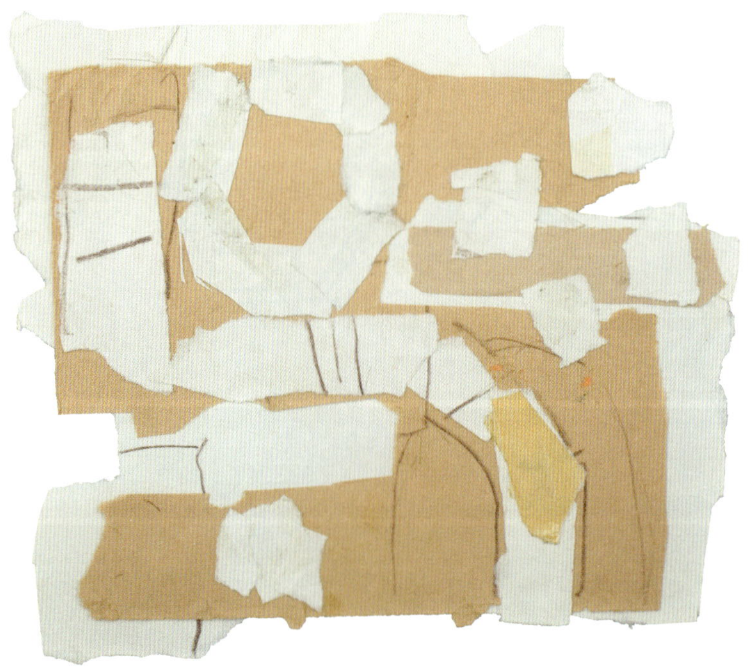

HL-27   1983   Collage with envelopes   17.7 × 20.3 cm (6.9 × 7.9")

HL-18   1983   Collage with envelopes   16.5 × 21.5 cm (6.5 × 8.6")

Conclusion

Art is an activity of fitting together and showing again under other forms, but for Davison it was principally a lyrical and exhilarated improvisation, a play of shapes. He was profoundly against the concept of art world success – perhaps an easier stance to assume as an impoverished East Anglian chicken farmer than as a hugely-fêted young metropolitan painter – and derided the kind of biographical self-obsession that today counts for art. This is wonderfully refreshing. He was also against containment. He didn't want his art to be categorized and safely stowed away in a pigeonhole. His collages duly break out of their confines, and explode beyond what might sensibly be expected to be their edges.

A statement found among Davison's papers after his death reads:

> People often ask what is the aim, what is the meaning of the collages, instead of looking to see what has been made with paper instead of paint. So I don't explain them. I look at them again and see that what was obviously a mess has taken shape. There's something, it's flat, there are empty spaces, there's slight relief, one piece of paper goes behind, another comes in front. There are false starts, crossings out, suggestions that are not followed up.
>
> This work the paper is doing gradually arrives at something 'made' cutting away what is not wanted, adding more and taking away, more of this colour, less of that, simplifying, messing until everything is lost or saved.
>
> The whole process is there, even what was cut out or what was used and discarded until something modest appears, a satisfactory balance and stillness, a suggestive form.

For Davison, collage was not about the juxtaposition of different realities to express the modern world's confusion and sense of dislocation. It was about making new harmonies from the overlooked and discarded, new patterns which would reflect our innermost needs and programmes. In effect, new realities and new worlds. He rehabilitated worn surfaces, going a bit deeper than the fashionable distressed look, and found, in the medium of used and commercially coloured paper, his unique language. As Margaret Mellis wrote in an undated fragment:

> You have to use the medium which releases you. It is nothing to do with ease or difficulty of a medium, it is entirely to do with allowing what is inside you to come out properly.

When he began making collages in 1952, Davison never again felt the need to paint, because his collage was a form of brushless painting. He continued to make drawings – mostly diagrammatic pencil studies of possible collages – but had no desire to push paint around. His collages remain some of the most painterly of any paper assemblages.

Michael Harrison writes:

> For me he vindicates the whole business of abstract art. Not for him the 'balance' of Ben Nicholson or Jim Ede, much more the 'dynamic equilibrium' of Mondrian. (Bridget Riley loathes any notion of balance.) It's the range he manages within one work. There are all sorts of forces at work, falling, leaping, pushing, pulling, hesitating, speeding. His work is entirely abstract, austere in its means, no seductive brushwork, while still evoking landscapes, internal as well as external. For all his personal reticence, he runs the risk of exposure to himself that George Fullard – another one who has been sidelined – insisted on – the work a 'survivor' – but everything ends up decided and particular. I'm pushed to thinking of anyone who manages anything equivalent: William Scott at his best, though rarely when he is fully abstract; Kenneth Martin in those late paintings.

In the end Davison's work manages successfully to resist commentary and analysis, and I can only commend you to the work itself. Go back to it, again and again: it will not disappoint.

Sources

There has been very little published about Francis Davison, apart from the exhibition catalogues listed in the bibliography on page 175 and my own monograph on Margaret Mellis, published by Lund Humphries in 2010. I have thus concentrated on primary sources, and in particular the archive maintained by Telfer Stokes, Mellis's son and Davison's step-son. Consisting primarily of letters and manuscripts, together with a treasure trove of loose drawings and sketchbooks, this is a rich resource, which needs to be more thoroughly investigated. I hope the present study will encourage others to research further into the work of this fascinating artist.

Notes

Quotations from the various catalogues (mostly unpaginated) are self-explanatory. Except where stated below, all other quotes come from Davison archive material. I'd like to thank all those who have assisted in my researches, but my greatest debt by far is to Telfer Stokes, who has supplied me with information and opinion, showed me Davison's work and allowed me to interpret the material as I saw fit.

pp52, 54 Patrick Heron's Matisse comments appear in his 1993 article 'Late Matisse', reprinted on p198 in *Painter as Critic, Patrick Heron: Selected Writings*, edited by Mel Gooding (Tate, 1998).

p100 The excerpt is taken from *Arp*, exh cat MOMA NY 1958, edited by James Thrall Soby, pp15–16.

p117 William Packer's comments come from an email to the author, March 2013.

p159 The phrase 'gracewillow ease' comes from a poem by Francis Davison, published under the pseudonym Francis Douglas, in *Now*, 'A Journal of Good Writing', no 7, dated Fall 1941.

p173 Michael Harrison's comments come from an email to the author, January 2013.

Bibliography

Francis Davison: Paper Collages, Hayward Gallery, London, 1983,
    text by Julian Spalding
Francis Davison, Redfern Gallery, London, 1986, texts by Patrick
    Heron and Julian Spalding
Francis Davison 1919–1984, Works with Green, Redfern Gallery,
    1988
The Experience of Painting: Eight Modern Artists, South Bank Centre,
    London, 1989, text by Mel Gooding
Margaret Mellis & Francis Davison, A Drift of Angels, Bede Gallery,
    Jarrow, !996
Margaret Mellis, Austin/Desmond Fine Art, London & Newlyn Art
    Gallery, Cornwall, 2001, with a foreword by Damien Hirst
Francis Davison: Paintings and Collages 1948–83, Austin/Desmond
    Fine Art, London, 2003, text by Alan Powers
Francis Davison: Early Paintings, Late Collages, Austin/Desmond
    Fine Art, London, 2006, text by Catriona Colledge
Francis Davison: Collages and Early Works, Kettle's Yard,
    Cambridge, 2007, text by Michael Harrison
Francis Davison 1919–1984, Goldmark Gallery, Rutland, 2010, text
    by Adrian Lewis
Francis Davison, Collages, Austin/Desmond Fine Art, London, 2012

Acknowledgements

Photographers
Douglas Atfield
John Christie
Colin Mills

Letter to Francis from Patrick Heron (p37). Copyright © The Estate
of Patrick Heron 2013. All Rights Reserved DACS

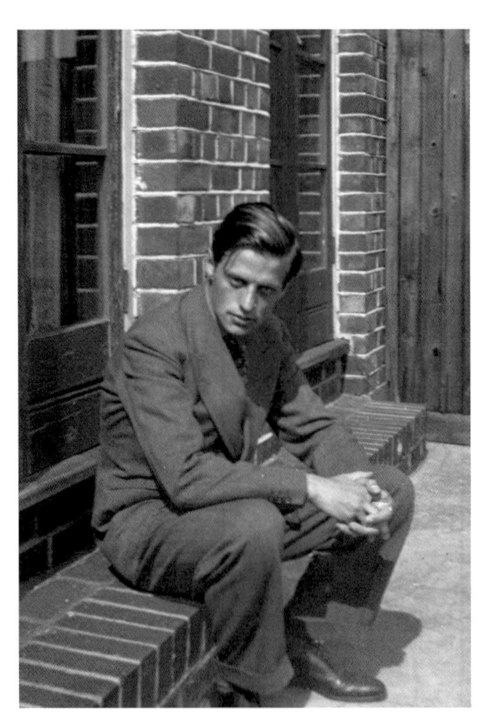